The Politically Correct University

The Politically Correct University

Problems, Scope, and Reforms

Editors
Robert Maranto
Richard E. Redding
Frederick M. Hess

The AEI Press

Publisher for the American Enterprise Institute

WASHINGTON, D.C.

Distributed to the Trade by National Book Network, 15200 NBN Way, Blue Ridge Summit, PA 17214. To order call toll free 1-800-462-6420 or 1-717-794-3800. For all other inquiries please contact the AEI Press, 1150 Seventeenth Street, N.W., Washington, D.C. 20036 or call 1-800-862-5801.

NRI NATIONAL RESEARCH INITIATIVE

This publication is a project of the National Research Initiative, a program of the American Enterprise Institute that is designed to support, publish, and disseminate research by university-based scholars and other independent researchers who are engaged in the exploration of important public policy issues.

Library of Congress Cataloging-in-Publication Data

The politically correct university : problems, scope, and reforms /
editors Robert Maranto, Richard E. Redding, Frederick M. Hess.

    p. cm.
 ISBN-13: 978-0-8447-4317-2
 ISBN-10: 0-8447-4317-8
 1. Education, Higher—Aims and objectives—United States. 2. Education, Higher—Political aspects—United States. 3. Political correctness—United States. I. Maranto, Robert, 1958– II. Redding, Richard E. III. Hess, Frederick M.

 LA227.4.P66 2009
 378'.01—dc22

2009025229

13 12 11 10 09   1 2 3 4 5 6 7

Printed in the United States of America

To the O'Brien family and to Kristin O'Brien,
whose untimely death puts these Ivory Tower issues in perspective

Contents

List of Illustrations

PART I

Diagnosing the Problem

1

The PC Academy Debate:
Questions Not Asked

Robert Maranto, Richard E. Redding, and Frederick M. Hess

After we launched this project exploring intellectual diversity in American higher education, a colleague of the lead editor playfully accused him of wasting time on "that stab-us-in-the-back book" rather than producing ever greater quantities of conventional social science. The remark was a joke, but it hints at the academic culture that led us to undertake this project, a culture in which any departure from the politically correct norm is viewed with suspicion. Our goal in this book is to explore and finally offer remedies to this culture of political correctness, the bugaboo that has most bedeviled American higher education in recent years. We focus on the problem of liberal political orthodoxy in teaching and scholarship and seek to understand how "diversity"—of race, ethnicity, gender, and sexual orientation, but not of ideas—has become the dominant ideology in higher education.

Charges of a leftist, politically correct environment in academia are nothing new. The famous Bennington College study of the 1930s presented evidence that even in that era, conservative students felt isolated from the larger campus atmosphere.[1] The father of modern American conservatism, William F. Buckley Jr., complained in 1951 that university professors had

We wish to thank the American Enterprise Institute for its vital support of this project. We must also thank Villanova University, particularly the Office of Sponsored Research, and the Department of Education Reform at the University of Arkansas. In addition, Jason O'Brien, Henry Olsen, and April Gresham Maranto played a vital role in critiquing this and other chapters. The usual caveats apply.

3

contempt for religion and capitalism, combined with reverence for central planning. More recent heirs to Buckley include Charles J. Sykes, Dinesh D'Souza, and Martin Anderson.[2] Each has savaged colleges and universities for lowering academic standards and fostering political correctness. Nor have all the critics come from the right. Centrist thinkers including Jonathan Rauch and Richard Bernstein have made essentially the same complaints.[3]

More recently, however, political entrepreneurs have turned a generalized complaint into a very specific political movement. The critics of academia, most notably conservative activist David Horowitz, have organized for reform. Horowitz has "outed" the "101 most dangerous professors" who proselytize for their political views in the classroom and has founded the activist group Students for Academic Freedom, which seeks to guarantee equal rights for conservative students and faculty. Proposals outlawing discrimination against conservative faculty and students have been under consideration in at least eighteen states.[4]

Mainstream academics have reacted to the Horowitz critique with denial and condescension: if conservatives are underrepresented in the academy, it is because they lack sufficient motivation or intelligence to survive professional peer review. Many academics seem even to deny that colleges and universities *should* play host to a variety of viewpoints. For an interesting example, see the American Association of University Professors report *Freedom in the Classroom*, which argues that any attempt at ideological diversity would inevitably lead to "'equal time' for Communist totalitarianism or Nazi fascism," given the "potentially infinite number of competing perspectives." Seemingly the AAUP finds Republican doctrines no more (or less) plausible than those of Hitler and Stalin.[5]

This volume begins from the premise that the response of mainstream academics to charges of political correctness has been empirically suspect and intellectually counterproductive. Substantial anecdotal and quantitative evidence indicates that there is a decided leftist bent to colleges and universities, particularly the most prestigious institutions. Former Harvard president and Clinton treasury secretary Larry Summers has said that in Washington he was "the right half of the left," while at Harvard he found himself "on the right half of the right."[6] Moreover, as several of the following contributions discuss, this political imbalance likely stems from practices within the academy that discourage conservatives from pursuing academic careers.

We do not regard this as an indictment of most college and university faculty and administrators, however. As Daniel Klein and Charlotta Stern show in a later chapter on majoritarian departmental politics, the sort of biases that disadvantage conservatives in academic job markets may be subtle and largely unintentional. Pressures to conform to group norms may have become particularly strong in recent years, given the weak academic job market.[7]

Such pressures have resulted in colleges and universities that drastically overrepresent the left and far left to the point of marginalizing alternative voices. In the social sciences, where one's ideology plays a far greater role in guiding teaching and research than in the sciences, we have observed the following firsthand:

- A senior professor urges a non-tenure-track political science professor to delete from his resume work on a Republican campaign, speculating that this "blotch" might explain the younger man's failure to land a tenure-track job.

- An undergraduate psychology student, a conservative, says he feels "alone with my views amid a sea of liberal graduate students and professors"—so much so that he doubts his ability to be successful in his chosen profession.

- A graduate student in the social sciences cites the frequency with which psychologists "write or say demeaning things about people with conservative political or religious views" without ever considering the views of their audience.

We maintain that the relative absence of conservative, libertarian, and neoliberal thinkers and thought from the academy is in part caused by discriminatory academic personnel practices. Further, we see this discrimination against conservatives as having four chief costs to academia and society.

First and most importantly, the lack of diversity in academia limits the questions we ask and the phenomena we study, retarding our pursuit of knowledge and our ability to serve society. We know, for instance, that the public had determined by the 1970s that the welfare program AFDC was not working, yet academic sociologists even now adamantly reject that conclusion and ostracize those who take it seriously.[8] Charles Murray's research on the problems caused by out-of-wedlock birth in general and AFDC in particular has influenced public policy—but from outside the academy. Murray is not an academic and could almost certainly not attain an academic position given his views.[9]

Similarly, criminology professors have worked tirelessly to deny the success of the New York City Police Department's reforms rather than encouraging other cities to adopt like reforms.[10] Despite New York City's fifteen-year decline in crime continuing through the tenure of three mayors and five police chiefs, criminologists still struggle to attribute increased safety to demographic shifts or even random statistical variation (which seemingly skipped other cities!) rather than to more effective policing. This failure to accept reality costs thousands of lives.[11]

A second, related problem is that limiting "critical" conservative or libertarian thought serves to delegitimize academic expertise and the academy in general among large swaths of voters and policymakers. It thus becomes harder for scholars to contribute effectively to policy debates. Indeed, the development of free-market-oriented think tanks such as those in the State Policy Network in part reflects the erosion of academics' technical authority.[12] It also becomes harder for citizens to believe in their public universities. As Hanna F. Pitkin has shown, most conceptions of democratic representation suggest that public organizations, including universities, should represent the ideals and demography of citizens.[13] Without a reasonable diversity of political opinion, public institutions of higher learning lose their legitimacy.

Third, a range of insightful critics, including Allan Bloom, Martin Anderson, Josiah Bunting III, C. John Sommerville, and Richard H. Hersh and John Merrow, has questioned whether universities as now constituted serve to make students more capable people and citizens.[14] Indeed, recent studies by the Intercollegiate Studies Institute report that even elite colleges and universities fail to teach students the basic information they need to make good decisions as voters, in matters such as where public money goes.[15] The lack of intellectual diversity on campuses itself harms undergraduates by limiting the depth and range of ideas to which they are exposed. The result is incalculable damage to the life of the mind, as the academy becomes ever more a mere credentials machine. Yet the days of growth without accountability may be coming to an end; academia is now under increasing scrutiny for permitting lower academic standards, substituting indoctrination for teaching, and raising costs, themes developed in the last section of this book.

Finally, such critics as Martin Anderson and David Lodge argue that our ideological monoculture makes universities intellectually dull places where careerism and profit seeking prevail and the energy of contending ideas is absent.[16] Such matters as the Iraq War and affirmative action are debated in newspapers and in Congress, but not in academia, where a single acceptable view is presumed. Dullness sounds like a minor problem, but in practice it bleeds academia of some of its best and brightest minds, a point made even by such nonconservative thinkers as David M. Ricci and Russell Jacoby.[17]

Although the lack of intellectual diversity in academia clearly has costs, the conservative critiques to date are unlikely to bring about desired changes. For starters, too much of the case suggesting that academia is hostile to conservative ideas has been anecdotal rather than systematic. Moreover, some "conservative" critics of academe appear to be more concerned with ideological balance on campus than with ensuring that higher education is equipped to pursue its intellectual, educational, and social mission.

What the debate needs—and what we offer in this volume—is empirically and historically grounded criticism of academia combined with ideas about how to make academia truer to its social purpose of gaining and disseminating knowledge. We have brought together a group of scholars and practitioners who care deeply about higher education, and who set about systematically answering the following questions: How rare are conservative professors? Why are they so rare? How does this vary by discipline? What are the effects of this political homogeneity on campus? What solutions are available for reforming the PC university?

This book is organized into four sections. Chapters in the first and most empirical section, "Diagnosing the Problem," establish that universities actually do need reform. This section begins with chapters providing the most current and comprehensive statistical analyses of the relative rarity of conservative and libertarian professors. Chapters follow that explore the psychological and sociological mechanisms by which such imbalance comes about; these chapters also consider how and why academia stresses demographic diversity while largely eschewing political diversity.

In "By the Numbers: The Ideological Profile of Professors," Daniel Klein of George Mason University and Charlotta Stern of Stockholm University summarize and critique all important survey research since the 1960s on the ideology, policy views, and voting behavior of humanities and social science faculty. They find that conservatives and libertarians are becoming increasingly rare in academia, outnumbered by liberals and radicals by nearly 3 to 1 in relatively conservative fields like economics, more than 5 to 1 in moderate fields like political science, and 20 to 1 or more in anthropology and sociology.

In "Left Pipeline: Why Conservatives Don't Get Doctorates," Matthew Woessner of Penn State–Harrisburg and April Kelly-Woessner of Elizabethtown College use a national survey of college and university seniors to show that conservative students are substantially less likely to want to pursue doctorates than similarly situated liberal peers. This is not because they are less intelligent (liberal and conservative students have identical mean GPAs) but because they have different life priorities and career goals. Yet the data also suggest that conservative students lack academic role models, have more distant relationships to faculty, and may have fewer opportunities to do research with their professors, all of which may also affect their decision to pursue graduate education.

That the academic job markets seem to discriminate against conservative PhDs is suggested in "The Vanishing Conservative—Is There a Glass Ceiling?" by Stanley Rothman of Smith College and S. Robert Lichter of George Mason University. They find strong statistical evidence that socially conservative academics must publish more books and articles to get the same jobs as liberal peers. While publication records have the most impact on academic success, it remains the case that conservatives seem to be underplaced within the academic meritocracy, with social conservatism having about a third of the statistical impact on career success as one's publishing record.

The second section, "'Diversity' in Higher Education," begins with a second piece by Daniel Klein and Charlotta Stern, "Groupthink in Academia: Majoritarian Departmental Politics and the Professional Pyramid." Klein and Stern suggest that anticonservative bias in the academy is likely explained by a psychological phenomenon known as "groupthink." Organizations that can both select members and control members' rewards tend to select and reward those like the original group, so that an initial liberal academic orientation has led to faculties that are increasingly less ideologically diverse. In developing their groupthink interpretation, Klein and Stern explore how a few especially prestigious departments shape majoritarian thinking in departments across the discipline.

In "The Psychology of Political Correctness in Higher Education," University of Nevada–Reno professor William O'Donohue and Chapman University professor Richard Redding explore the psychological goals and assumptions underlying diversity programs and political correctness. They challenge the assumption that disadvantaged groups suffer harm from certain speech or actions, and that ameliorative interventions are necessary to correct the harm. Drawing on psychological research, they argue that sociopolitical diversity may actually be the most important form of diversity for achieving the stated goals of diversity in higher education.

How demographic diversity came to trump ideological diversity on campus is the subject of "College Conformity 101: Where the Diversity of Ideas Meets the Idea of Diversity," by National Association of Scholars executor director Peter Wood. Wood shows how demographic diversity has come to dominate higher education through its application in faculty hiring, student admissions, curricula, student orientation, residence hall policies, and virtually every other aspect of college life. Wood refers to a "new kind of aristocracy" created by this understanding of diversity, with a hierarchy of privilege based on perceived victimization, but he holds out the hope that inherent tensions in the diversity doctrine, combined with state ballot initiatives outlawing affirmative action, may ultimately chip away at the diversity regime.

Finally, in "The American University: Yesterday, Today, and Tomorrow," James Piereson, president of the William E. Simon Foundation and a former academic, sees the modern university as the product of twentieth-century liberalism, and suggests that the break-up of the foundational assumption of liberalism—free thought—poses the most profound challenge of all to the modern university. He suggests that the nationalization and internationalization of higher education is working to increase political uniformity among faculty, and that the very financial success of universities may insulate them from reform impulses.

In the third section, "Different Disciplines, Same Problem," leading scholars explore how political correctness affects scholarship and teaching across core liberal arts and social science disciplines. While the AAUP holds that "it is not indoctrination for professors to expect students to comprehend ideas and apply knowledge that is accepted as true within a relevant discipline,"[18] these essays illustrate how liberal political biases and agendas color what is accepted and acceptable within a discipline.

In "When Is Diversity Not Diversity: A Brief History of the English Department," University of Virginia professor Paul Cantor shows that literature departments were much more intellectually diverse in the 1950s, when discrete schools of literary study dominated individual campuses and competed with one another in the broader academic universe. Today, a depressing uniformity of approach prevails, as literature departments may study a wider variety of works but generally do so through the narrower lenses of race, class, and gender.

In "Linguistics from the Left: The Truth about Black English That the Academy Doesn't Want You to Know," Manhattan Institute scholar and former University of California, Berkeley professor John McWhorter looks at the study of Black English to show how identity politics has managed to drive linguistics from its original mission, the nonpartisan description and analysis of languages and dialects. Dishonest linguists, McWhorter shows, are influencing elementary educators, and in turn making it harder for struggling black children to learn to read.

The field of history shows a similar dynamic. In "History Upside Down," Hoover Institution scholar Victor Davis Hanson defines politically correct history as those efforts to use the past to achieve social change in the present. The goal of such history is to indict the West—and the United States in particular—as an inherently pathological oppressor of the "other." Hanson describes numerous examples of such demonization, which increasingly replaces more nuanced and accurate understandings of the past. The resulting weaknesses of modern academic history have left the field ripe for takeover: increasingly, journalists fill the roles previously held by historians.

Political science may be in better shape than history, the next chapter suggests. In "Why Political Science Is Left But Not Quite PC: Causes of Disunion and Diversity," University of Virginia professor James Ceaser and University of Arkansas professor Robert Maranto demonstrate that political science is less rigidly liberal than many other disciplines. The cause: certain subfields such as constitutional law, traditional political philosophy, political economy, and international relations require skills and attitudes that permit moderates and conservatives to compete effectively for jobs. In addition, the pluralist ideology of American political science argues for tolerance of a range of viewpoints. Nevertheless, roughly 80 percent of political scientists are liberal or progressive, and this limits the sorts of questions those in the field ask.

In the final section, "Needed Reforms," practitioners describe the history of political correctness in universities and outline possible ways to reform academia.

In "The Route to Academic Pluralism," National Association of Scholars president Stephen Balch calls for more active trustees and the creation of centers within universities to explore and represent conservative, traditional liberal, and libertarian perspectives. Such centers now exist at Princeton, Duke, Brown, and other schools. They lay the groundwork for eventually creating intellectually diverse departments, which, through their ability to hire and train, could reopen the academic marketplace to intellectual dissidents.

In "The Role of Alumni and Trustees," Anne Neal of the American Council of Trustees and Alumni argues for the involvement of informed alumni and trustees in overseeing colleges and universities. Alumni and trustees have abdicated their proper role out of deference to faculty and presidents, but they must be willing to articulate their concerns about trends in the academy that threaten its future stature, rather than merely delegate to academics.

In "Openness, Transparency, and Accountability: Fostering Public Trust in Higher Education" former U.S. senator and University of Colorado president Hank Brown, and his colleagues John Cooney and Michael Poliakoff, point out that both America's preeminence in, and public trust of, higher education are eroding. The authors explain that only by adhering to principles of openness, transparency, and accountability can the academy regain public trust. The authors discuss such policies in the context of perceived fiscal mismanagement, political bias, declining academic rigor, and low standards for awarding tenure.

Finally, John Agresto, former National Endowment for the Humanities chairman and former president of St. John's College in New Mexico, explains that PC problems mainly affect the liberal arts, in part for reasons inherent in their very nature. In "To Reform the Politically Correct University, Reform the Liberal Arts," he advocates restoring balance and openness to our colleges and universities by deliberately exploring the vital middle ground between those who see the liberal arts as necessarily in opposition to reigning orthodoxies, and those more libertarian scholars who know that some apparent attempts to smash all idols are actually efforts to substitute a new orthodoxy for the old. In effect, Agresto wants academics to heal themselves by changing the culture of academia from one of smugness to one of seeking.

This volume will not be the last word on the PC university. In particular, we have hardly begun to explore the costs of ideological consensus—to look, that is, at how academia's left-oriented status quo harms students and society. Still, we hope this work will start a dialogue between groups such as the AAUP, which defend that status quo, and critics mainly from the right and center. (In that debate, we trust that civility and data will prevail over passions and interests.) If the empirical evidence this volume offers persuades many well-meaning scholars on the left that higher education really has a PC problem, academia may begin to reform itself from the inside. One thing is near certain: reform will come—only its timing and nature are in doubt.

Notes

1. T. M. Newcome, *Personality and Social Change* (New York: Dryden, 1943).

2. William F. Buckley Jr., *God and Man at Yale* (Chicago: Regnery, 1951). See also Charles J. Sykes, *ProfScam* (Washington, DC: Regnery Gateway, 1988); Dinesh D'Souza, *Illiberal Education* (New York: Vintage, 1991); and Martin Anderson, *Impostors in the Temple* (Stanford, CA: Hoover Institution Press, 1996).

3. See Jonathan Rauch, *Kindly Inquisitors* (Chicago: University of Chicago Press, 1993); Richard Bernstein, *Dictatorship of Virtue* (New York: Vintage, 1994).

4. See David Horowitz, *The Professors: The 101 Most Dangerous Academics in America* (Washington, DC: Regnery, 2006); see also "Students for Academic Freedom," http://www.studentsforacademicfreedom.org/. Horowitz is an institution builder in the mode of Ralph Nader, though with notably different goals. He has also founded the Center for the Study of Popular Culture (now called the David Horowitz Freedom Center) and *FrontPage Magazine*.

5. American Association of University Professors, *Freedom in the Classroom*, September 11, 2007, http://www.aaup.org/AAUP/comm/rep/A/class.htm. See also Michael Berube, "Freedom to Teach," *Inside Higher Ed*, September 11, 2007, http://www.insidehighered.com/views/2007/09/11/berube.

6. Lawrence Summers, cited in Scott Jaschick, "The Liberal (and Moderating) Professoriate," *Inside Higher Ed*, October 8, 2007, http://www.insidehighered.com/news/2007/10/08/politics.

7. As Zachary Karabell states in *What's College For?* (New York: Basic Books, 1998), a poor academic job market since the 1970s has limited intellectual innovation in the academy: "Because of the pressure to get a job and the odds against landing one, graduate students are becoming ever more likely to conform to the orthodoxies of their field and ever less likely to be able to communicate with the world outside of the academy" (67).

8. Stephen Teles, *Whose Welfare? AFDC and Elite Politics* (Lawrence: University Press of Kansas, 1998), makes clear that the failures of AFDC were apparent early on.

9. See, for example, Murray's *Losing Ground* (New York: Basic Books, 1984). Murray was anathema to the academy even before he wrote (with R. J. Herrnstein) *The Bell Curve: Intelligence and Class Structure in American Life* (New York: Free Press, 1994).

10. See William Bratton and Peter Knobler, *Turnaround* (New York: Random House, 1998); and George L. Kelling and William H. Sousa, *Do Police Matter?* (New York: Manhattan Institute, 2001).

11. Examples of this type are rampant. In the area of comparative politics, scholars eager to see U.S. and Israeli failings but reluctant to acknowledge problems within Arab societies could neither anticipate nor understand the potent threat of political Islam, a point developed by, among others, Martin S. Kramer, *Ivory Towers on Sand* (Washington, DC: Washington Institute for Near East Policy, 2001). While most of the critics of the academy are conservatives or libertarians, the left-of-center E. D.

Hirsch argues in *The Schools We Need and Why We Don't Have Them* (New York: Anchor, 1999) that academics in schools of education have harmed young people by promoting progressive dogma rather than examining what works in real classrooms, a theme also developed later in this volume by John McWhorter.

12. In the interest of full disclosure, the first author of this chapter is associated with two SPN institutions.

13. Hanna F. Pitkin, *The Concept of Representation* (Berkeley and Los Angeles: University of California Press, 1967).

14. See Allan Bloom, *The Closing of the American Mind* (New York: Simon and Schuster, 1987); Anderson, *Impostors in the Temple*; Josiah Bunting III, *An Education for Our Time* (Washington, DC: Regnery, 1998); C. John Sommerville, *The Decline of the Secular University* (New York: Oxford University Press, 2006); and Richard Hersh and John Merrow, *Declining by Degrees* (New York: Palgrave, 2005).

15. T. Kenneth Cribb Jr., *Failing Our Students, Failing America* (Wilmington, DE: Intercollegiate Studies Institute, 2007).

16. Anderson, *Impostors in the Temple*; David Lodge, *Small World* (New York: Penguin, 1984). Lodge's work is fiction, inspired by real people and events.

17. David M. Ricci, *The Tragedy of Political Science* (New Haven, CT: Yale University Press, 1984); Russell Jacoby, *The Last Intellectuals* (New York: Basic Books, 1987).

18. America Association of University Professors, *Freedom in the Classroom*.

2

By the Numbers:
The Ideological Profile of Professors

Daniel B. Klein and Charlotta Stern

There have been two peaks in interest in the ideology of professors, the first in the 1960s and '70s, the second in the beginning of the twenty-first century. In both periods studies found that professors tended to be radical; and in both periods the findings were challenged by scholars who claimed that professors were less radical than the studies showed. But there is one difference between the periods: in the earlier period the critics were openly disappointed that professors were not more radical, whereas in the later period the critics defensively argued that professors are more like ordinary people, more "moderate," than the studies show.

The change in attitude partly has to do with the researchers themselves. In the earlier period the studies were conducted by prominent liberal academics such as Ladd and Lipset and openly left sympathizers such as Faia,[1] whereas the later studies come from conservative and classical liberal/ libertarian academics. The change in attitude may also be an indication of the decline of professors with definite nonleftist views. This chapter summarizes the evidence on the ideology of professors and shows that few professors in the social sciences and humanities today are not on the left, and that there has been a decline since the 1960s in professors who are not on the left, as indicated by Republican voting, self-identified conservative leanings, or policy views.

We thank Richard Redding for detailed feedback that significantly improved this chapter.

TABLE 2-1

DEMOCRAT:REPUBLICAN RATIOS FOUND IN VOTER REGISTRATION STUDIES

	Cardiff and Klein[a]	Five Misc. Studies[b]	Center for Study of Popular Culture[c]
Anthropology	10.5	NA[d]	—
Economics	2.8	1.6	4.3
English	13.3	19.3	18.6
History	10.9	75.0	20.7
Philosophy	5.0	24.0	8.9
Political science	6.5	7.9	7.9
Sociology	44.0	NA[e]	30.4

NOTES: a. Cardiff and Klein, "Faculty Partisan Affiliaton," 239, based on 2004–5 data; b. 2003–5 voter registration data pooled from separate investigations at Capital University, Dartmouth College, Duke University, Ithaca College, and the University of Nevada–Las Vegas, detailed in "Other Schools" worksheet, http://www.gmu.edu/departments/economics/klein/Voter/California%20Voter%20Reg%20CORRECTED%2013%20Oct%202007.xls; c. 2001–2 voter registration data for thirty-two elite schools reported in David Horowitz and Eli Lehrer, "Political Bias in the Administrations and Faculties of 32 Elite Colleges and Universities," Center for the Study of Popular Culture, 2002, http://www.frontpagemag.com/Content/read.asp?ID=55; d. This group consisted of twenty-one Democrats and zero Republicans; e. This group consisted of thirty-two Democrats and zero Republicans.

We focus on the humanities and social sciences (abbreviated here as h/ss) because in those disciplines, where professors deal with political matters in the classroom, ideological sensibilities likely play a significant role. Political views play a much smaller role in fields like math or chemistry.

Voter Registration Studies

Voter registration studies are in some ways more useful than survey studies as a means of understanding individuals' political beliefs. Voter registration studies avoid response bias and membership bias. However, the approach is obviously limited by America's two-party system—specifically, the crudeness of what can be inferred from support for either of those two parties and the problem that a large percentage of any faculty sample cannot be identified as being either Democrat or Republican.[2] Of course, there is also the concern that the faculties investigated may not be representative of academia in general.

TABLE 2-2

DEMOCRAT:REPUBLICAN RATIOS IN ELEVEN CALIFORNIA UNIVERSITIES,
2004 TO 2005

Division	N	D	R	D:R Ratio
Humanities	1,153	600	60	10.0
Arts	313	151	20	7.6
Social sciences	1,039	529	78	6.8
Hard sciences/math	1,635	792	126	6.3
Medicine/nursing/health	489	233	49	4.8
Social professional[a]	662	315	71	4.4
Engineering	700	213	85	2.5
Business	389	116	86	1.3
Military/sports	69	11	15	0.7
Total	*6,449*	*2,960*	*590*	*5.0*

SOURCE: Cardiff and Klein, "Faculty Partisan Affiliation."
NOTE: a. Social professional includes fields of education, communications, law, social welfare, and policy.

Even given these limitations, voter registration data are still informative. Table 2-1 provides a summary of voter registration studies since 2001. The data show that h/ss faculties are dominated by registered Democrats.

A 2005 study by Klein and Stern suggests that h/ss faculties in the United States, excluding those at two-year colleges, have an overall D:R ratio (in terms of either usual voting behavior or voter registration) of at least 7:1 and more likely about 8:1.[3] This chapter finds that such estimates continue to appear sound.

Consider table 2-2, which presents information from a study by Cardiff and Klein about a range of academic divisions at eleven California institutions, including two that are reputed to be relatively conservative, Pepperdine and Claremont-McKenna.[4] Significant variations across academic divisions are evident when the eleven institutions are treated as a single pool. To be sure, Democratic preponderance is not the case at every school. Among the eleven schools investigated, the faculty *overall* at Pepperdine had a D:R ratio of 0.9, Point Loma Nazarene 1.0, and Claremont McKenna 1.3. However, those schools were deliberately included in the investigation because they have reputations for being conservative.

Table 2-2 shows that the only category that favors Republicans is military/sports, which is the smallest. The surprise is not that military/sports is less Democratic than other divisions, but that it is not more Republican than it is. The same is true of business, where the ratio of 1.3 Democrats per Republican indicates that the latter are not marginalized in business education, but that they are not dominant, either.

The high D:R ratios in h/ss echo studies from the 1960s. Older studies (which relied on self-reports of voting, not voter registration) often discussed an ideological divide in academia between h/ss and the "hard" sciences.[5] Voter registration studies do not find such a divide. The hard sciences in these eleven California faculties are preponderantly Democratic.

Cardiff and Klein analyze the data by gender and academic rank. They find that female professors generally have significantly higher D:R ratios than male professors, except at Caltech and the two Protestant schools (Pepperdine and Point Loma Nazerene). The pattern for academic rank is not uniform across the eleven schools, but on the whole, the Republicans who can be found among the faculty are disproportionately full professors (not associate or assistant professors).[6] Such is the case at all but two of the smaller schools, Pepperdine and Caltech, and dramatically so at Berkeley and Stanford. The implication is that, unless young Democratic professors occasionally mature into Republicans, the D:R ratios will become more lopsided in the future.

Democrat versus Republican by Self-Reporting

Another kind of party-affiliation data comes from survey questions that ask the respondents to report their own voting behavior, party identification, or party leanings. The phrasings of such questions differ, and the differences can be significant. For example, response might be sensitive to the moment or referent election (consider the 1964 Johnson landslide against Goldwater). Here we treat different formulations as asking the same basic question. Because such surveys have been conducted for decades, we can compare data over time.

Data indicate that in the period around 1970 the D:R ratio in the h/ss was about 4:1 (excluding two-year colleges). Thus, roughly speaking, over the thirty-five-year period from 1970 to 2005, the h/ss D:R ratio has probably

TABLE 2-3

DEMOCRAT:REPUBLICAN RATIOS FOUND IN SURVEYS OF ENTIRE FACULTY,
1960 TO 1972

Survey	Yee 1963[a]	Joyner 1963[b]	Eitzen and Maranell 1968[c]	Faia 1967[d]	Ladd and Lipset 1973[e]
Year of data	1960	1962	1962	1965	1972
	Faculty, three state colleges, WA	Faculty, University of Arizona	Behavioral and physical sciences, fine arts	Faculty, universities and colleges, CA	Faculty, national sample
Average	2.04	1.3	1.3[f]	1.3	2.6

SOURCE: Faia, "Myth of the Liberal Professor," 174.
NOTES: a. Robert Yee, "Faculty Participation in the 1960 Presidential Election," *Political Research Quarterly* 16 (March 1963): 213–20; b. Conrad Joyner, "Political Party Affiliation of University Administrative and Teaching Personnel," *Southwestern Social Science Quarterly* 40 (March 1963): 353–56; c. D. Stanley Eitzen and Gary M. Maranell, "The Political Party Affiliation of College Professors," *Social Forces* 47, no. 2 (1968): 145–53; d. Michael A. Faia, "Alienation, Structural Strain, and Political Deviancy: A Test of Merton's Hypothesis," *Social Problems* 14 (Spring 1967): 389–413; e. Everett Carll Ladd Jr., and Seymour Martin Lipset, *Academics, Politics, and the 1972 Election* (Washington, DC: American Enterprise Institute for Public Policy Research, 1973); f. Eitzen and Maranell found that in the behavioral sciences the D:R ratio was about 2:1; in the physical sciences and in the fine arts there was no Democratic dominance.

about doubled. Here we review the survey-based D:R data, but space constraints require the omission of exact wording, sampling size, method, etc.

D:R during the Earlier Period. Table 2-3 presents an overview of results on faculty voting from 1955 to 1972. Note that the overview compares only Democratic and Republican voters and excludes other party identifications, independents, and unaffiliated voters.

Overall, the results suggest that across campus in those days there was a Democratic lead, with the D:R ratio ranging between 1.3 and 2.6. Nowadays, faculty surveys on voting report ratios of 4.5:1,[7] 2.9:1,[8] and 3.6:1.[9]

Humanities and Social Sciences. In h/ss the Democratic lead has always been larger, as shown in table 2-4, with earlier discipline surveys (between

TABLE 2-4

DEMOCRAT:REPUBLICAN RATIOS FOUND IN SURVEYS OF CERTAIN
DISCIPLINES IN SOCIAL SCIENCES AND HUMANITIES, 1959 TO 1964

	Turner et al. 1963a[a]	Turner et al. 1963b[b]	Source Spaulding and Turner 1968[c]	Eitzen and Maranell 1968[d]	McClintock et al. 1965[e]
Year	1959	1960	1959–64	1962	1962
History			2.6 (72% D)		
Philosophy			3.8 (79% D)		
Political science	4.5				
Psychology				2.3	3.4
Sociology		7.5			

NOTES: a. Henry A. Turner, Charles B. Spaulding, and Charles G. McClintock, "Political Orientations of Academically Affiliated Sociologists," *Sociology and Social Research* 47 (1963): 273–89. This study also reports on botanists (50 percent Democratic), geologists (35 percent), mathematicians (29 percent), and engineers (27 percent); b. Henry A. Turner, Charles B. Spaulding, and Charles G. McClintock, "The Political Party Affiliation of American Political Scientists," *Western Political Quarterly* 1 (1963): 650–65; c. Charles B. Spaulding and Henry A. Turner, "Political Orientation and Field of Specialization among College Professors," *Sociology of Education* 41, no. 3 (1968): 247–62. Spaulding and Turner's table reports only the percentage of Democrats, noted in the cells in parentheses. To make comparisons easier, we present ratios assuming that the remainder of the respondents reported voted Republican. When compared with numbers reported in the discipline-specific articles (see table footnotes a and b), we find that the assumption overrepresents the number of Republicans; d. D. Stanley Eitzen and Gary M. Maranell, "The Political Party Affiliation of College Professors," *Social Forces* 47, no. 2 (1968): 145–53. This study lumps sociologists and psychologists together; e. Charles G. McClintock, Charles B. Spaulding, and Henry Turner, "Political Orientations of Academically Affiliated Psychologists," *American Psychologists* 20 (March 1965): 211–21.

1959 and 1964) showing D:R ratios in the range of 2.3 to 7.5. An even earlier survey of social scientists, conducted in 1955 by Lazarfeld and Thielens, found an overall ratio of 2.9.[10]

Ladd and Lipset present data specifically on presidential voting by the entire social science and humanities categories, as shown in table 2-5. The smattering of data seems to sustain the conclusion that around 1970 the overall D:R ratio in h/ss was probably somewhere between 3.5 and 4.

TABLE 2-5

DEMOCRAT:REPUBLICAN VOTING IN PRESIDENTIAL ELECTIONS, 1964, 1968, 1972

	1964 Presidential Election	1968 Presidential Election	1972 Presidential Election
Social science	8.9	3.8	3.5
Humanities	6.6	3.1	2.4

SOURCE: Ladd and Lipset, *Divided Academy,* 62–84.

Recent D:R Survey Data. Surveys of recent years, shown in table 2-6, indicate a substantial increase in D:R ratios. Rothman et al. find for the humanities as a whole a ratio of 10.3, and for the social sciences 7.9.[11] Tobin and Weinberg report that in the 2004 election the ratio of Kerry to Bush voters was 5.4 in the humanities and 4.8 in the social sciences.[12]

The survey results may be compared to voter registration results only for the recent period, where the two methods generally line up and reinforce each other. Gross and Simmons report that humanities professors in 2004 voted 83.7 percent for Kerry, 15.0 percent for Bush; and that social science professors voted 87.6 percent for Kerry, 6.2 percent for Bush. Thus "averaging the figures for the social sciences and humanities generates a ratio of Democratic to Republican voters of 8.1 to 1."[13]

D:R by Cohorts. Another way to detect changes over time is by comparing cohorts at the same point in time. That younger faculty are usually somewhat more likely to vote for Democratic (or left) candidates is a finding of long standing—Ladd and Lipset show it occurring in the 1948 presidential election.[14] Klein and Stern find that in each of the six h/ss associations surveyed, older respondents are on the whole more likely to vote Republican as opposed to Democratic.[15] Using multivariate regression analysis, they also find an increase in the likelihood of voting Democratic with the year of one's degree—that is, the longer ago one received his degree, the more likely he is to vote Republican; this relation holds statistically (at 0.01) even with a number of variable controls.[16] The size of the effect is not big, but it is statistically strong. Gross and Simmons also indicate that Republican voters are more common among full professors.[17]

TABLE 2-6

DEMOCRAT:REPUBLICAN RATIOS FOUND IN SURVEYS OF FACULTY
IN SOCIAL SCIENCES AND HUMANITIES, 1999 TO 2003

	Source			
	Rothman et al. 2005[a]	Brookings 2001, Light 2001[b]	Klein and Stern 2005[c]	Gross and Simmons 2007[d]
Year	1999	2001	2003	2006
Economics	2.1	3.7	2.9	3.0
Philosophy	5.6		9.1	
History	17.5	4.1	8.5	18.9
Political science	7.3	4.8	5.6	18.8
Psychology	9			
Sociology	59	47	28[e]	19.5

NOTES: a. Rothman, Lichter, and Nevitte, "Politics and Professional Advancement among College Faculty"; b. Brookings Institution, "National Survey on Government Endeavors," prepared by Princeton Survey Research Associates, November 9, 2005, http://www.brook.edu/comm/reformwatch/rw04_surveydata.pdf; Paul C. Light, "Government's Greatest Priorities of the Next Half Century," *Reform Watch*, no. 4, Brookings Institution, Washington, DC, December 2001, http://www.brook.edu/comm/reformwatch/rw04.htm; c. Daniel B. Klein and Charlotta Stern, "Professors and Their Politics: The Policy Views of Social Scientists," *Critical Review* 17, no. 3–4 (2005): 257–303; d. Gross and Simmons, "Social and Political Views of American Professors." We are using this study's data on Kerry versus Bush voting in 2004. This study reports self-described party affiliation by departments, but only in a way such that 38.9 percent of faculty overall are independents; e. This ratio of 28 for sociology is from Daniel B. Klein and Charlotta Stern, "Sociology and Classical Liberalism," *Independent Review* 11 (Summer 2006): 37–52, which treats sociologists only.

The results agree with the voter registration data that generally found a lower D:R ratio among the full professors. Republican representation will likely decline as the older professors pass from the scene.

"Liberal versus Conservative"

Our analysis of D:R ratios thus far has proceeded with only minor points of controversy: Are we excluding the two-year colleges? Are we talking about h/ss or the entire faculty? These points are readily resolved. Discussion of political or ideological views, on the other hand, has been more troubled.

Some Conceptual Issues. Controversy surrounds the ways in which researchers read the data in terms of ideological attributions. Most scholars have employed America's dominant one-dimensional framework, "liberal versus conservative" (sometimes "left versus right"), which is often vague code for "Democrat versus Republican." That framework has a number of problems.

There is a tendency to treat Democratic as identical to "liberal" and Republican as identical to "conservative." One problem is that—third parties, etc. aside—voting behavior amounts to a binary variable with no in-between, whereas "liberal versus conservative" self-identification invariably allows for a substantial middle or center. There then arises confusion over how to categorize this middle.

There are other problems with "liberal versus conservative" (or "left versus right"): (1) "middle-of-the-road" as an option for self-identification is sensitive to the respondent's reference group—that is, not everyone lives on the same road; (2) politics has more than one dimension, so that what exactly is being measured in the "liberal to conservative" dimension is not clear; (3) the terms "liberal" and "conservative" have disparate connotations; (4) liberalism originally suggested laissez-faire, and that classical meaning has been rejuvenated ("liberalization," "liberal" drug or immigration policy, etc.), so that self-identification as "liberal" means more than one thing;[18] (5) conservatism has traditionally meant establishment interests. Given that academe is one of the most established, caste-based domains of American society, and that extensive government interventions and welfare-state programs are now pervasive and entrenched, why shouldn't professors who support the status quo think of themselves as moderates or even conservatives?[19]

If you stick your finger into a glass of water it appears bent, because when light passes through a different medium it is refracted. Likewise, Democrat:Republican ratios do not exactly mirror ratios of self-identified "liberals" to self-identified "conservatives." Rather, because of the problems just listed, one is a kind of social refraction of the other.

Those who highlight the preponderance of Democrats (as well as certain policy opinions) naturally impute ideological content to the findings. There has been a recurrent response by other scholars, who represent the highlighters as saying that there is a corresponding preponderance, more or less, of "liberals." Academically well-placed examples of this kind of response are the following four papers:

1. Faia, "Myth of the Liberal Professor."

2. Hamilton and Hargens, "Politics of the Professors: Self-Identifications, 1969–1984."

3. Zipp and Fenwick, "Is the Academy a Liberal Hegemony?"

4. Gross and Simmons, "Social and Political Views of American Professors."[20]

Papers 2, 3, and 4 use political self-identification data to show that the liberals are less dominant than "right-wing activists and scholars" suggest.[21] One reason is that a lot of Democratic-voting professors self-identify as "middle/center" or "moderately conservative," as in "conservative Democrat." Another reason is that the authors include faculties of two-year colleges, weighted to represent their large numbers throughout the United States—a controversial method, as clearly, beyond the classroom, faculty at two-year colleges have very little influence on research, scholarship, and public discourse. The first and second papers also include results of attitude questions about policy or university issues, and tend to show that only a minority of professors adopts the conspicuously "liberal" positions. Faia doubts whether self-identified "liberals" are really liberal.[22]

The upshot is that different voices use terms differently. The "liberal" attribution, for example, can mean a range of things, here listed from widest to narrowest:

- All professors who do not show themselves to be Republican or "real" conservatives or classical liberals.
  - Professors who vote Democratic.
    - Professors who self-identify as "liberal."
      - Professors who take "liberal" positions on issues.

We should expect scholars of different perspectives to use terms differently, since ideological differences entail differences over the understanding of the most important words. That said, communication with ideological "others" works best when it sticks to relative concretes, such as reported voting and policy views. Acknowledging various limitations, we review the "liberal versus conservative" findings here.

TABLE 2-7

PERCENTAGES OF LIBERALS AND CONSERVATIVES, ALL FACULTY
(CARNEGIE SURVEYS OVER TIME, INCLUDING TWO-YEAR COLLEGES)

	1969	1975	1984		1989	1997
Left and liberal	46	41	40	Liberal and moderately liberal	56	56
Middle-of-the-road	27	28	27	Middle-of-the-road	17	20
Moderately and strongly conservative	28	31	34	Moderately conservative and conservative	28	24

SOURCES: For 1969, 1975, and 1984: Hamilton and Hargens, "Politics of the Professors"; for 1989 and 1997: Zipp and Fenwick, "Liberal Hegemony?"

"Liberal versus Conservative": Self-Identification. Survey research commonly asks about political views in terms of "liberal versus conservative." One group of surveys that has done so is the Carnegie surveys of faculty, which collected data on academics in 1968, 1975, 1984, 1989, and 1997.[23] Published findings using these surveys appear in table 2-7.

Similar approaches were used in surveys by the Higher Education Research Institute (HERI) of the University of California–Los Angeles,[24] by the North American Academic Study Survey (NAASS) in 1999,[25] and by the Institute of Jewish Community Research (IJCR) in 2005.[26] Results for these, as well as for the survey of Gross and Simmons, are summarized in table 2-8.[27]

Some of the variation in findings reported in table 2-8 probably depends on wording and how the researchers bunch multipoint responses into three categories. Some of the variation also depends on different sampling strategies; the Carnegie, HERI, and Gross and Simmons surveys include two-year colleges, where conservative self-identification is substantially higher than for any other category of higher education, while the NAASS and IJCR do not.[28] Despite these kinds of discrepancies, the recent Gross and Simmons study helps to support the conclusion that self-identified conservatives have been declining.

TABLE 2-8

PERCENTAGES OF LIBERALS AND CONSERVATIVES, ALL FACULTY
(HERI, NAASS, IJCR, GROSS AND SIMMONS SURVEYS)

	1989	2001	1999	2005	2006
	——HERI[a]——		NAASS[b]	IJCR[c]	Gross and Simmons[d]
Liberal, left	42	48	62	50	44.1
Moderate, middle	40	34		32.3	46.6
Conservative, right	18	18	12	17.7	9.2

NOTES: a. HERI, "UCLA Study Finds Growing Gap in Political Liberalism between Male and Female Faculty," UCLA Higher Education Research Institute, 2002, http://www.gseis.ucla.edu/heri/act_pr_02.html; b. Rothman, Lichter, and Nevitte, "Politics and Professional Advancement"; c. Tobin and Weinberg, *Profile of American College Faculty*; d. Gross and Simmons, "Social and Political Views of American Professors." Columns except NAASS sum to 100 percent: missings, others, don't knows, etc. have been suppressed. The NAASS column is incomplete because of insufficient reporting. Also, the NAASS numbers are the interpolations made by Rothman and Lichter as described in their chapter in this volume.

Humanities and Social Sciences. If we exclude the two-year colleges from the Carnegie 1997 data, the results line up quite well with the 1999 NAASS data on h/ss, as noted by Rothman and Lichter in their chapter in the present volume. Gross and Simmons provide the most recent data (which includes data for two-year colleges): humanities professors self-identify 52.2 percent liberal, 44.3 percent moderate, 3.6 percent conservative; social science professors self-identify 58.2 percent liberal, 36.9 percent moderate, 4.9 percent conservative.[29] Again, the findings of Gross and Simmons support the conclusion that self-identified conservatives have been in decline.

The Refraction between D:R and L:C. Rothman, Lichter, and Nevitte present Harris Poll data showing patterns in the U.S. public. We have pursued this line of inquiry using Harris and Gallup data from 1989 to 2004 in a response to Zipp and Fenwick.[30] We found that Democrats were more likely than Republicans to call themselves middle/center; called themselves "liberal" less often than Republicans call themselves "conservative;" and called themselves "conservative" more often than Republicans call themselves "liberal." Those are findings about the public at large, but presumably they carried over at least weakly to professors as well. The upshot would be that social refraction causes D:R ratios to be substantially higher than liberal:conservative self-identification ratios.[31]

That refraction from D:R to L:C takes place is reinforced by Tobin and Weinberg.[32] They find that among faculty describing themselves as moderates, in the 2004 presidential election 68 percent voted for Kerry and 27 percent for Bush. Also, they found that only 1 percent of professors who self-identify as liberal/very liberal voted for Bush, while 8 percent of professors who self-identify as conservative/very conservative voted for Kerry.[33]

To summarize: (1) Self-identified "liberals" substantially outnumber "conservatives," especially in h/ss and especially when two-year colleges are excluded.[34] (2) L:C ratios are much lower than D:R ratios. We would add that tracking "liberal versus conservative" through the years is fraught with problems, even when confined to self-identification data. Evidence from Gross and Simmons indicates that being "moderate" is on the rise.

An Aside on Marxism. Gross and Simmons included a question that gave respondents opportunity to characterize themselves as "Marxist." We were surprised at how many did: 17.6 percent in the social sciences (including 25.5 percent of sociologists), 5.0 percent in the humanities, and 12.0 percent of all faculty at liberal arts colleges. Of the overall faculty of all kinds of schools, Marxists were 3.0 percent.[35]

Surveys of Policy Views: Laissez-Faire versus Intervention

Party affiliation and political labels are valuable only to the extent that they usefully summarize substantive views about policy and social affairs. The ambiguity and controversy surrounding labels argue for focusing on such views.

Surveys ask professors about a wide variety of social issues—not just basic issues of public policy, but also contemporary events (such as wars), morals and culture, and university affairs. An individual "issue" question is of limited importance in isolation. Usually, researchers ask a set of questions. But a set will generate confusion unless it is part of a *conceptual scheme*.

Almost invariably, researchers have imposed on sets of questions a "liberal versus conservative" scheme. We think that this scheme is inadequate, and ultimately represents a kind of society-wide groupthink that encompasses and joins "liberals" and "conservatives." We offer an alternative scheme for questions of public policy: laissez-faire versus government intervention/activism, on an issue-by-issue basis. Over the range of issues, researchers can then categorize respondents in ways that defy the "liberal versus conservative" framework.

Policy Questions from Earlier Surveys. Earlier surveys included interesting policy questions. Unfortunately, the only reporting on responses takes the minimal form of constructed index scores.

In surveys conducted between 1959 and 1964, Spaulding and Turner asked fourteen excellent policy questions, very much along a laissez-faire–intervention spectrum, and called being more laissez-faire "conservative."[36] They found (based on a policy index cutpoint) that the percentage of faculty who were conservative was 9 in philosophy, 10 in political science, 12 in sociology, 17 in history, 26 in psychology, 51 in botany, 54 in math, 61 in geology, and 66 in engineering. Thus, in the early 1960s, the sciences and math were laissez-faire-oriented to an extent that was very high relative to the h/ss fields, and surely high relative to today. Another survey conducted around 1963, summarized by Maranell and Eitzen, also shows science professors to be more "conservative."[37]

The 1969 Carnegie survey of professors asked about agreement with the statement "Marijuana should be legalized."[38] The "strongly agree" percentages by self-identified political view were 59 for left, 17 for liberal, 5 for middle-of-the-road, 3 for moderately conservative, and 4 for strongly conservative. The left professors were the most laissez-faire on the issue, by far.

Some Recent Policy Questions. The 1999 NAASS survey included a few policy questions and reported for all faculty.[39] "Agree" percentages (combining "strongly agree" and "somewhat agree") are as follows: "Government should work to ensure that everyone has a job," 66; "Government should work to reduce the income gap between rich and poor," 72; "More environmental protection is needed, even if it raises prices or costs jobs," 88. The questions are a bit ambiguous, but the results indicate that on those issues, professors mostly support government intervention. The survey also asked about abortion; 84 percent agreed that "it is a woman's right to decide whether or not to have an abortion." On that issue, there is special difficulty in applying a "laissez-faire versus intervention" framework, but we see pro-choice as the laissez-faire position.

The 2001 survey of economists, historians, political scientists, and sociologists sponsored by Brookings asked respondents to complete the statement "Generally speaking, government programs should be . . ." by choosing along a six-point range from "cut back to reduce the power of government" to "expanded to deal with important problems." Even economists leaned toward "expanded," the others strongly so—sociologists, super strongly.[40]

The IJCR survey of Tobin and Weinberg focused on foreign affairs but also contained a few "laissez-faire versus intervention" questions.[41] One asked whether the powers granted to the government under the Patriot Act should be strengthened, reduced, or left pretty much unchanged, and among all professors, 83 percent of Democrats responded "reduced" and 1 percent "strengthened," while for Republicans the percentages were 22 and 17, respectively. On that issue the Democrats are more laissez-faire. On other issues, Republicans are more laissez-faire. Two-thirds (66 percent) of Republicans agree and 16 percent disagree with the statement "People in developing countries benefit more than they lose from involvement of global corporations," while 27 percent of Democrats agree and 44 percent disagree.[42] Almost three-quarters (74 percent) of Republicans disagree and 17 percent agree with the statement "Although capitalism helped bring prosperity to this country, it is not well-suited to accomplish the same thing today in most developing nations," compared to 43 percent of Democrats who agree and 38 percent who disagree.[43]

Summary of the 2003 Policy Survey of Six Associations. We conclude with a summary of results from our 2003 survey.[44] We asked eighteen policy questions, each positing an existing government intervention and providing a five-point scale from "support strongly" to "oppose strongly." The format of the questions was uniform and lent itself to the construction of an index, with lower numbers being more interventionist, higher being more laissez-faire. The survey was sent to random samples of six scholarly associations. The lists of anthropologists, economists, historians, political scientists, and sociologists all came from the major American association for each group. The philosophers came from the American Society for Political and

Legal Philosophy. We treated those employed in academia as professors, and restricted the results to that group (n = 1208).

The eighteen policy issues were tariffs, minimum wage, workplace safety regulation, FDA drug approval, air and water regulation by the EPA, discrimination by private parties, "hard" drugs, prostitution, gambling, guns, government ownership of industry, redistribution, government schooling, monetary policy, fiscal policy, immigration, military aid or presence, and foreign aid.

The important results are as follows:

- On twelve of the eighteen policy issues, the Democrats were at least noticeably, often substantially, more interventionist than the Republicans.

- But Republicans were more interventionist on immigration, military action, prostitution restrictions, and drug prohibition.[45]

- Generally, the Democrats and Republicans fit the stereotypes, except that neither group is strongly laissez-faire on the issues that one might expect. The policy-index averages (which can range from 1 to 5, with lower being more interventionist, higher more laissez-faire) were Democrats 2.12, Republicans 2.69.[46] On the whole, Republicans gave laissez-faire supporters nothing to write home about, except perhaps their disappointment.

- The Democrats not only dominate, but they have a significantly narrower tent. Summing the standard deviation for each group's eighteen policy responses yields the contrast: Democrats 17.1, Republicans 23.1. Thus, whereas the Republicans usually have diversity on a policy issue, the Democrats very often have a party line—with almost no support for laissez-faire. It is clear that there is significantly more diversity under the Republican tent.

- Economists are measurably less interventionist than other disciplines but still, on the whole, lean toward intervention; rumors of widespread laissez-faire support among economists are very wrong. Only in relative terms does economics stand out.

- Economists show the least consensus on policy issues. The differences between Democrats and Republicans are largest in economics, and the standard deviations are largest. A lack of consensus is a curious thing for the so-called queen of the social sciences.

- Younger professors tend to be slightly less interventionist than older professors. This result suggests that, although faculty in h/ss have grown increasingly Democratic, they have not necessarily grown increasingly interventionist.

- The cluster analysis based on the policy questions sorted the respondents into five groups, four of which correspond to familiar ideological categories: establishment Left (n = 470), progressive (n = 413), conservative (n = 35), and classical liberal/libertarian (n = 35).[47] (These are labels we attribute to the groups; they are not self-identifications.)[48] *The cluster-analysis results suggest that people tend to cluster as certain ideological types, as opposed to being spread more or less uniformly between convex combinations of those types.*

- Of the one thousand academic respondents from the six associations with sufficient data to be included in the cluster analysis, therefore, thirty-five can appropriately be called "real" conservatives and thirty-five can be called "real" libertarians, facts that call for two important remarks: (1) Conservatives and libertarians, so defined, are rare. Of those seventy professors, forty-eight (68.6 percent) were in either economics or political science. In the other four fields surveyed, substantive conservatives and libertarians are close to absent. (2) Libertarians are as numerous as conservatives. In some ways, the h/ss fields are more congenial to libertarians, who tend to be culturally liberal and not religious.

- On immigration, drugs, prostitution, and the military, the conservatives are the most interventionist of the four familiar groups.

- The policy-index averages were as follows: establishment Left 1.99, progressive 2.26, conservative 2.75, libertarian 4.12.[49] In other words, the people who often stand strongly opposed to status quo interventions tend to be those whose views fit a libertarian pattern.[50]

Conclusion

Survey evidence and voter registration studies support the view that Democratic voters greatly outnumber Republican voters in academe. The estimate of 7:1 or 8:1 in the humanities and social sciences continues to hold up. There is evidence that the Democratic preponderance has increased greatly since around 1970 and is likely to continue to increase. In policy views, humanities and social science professors are mostly highly supportive of status quo interventions and lean left on issues such as redistribution and discrimination controls. Indeed, Gross and Simmons find a surprisingly high percentage of Marxists. Professors who vote Republican or self-identify as conservative seem to be in decline. Professors fitting a substantive conservative profile or a libertarian profile are very few in h/ss. Our analysis suggests that the substantive conservatives and libertarians are about equal in number. Economics is exceptional among h/ss for having a small but nonminiscule number of definite non-left professors.

Gross and Simmons report that moderates are on the rise and radicalism on the decline.[51] One may discount their report of increases among moderates on several grounds.[52] Meanwhile, however, Klein and Stern found a slight slope that says that the younger the professor, the less he supports government intervention overall.[53] Academe is a Democratic stronghold, but aggressive ideologies of state collectivism, such as socialism, continue to wane. Klein and Stern found that about 70 percent of humanities and social science professors who vote Democratic do *not* support government ownership of industrial enterprises.[54]

Increasingly, academe is best understood as an agglomeration of disciplinary tribes and subfields, each consisting of individuals primarily interested in making a career and enjoying personal comfort and security. The academic agglomeration is one of America's most established, static, and caste-based domains. Like pragmatic people in business careers, social-democratic academics need to be "moderate," and most of them seem to give the presumption to mainstream Democratic views. It is quite possible that fervent idealists for solidarity, equality, and social justice get disproportionate attention, and that even they are often unwilling to advocate radical reforms of greater government control.

Conservatives and libertarians have great reason to complain about the ideological climate of academe. But to conclude on a note of slight optimism: perhaps a growing pragmatism among the professoriate will allow for better discourse about public policy and, in time, will offer to people who favor individual liberty slightly more opportunity in the academic establishment.

Notes

1. Everett Carll Ladd Jr. and Seymour Martin Lipset, *The Divided Academy: Professors and Politics* (New York: McGraw-Hill, 1975); Michael A. Faia, "The Myth of the Liberal Professor," *Sociology of Education* 47 (1974): 171–202.

2. Christopher F. Cardiff and Daniel B. Klein, "Faculty Partisan Affiliation in All Disciplines: A Voter-Registration Study," *Critical Review* 17, no. 3–4 (2005): 237–55. In the Cardiff and Klein study, which achieved a high identification rate (about 71 percent) compared to other voter registration studies, 55 percent identified as either Democrat or Republican; the other 45 percent of the sample was divided among "not found" (19 percent), "decline to state/nonpartisan" (13 percent), "indeterminate because of multiple and conflicting listing of the name" (10 percent), "Green Party" (1 percent), and "other third parties" (1 percent). The indeterminates are white noise, but not-founds and decline-to-state/nonpartisans may invite speculation.

3. Daniel B. Klein and Charlotta Stern, "Political Diversity in Six Disciplines," *Academic Questions* 18, no. 1 (Winter 2005): 40–52. This article did not originally specify exclusion of two-year colleges; the authors do so here following John F. Zipp and Rudy Fenwick, "Is the Academy a Liberal Hegemony? The Political Orientations and Educational Values of Professors," *Political Opinion Quarterly* 70, no. 3 (2006): 304–26.

4. Cardiff and Klein, "Faculty Partisan Affiliation."

5. Ladd and Lipset, *Divided Academy*.

6. Incidentally, we'd like to take this opportunity to note a minor error in Cardiff and Klein, "Faculty Partisan Affiliation," 252. In reporting data by rank, the authors transposed the data for assistant and associate professors at Stanford and Berkeley. The data came from, and were reported correctly in, Daniel B. Klein and Andrew Western, "Voter Registration of Berkeley and Stanford Faculty," *Academic Questions* 18, no. 1 (2004–2005): 53–65.

7. Stanley Rothman, S. Robert Lichter, and Neil Nevitte, "Fundamentals and Fundamentalists: A Reply to Ames et al.," *Forum* 3, no. 2 (2005), http://www.bepress.com/forum/vol3/iss2/art8/.

8. Gary A. Tobin and Aryeh K. Weinberg, *A Profile of American College Faculty*, vol. 1, *Political Beliefs and Behavior* (San Francisco: Institute of Jewish and Community Studies, 2006).

9. Neil Gross and Solon Simmons, "The Social and Political Views of American Professors" (paper presented at the Harvard University Symposium on Professors and Their Politics, Cambridge, MA, October 6, 2007). Incidentally, regarding voting in the 2004 presidential election, Gross and Simmons report a quite surprising finding: among health sciences faculty—meaning mostly professors of nursing—48.1 percent voted for Kerry, 51.9 percent for Bush.

10. Paul F. Lazarsfeld and Wagner Thielens Jr., *The Academic Mind: Social Scientists in a Time of Crisis* (Glencoe, IL: Free Press of Glencoe, 1958).

11. Stanley Rothman, S. Robert Lichter, and Neil Nevitte, "Politics and Professional Advancement among College Faculty," *Forum* 3, no. 1 (2005), http://www.bepress.com/forum/vol3/iss1/art2/.

12. Tobin and Weinberg, *Profile of American College Faculty*, 1:24. We are surprised that this study did not find higher Kerry:Bush numbers. We do not know the composition/sampling of its "humanities" and "social sciences."

13. Gross and Simmons, "Social and Political Views of American Professors," 37.

14. Ladd and Lipset, *Divided Academy*, 193.

15. Klein and Stern, "Professors and Their Politics," 265.

16. Ibid., 288.

17. Gross and Simmons, "Social and Political Views of American Professors," 33.

18. The rejuvenation we speak of refers to the movement led by such figures as Ludwig von Mises, Friedrich Hayek, and Milton Friedman, who called themselves "liberal" and never "conservative." That movement is now often called "libertarian" in the United States, and "neoliberal" in Europe. In Continental Europe, especially Eastern Europe, "liberal" usually still largely means what it originally did.

19. For a more thorough criticism of "liberal versus conservative," see Daniel B. Klein and Charlotta Stern, "Liberal Versus Conservative Stinks," Society 2008, vol. 45: 488–95, which makes a thorough reply to Zipp and Fenwick on the ideological profile of faculty. The piece is available online at http://www.gmu.edu/departments/economics/klein/papers.html.

20. The second paper is Richard Hamilton and Lowell L. Hargens, "Politics of the Professors: Self-Identifications, 1969–1984," *Social Forces* 71, no. 3 (1993): 603–27; the other three papers have been cited in full above.

21. Zipp and Fenwick, "Is the Academy a Liberal Hegemony?" 304.

22. Faia, "Myth of the Liberal Professor," 171, 197.

23. The data collected within the framework of the Carnegie surveys are available to scholars through the Roper Center, http://www.ropercenter.uconn.edu/.

24. Data collected by the HERI are available for scholars at http://www.gseis.ucla.edu/heri/index.php.

25. Rothman, Lichter, and Nevitte, "Politics and Professional Advancement."

26. Tobin and Weinberg, *Profile of American College Faculty*.

27. The 2001 Brookings-sponsored survey of political scientists, economists, historians, and sociologists found that 58 percent of each group on average self-identified as very liberal/liberal, while 8 percent on average self-identified as very conservative/conservative. See Paul C. Light, "Government's Greatest Priorities of the Next Half Century," *Reform Watch*, no. 4 (December 2001), Brookings Institution.

28. Gross and Simmons, "Social and Political Views of American Professors," 29.

29. Ibid., 28.

30. Klein and Stern, "Liberal Versus Conservative Stinks."

31. Gross and Simmons, "Social and Political Views of American Professors," 35, reports findings at variance with the tendencies we find in the poll data. It should be

noted, however, that Gross and Simmons asked questions and categorized data in ways that tended to swell the ranks of the "moderates" and "independents," and they have not as yet provided the more refined data, nor, it seems, reported what percentage of "moderates" voted for Kerry in 2004.

32. Tobin and Weinberg, *Profile of American College Faculty*, 27.

33. Tobin and Weinberg also found that only 1 percent of professors who self-identify as Democrat voted for Bush, while 13 percent of the self-identified Republicans voted for Kerry. This remarkable asymmetry may say something about how professors self-identify by political party, something about the 2004 contest between Kerry and Bush, or both.

34. Similar findings for Canadian professors are reported in M. Reza Nakhaie and Robert J. Brym, "The Political Attitudes of Canadian Professors," *Canadian Journal of Sociology* 24, no. 3 (1999): 329–53.

35. With each label, Gross and Simmons, "Social and Political Views of American Professors," asked respondents to indicate how well, on a seven-point scale ranging from not at all to extremely well, the label fit them. They reported Marxists were those who marked a score of 4 or higher.

36. Charles B. Spaulding and Henry A. Turner, "Political Orientation and Field of Specialization among College Professors," *Sociology of Education* 41, no. 3 (1968): 247–62. In those days, with the New Deal only a few decades old and the rejuvenation of classical liberalism just beginning, the "conservative" attribution made more sense than it does today. These authors consider interventionists to be liberal. Note that they never present "liberal versus conservative" numbers.

37. Gary M. Maranell and D. Stanely Eitzen, "The Effect of Discipline, Region, and Rank on the Political Attitudes of College Professors," *Sociological Quarterly* 11, no. 1 (1970): 112–18. The exact year of the sampling is not specified, but Eitzen and Maranell, "Party Affiliation of Professors," noted that the sampling was based on college catalogues of 1962 (147).

38. Faia, "Myth of the Liberal Professor," 171, 194.

39. Rothman, Lichter, and Nevitte, "Politics and Professional Advancement."

40. Light, "Government's Greatest Priorities," 55.

41. Tobin and Weinberg, *Profile of American College Faculty*, 35–39.

42. Only 21 percent of humanities professors and 38 percent of social science professors agreed that global corporations offered net benefits.

43. Gross and Simmons, "Social and Political Views of American Professors," 43–44, asks a few questions about government policy, but we omit this study because it is more concerned with goals rather than specific policy measures. Also, in two cases, the "neither" response is so large as to make the results hard to interpret.

44. Klein and Stern, "Professors and Their Politics." We say "our" survey, but Stern did not become involved until after the survey was conducted. Blame Klein for all survey-design flaws.

45. On two issues—gambling and using monetary policy to fine-tune the economy—the parties appeared about evenly divided; the latter issue isn't clearly of the laissez-faire type, anyway.

46. The twenty respondents who reported voting mostly Green had an average policy-index score of 2.30, while the thirteen who reported voting mostly Libertarian had 4.24.

47. The fifth group, n = 47, is odd: center-left on most issues, but with rather permissive views on personal issues and somewhat hawkish.

48. Of the thirty-five attributed libertarians, fourteen (40 percent) vote Republican and twelve (34 percent) vote Libertarian. Of the thirty-five attributed conservatives, twenty-three (66 percent) vote Republican and none votes Libertarian.

49. The average for the other group (of forty-seven), which did not fit a familiar ideological type, was 2.53.

50. In fact, the minimum of the sum of position dissimilarity on each issue between the libertarians and any other group is greater than the maximum of sums of dissimilarity between any pair of other groups.

51. Gross and Simmons, "Social and Political Views of American Professors," 40–41.

52. See Klein and Stern, "Liberal Versus Conservative Stinks."

53. Klein and Stern, "Professors and Their Politics," 288.

54. Ibid., 268.

3

Left Pipeline: Why Conservatives Don't Get Doctorates

Matthew Woessner and April Kelly-Woessner

When attempting to explain the dominance of the political left among college faculty, one must grapple with the dearth of conservatives in the academic pipeline. Every year, self-identified liberals apply to PhD programs in far greater numbers than do conservatives. However, the reasons for this ideological imbalance are far from clear. Those on the political right tend to regard academia's liberal slant as evidence of discrimination against conservatives. By contrast, those on the political left often conclude that their overrepresentation in the academy is either a function of their acute interest in the liberal arts or evidence of superior intelligence.

Explaining the ideological imbalance in academia requires that researchers move beyond small-scale observations and anecdotal experiences. While individual tales of misfortune may provide clues to the overall cause of liberal dominance, they cannot tell us if those experiences are common. To examine the problem systematically, we turn to a set of surveys developed by the UCLA Higher Education Research Institute (HERI). Administered at both the beginning and the end of students' college careers, the HERI surveys ask students to assess their educational experience, career goals, personal values, ideological dispositions, and views on a number of important political controversies. The specific data used in our analysis are from a 2004 survey of 15,569 college seniors, attending 149 U.S. colleges throughout the United States. While the surveys, administered to the same students both at the beginning and the end of their college careers, cannot definitely explain why

FIGURE 3-1
COLLEGE SENIORS INTERESTED IN PURSUING A PhD

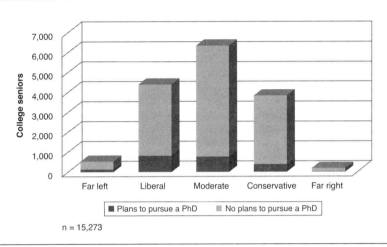

n = 15,273

SOURCE: *HERI 2004 College Student Survey.*

liberals pursue doctoral degrees more often than conservatives do, the results provide important clues to the underlying cause of the disparity.

The ideological imbalance among college students is evident immediately in figure 3-1. Overall, liberals and the far left constitute 32 percent of respondents, while conservatives and the far right make up 26 percent of respondents. Additionally, the figure shows that those on the political left are more likely than those on the right to express an interest in pursuing a PhD. Overall, 13 percent of respondents indicated that they planned to seek a doctorate. However, of those on the political left, 19 percent indicated that they planned to pursue a PhD, including 18 percent of liberals and 24 percent of the far left. Among students on the political right, slightly fewer than 10 percent indicated that they planned to get a doctorate, including 9 percent of conservatives and 11 percent of the far right. The college faculty pipeline is indeed slanted; in addition to being the minority, conservatives aspire to pursue doctoral degrees only half as often as liberals.

Drawing on theories espoused by both liberals and conservatives, we use the HERI data to examine several explanations for conservatives' relative lack of interest in pursuing doctoral degrees. We consider whether liberals and conservatives differ in four measures, each of which has the potential to influence educational aspirations and career goals: satisfaction with the college experience, academic performance, relationships with faculty, and personal goals and values.

Overall College Experience

There is reason to assume that liberals and conservatives have different experiences in college. If critics of the academy are correct, the liberal enclave provides a chilly environment for conservatives. This may not be the result of intentional discrimination. Rather, conservatives may simply find themselves to be in the minority and disconnected from the rest of the campus. According to previous research, satisfaction with the college experience does help to predict whether a student will complete an advanced degree,[1] so we might expect to find that conservative students were less satisfied with college than liberal students.

Figure 3-2 provides six distinct measures of college seniors' assessments of their undergraduate experience, broken down by self-reported ideology.[2] Each of the assessment scores is based on a four-point scale, with a higher score indicating greater satisfaction. By all six measures, students were, on balance, satisfied with their college experience. What small differences do exist between liberal and conservatives are in the opposite direction from what one might expect. Conservatives and those on the far right actually report a slightly higher satisfaction with college (3.29) than do liberals and those on the far left (3.21). Accordingly, the measures of college satisfaction shown in figure 3-2 fail to explain the ideological imbalance among PhDs.[3] While conservatives may still experience some hostility in individual courses or among certain disciplines, it appears that, if discrimination does occur, it does not profoundly affect their overall assessments of the college experience.

Academic Performance

One of the more straightforward theories concerning the ideological slant among PhDs is that ideology reflects intelligence or academic performance,

FIGURE 3-2

ASSESSMENTS OF THE COLLEGE EXPERIENCE

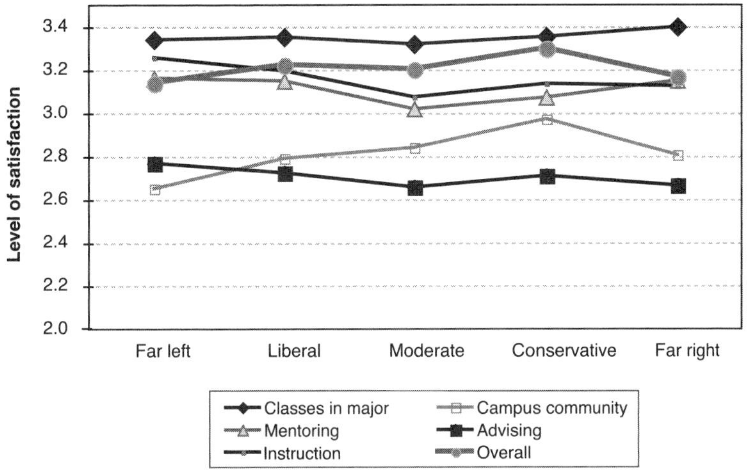

SOURCE: *HERI 2004 College Student Survey.*

such that conservatives are not able to compete in the graduate school admission process. It is worth noting that grades alone are not a perfect indication of intelligence. Differences in academic performance between liberals and conservatives could be a reflection of students' interest in the course material, their effort in school, or even discrimination in grading. Nevertheless, universities rely heavily on college grades as an indicator of candidates' preparation for graduate study. If conservatives earn lower marks than liberals do, their exclusion from academia may be justifiable.

The HERI College Senior Survey asks students to mark a box that best represents their college grade point average. Listed on a six-point scale, categories range from 1, indicating that the student scored a C- or less, to 6, indicating that the student maintained a nearly perfect A average. Figure 3-3 breaks down the survey responses by both ideology and four broad academic categories of college major: hard sciences, social sciences, humanities, and professional studies. (Lines representing the average grades of students majoring in each discipline are drawn only if the survey sample was sufficiently large—thirty or more students responding in each category of the survey—to provide reliable estimates. For example, only twenty-eight of the nearly three thousand humanities students indicated that they fell on the far right of the ideological spectrum, so we omitted their responses.)[4]

The thick gray line running near the middle of the chart indicates the overall breakdown of grades by ideology.

At first glance, one pattern becomes immediately clear. Variations in reported grades are not a function of conservatism, but rather a function of moderation. Moderates—defined in the HERI survey as being "middle-of-the-road"—consistently report lower grades than do their liberal and conservative counterparts.[5] Of the approximately seven hundred students on the far edges of the ideological spectrum, students on the far left enjoy a grade advantage of two-tenths of a point over students on the far right. Eight thousand students identify themselves as merely liberal or conservative; their reported college grades are effectively identical. Taken together, students who identify as either liberal or far left do enjoy a slight advantage over students who see themselves as conservative or far right. However, this three one-hundredths of a point difference hardly explains the abundance of liberals who seek doctoral degrees. Furthermore, in light of the fact that the more scholastically challenged moderates pursue doctoral degrees in higher numbers than their conservative classmates (see figure 3-1), it is clear that academic performance does not explain the shortage of conservatives in graduate school.

Faculty Mentoring

When deciding on whether to pursue a PhD, undergraduates may be heavily influenced by their relationship with their professors. We hypothesize that faculty-student relationships depend, in part, on the identification of shared values. According to Erkut and Mokros, "people emulate models who are perceived to be similar to themselves in terms of personality characteristics, background, race, and sex."[6] Students who find themselves ideologically at odds with the majority of their professors may be less likely to initiate out-of-class contact with faculty and form close mentoring relationships. In a number of studies, researchers find that individuals generally avoid disagreement, choosing to associate with politically like-minded individuals.[7]

Even if students are not aware of faculty members' ideologies, they will likely seek mentors who have interests and values that reflect their own. For

FIGURE 3-3
COLLEGE GRADES BY IDEOLOGICAL ORIENTATION

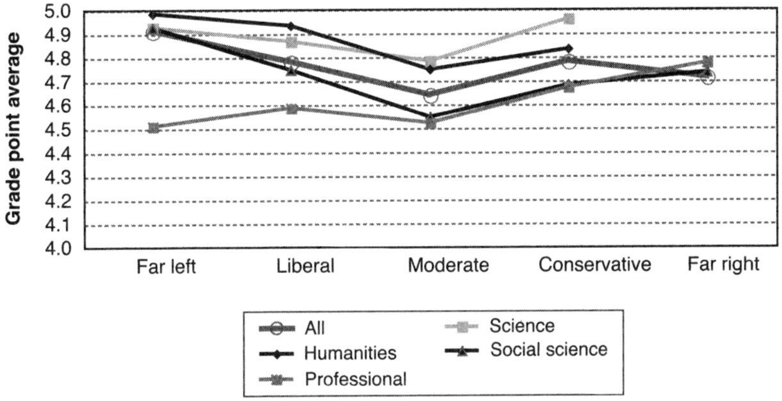

SOURCE: *HERI 2004 College Student Survey.*

example, students interested in peace studies are likely to seek mentors in this area. The overrepresentation of liberals among college professors means that liberal students have a larger pool of possible mentors from which to choose and are more likely to find one with whom they have something in common. There is evidence that relationships with faculty mentors have positive effects on students' success during college.[8] Hence, students who form close bonds with their instructors may be more likely to be interested in obtaining a doctoral degree.

To assess whether ideological differences meaningfully influence the student-faculty relationship, we examined the responses to seven HERI survey questions on students' interaction with faculty. The questions measured the following:

1. Student success in getting to know faculty

2. How often faculty provided emotional support and encouragement

3. Student ability to find faculty or staff mentor

4. How frequently the student met with faculty during office hours

5. How frequently the student had been a guest in a professor's home

6. How frequently the student worked on research projects with faculty

7. How frequently the student met with faculty outside of class or office hours

In order to claim that any of these factors contributes to the relative dearth of conservatives with PhDs, one needs to establish that the measure of student-faculty relationship is related to a student's interest in acquiring a PhD, and that this measure varies between liberals and conservatives.

When placed in a statistical model alongside measures of each student's ideology, sex, general assessment of college, grades, and various measures of personal goals, only three of the faculty-student relationship variables turn out to be important: being a guest in a professor's home, having opportunities to work on research projects, and meeting with the professor outside of class. (See table 3-1 for details on the full regression model.) The first three factors (getting to know the faculty, receiving emotional support or encouragement, and finding a faculty or staff mentor) are completely unrelated to a decision to pursue a PhD. The fourth factor (meeting with faculty during office hours) is related to the decision to pursue a doctorate, but the magnitude of the difference is so small that it is not theoretically meaningful.

Figure 3-4 illustrates the responses to the three student-faculty relationship measurements that do predict interest in a PhD.[9] For each of these, students on the political left enjoy a small advantage over students on the political right. Somewhat surprisingly, the measure of students' visits to professors' homes shows the least evidence of ideological bias. Moderates are the least likely to have been the guests of their instructors. Overall, the liberals and conservatives report almost the same propensity to visit their professors' homes. However, those on the far left report a higher visitation rate than those on the far right. At least among strong ideologues, those on the left do appear to have better relationships with faculty.

Although the survey responses on the remaining two measurements are not dramatically different, they further indicate that ideological factors may genuinely inhibit the student-faculty relationship. Whereas moderates are the least likely to visit a professor's home, conservatives are the least likely to meet with a professor outside of class or office hours. When it comes to conducting research—a pivotal experience for any undergraduate seriously

FIGURE 3-4

ASSESSMENTS OF THE STUDENT-FACULTY RELATIONSHIP

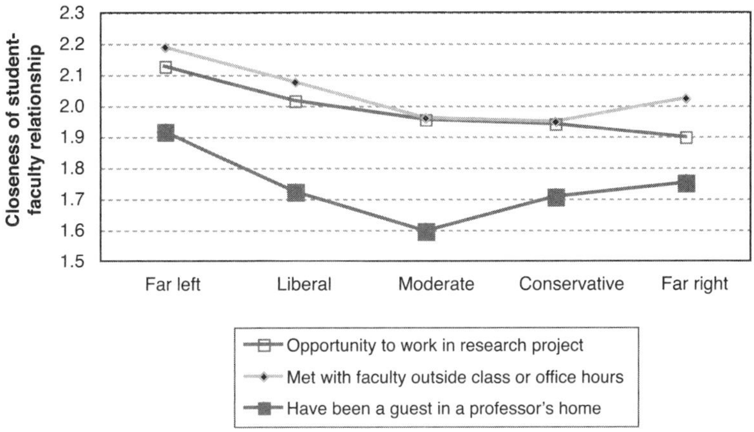

SOURCE: *HERI 2004 College Student Survey.*

considering a doctoral program—those on the far right come in dead last. The difference in scores is relatively small; but since the opportunity to conduct research is a relatively important predictor of interest in a doctoral degree, this distinction probably matters.

Figure 3-4 indicates that students on the political left (particularly on the far left) appear to enjoy somewhat closer relationships to their professors. These relationship variables are correlated with a desire to pursue a doctoral degree. However, the relative influence of these variables on the statistical model is small, indicating that the liberal advantage in faculty-student mentoring cannot fully explain why liberals are more drawn to graduate study.

Money, Creativity, and Family Values

Although there has been little direct study of the role that ideology plays in decisions to pursue doctoral degrees, there is indirect evidence that ideological differences probably do relate to career choice. Ideological differences are, in part, a reflection of differences in personality traits and values. There is a growing field of research on the relationship between inherent personality traits and political dispositions. Early research revolved around the concept of an "authoritarian personality,"[10] which was understood to exhibit a high level of submission to authority and loyalty to existing institutions and social conventions, and hence to be drawn to conservative political ideology.[11] Other research has argued that the New Left ideologues show "tendencies toward rebellion . . . expressed through reactive opposition to social authority and identification with its opponents."[12]

Liberal and conservative ideologies reflect not only specific responses to authority but also a number of competing values. According to Conover and Feldman, the core meaning of these ideological labels is focused on "change vs. the preservation of traditional values."[13] Whatever the basis of ideological identification, however, the differences between liberals and conservatives translate into differences in policy attitudes, behaviors, and dispositions, not all of which have direct political implications. For example, liberals and conservatives tend to differ on measures of the widely used NEO Personality Inventory.[14] Liberals tend to score higher in creativity and excitement seeking, while conservatives outperform in orderliness and striving for achievement.[15]

It is reasonable to assume that these differences in personalities and values translate into differences in career goals. For example, if liberals and conservatives have different notions of authority, this would theoretically translate into liberals selecting careers that are less hierarchical and that allow greater personal autonomy. In fact, Lindholm argues that the need for autonomy, independence, and intellectual freedom is the most cited reason college professors give for choosing academic careers.[16] Similarly, if liberals are more likely to value creativity, as Carney et al. suggest, they may be more likely to self-select into the arts and humanities, with the more practical conservatives opting for professional fields.[17]

Choice of a college major may itself direct students toward or away from further education. Students who choose college majors that translate easily into concrete, marketable skills are less likely to pursue a PhD. This tendency is no more evident than in comparisons of business students to those majoring in the humanities. For example, of the HERI respondents who majored in philosophy, 39 percent indicated an interest in obtaining a PhD (n = 105) while only 5 percent of accounting majors (n = 399) and 13 percent of computer science majors (n = 100) had similar intentions. Overall,

FIGURE 3-5
DISTRIBUTION OF STUDENTS WITHIN MAJOR FIELDS OF STUDY

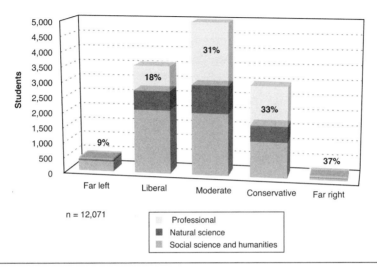

SOURCE: *HERI 2004 College Student Survey.*

one in four students who majored in the natural sciences, the social sciences, or the humanities expressed an interest in obtaining a doctorate, as compared to one in fourteen students in the professional majors (communications, law enforcement, marketing, finance, business administration, etc).

The causal direction of this relationship is still unclear. It may be that students select college majors depending on their inclination for graduate study: those who are not inclined toward further education may look to acquire skills that are immediately marketable, whereas those inclined toward graduate study select fields that emphasize abstract reasoning and other less tangible skills. It may also be that students consider graduate school when their undergraduate degree fails to produce attractive employment opportunities. Whichever the case, it appears that conservatives are more likely to enter the professional fields, which generate less interest in graduate school.

Figure 3-5 illustrates just how significantly liberals and conservatives differ in their propensity to major in a professional field. Only 9 percent of the far left and 18 percent of liberals major in professional fields, as compared to 33 percent of conservatives and 37 percent of the far right. Since liberals already outnumber conservatives among college students, this tendency for conservatives to congregate in professional degree programs means that liberals outnumber conservatives two to one in the humanities and social sciences—fields most likely produce interest in doctoral study.

There is some question about what the distribution of ideology across majors really means. Do conservatives generally enjoy the humanities and social sciences but allow practical considerations to push them into professional fields, or are these fields simply less appealing to them? Would conservatives find these courses more appealing if the faculty who taught them better represented their own viewpoints?

Figure 3-6 indicates that the choice of major is more than a practical consideration. Since students are often required to take general education courses across the curriculum, conservatives do get a taste of the humanities and social sciences. As figure 3-6 clearly illustrates, conservatives are less satisfied with their experiences in social science and humanities courses than are their liberal counterparts.[18] In light of the fact that conservatives tend to have a more positive assessment of science and math courses, as well as of classes within their major, than of humanities and social science classes, it is clear that their pockets of dissatisfaction are not simply the by-product of a negative disposition. While it is difficult to know what precisely is driving their opinions, some of our earlier research on the effects of politics in the classroom may provide important clues. Within political science courses, we found clear evidence that students who believed they were at odds with their professor's politics were generally more critical of the professor, the course, and the subject matter.[19] Perhaps it should come as no surprise that conservatives tend to be less satisfied with their coursework in fields notoriously dominated by the political left. It is also possible that liberals simply enjoy abstract courses in the arts, where creativity is more widely encouraged. Yet, regardless of the underlying cause, conservatives' preference for certain topics and specialties clearly contributes to their relative scarcity among doctoral candidates.

The conservative propensity to seek professional degrees tells only part of the story. Even within a given field, conservatives are still less likely to express an interest in a doctoral degree. Among humanities majors, 19 percent of students to the right of center expressed an interest in pursuing a PhD, as compared to 30 percent of those to the left of center. The same

FIGURE 3-6
SATISFACTION WITH CLASSES

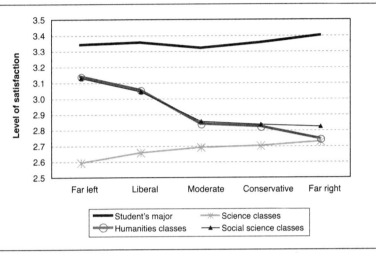

SOURCE: *HERI 2004 College Student Survey.*

pattern holds within the social sciences, where 16 percent of those on the right expressed an interest in pursuing a PhD, as compared to 30 percent of those on the left.

Suspecting that fundamental differences between liberals and conservatives might contribute to the left's dominance of academia, we compared student preferences on five issues associated with pursing a PhD.[20] The first factor, the importance given to raising a family, is a useful predictor of educational goals, since pursing a doctorate usually involves postponing children for four to six years. Statistically, those who rate family as a priority are less likely to express an interest in pursuing a doctorate. The second factor, the importance of writing original works, provides some indication of a student's desire to work in a creative environment. Students who indicate that writing original works is a priority are typically more interested in getting a PhD. The third factor, being well-off financially, is an important predictor of seeking a doctorate, for a number of reasons. The most prized PhD students enjoy university support for tuition, books, and a humble monthly stipend. However, many doctoral students spend their graduate years slowly accumulating a mountain of debt. While the salaries offered to PhDs may be

FIGURE 3-7

PERSONAL PRIORITIES AND IDEOLOGY

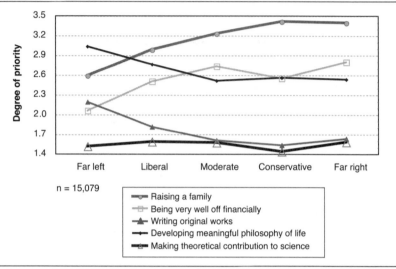

SOURCE: *HERI 2004 College Student Survey.*

attractive, the road to graduation is long and financially burdensome. Not surprisingly, students who place a high priority on being well-off financially are less likely to express an interest in attaining a doctoral degree. The fourth factor, developing a meaningful philosophy of life, captures a segment of the student population that seems particularly enamored with the intellectual exercises so often associated with academics. Not surprisingly, students who place a premium on developing a meaningful life philosophy are more interested in pursuing a PhD than their more practically oriented counterparts. The final factor, a desire to make a theoretical contribution to science, reveals a student's interest in research, which is the factor most closely associated with a desire to seek a PhD. (See table 3-1 for the relative importance of these factors.)

The results listed in figure 3-7 tell an important story. Unlike the previous figures, where the measurements hardly varied across the spectrum from the far left to the far right, all but one of the personal priority measures indicate relatively sharp differences between liberals and conservatives. More significantly, all of the differences highlighted in figure 3-7 run in the same direction, discouraging conservatives from pursuing a doctoral degree. Conservatives are simultaneously more family oriented, less interested in writing original works, more focused on financial success, less interested in developing a meaningful philosophy of life,[21] and less interested in making a theoretical contribution to science. It seems that, overall, the personal priorities of those on the left are more compatible with pursing a PhD. Personal preferences in combination seem to have a greater impact on conservatives' educational aspirations than any other factors in the statistical model.

The relative importance of money, family, and professionally oriented (practical) degree programs to liberals and conservatives does have one important implication. These underlying values are not likely to be the consequence of students' collegiate experience, but rather to reflect differences between liberals and conservatives that occur as the result of early socialization and/or innate personality differences. There is some indication that, as it pertains to their interest in pursuing a doctoral degree, the difference between liberals and conservatives predates their college experience.

Figure 3-8 provides snapshots of students' interest in obtaining a doctorate taken at two different points in time.[22] The black line shows the comparative interest of students as they enter college, broken down by ideology. The gray line denotes the intentions of the same individual students four years later, as they are about to graduate. The results from the freshman survey indicate that, even before they begin their college career, those on the left are most likely to indicate interest in a doctoral degree. At the beginning of their first year, 26 percent of left-leaning respondents expressed an interest in pursuing a doctorate, compared with 15 percent of those on the right. Some four years later, the left's advantage has grown.

It should come as no surprise that, over the course of four years, students often change their minds about their educational objectives. Looking to individual responses, most of the students who came to college intending to pursue a doctorate changed their minds by their senior year. Whereas two-thirds of moderates, conservatives, and those on the far right changed their mind about pursuing a doctorate by their senior year, just under half of those on the left altered their educational goals. On the opposite end of the spectrum, a vast majority of those who entered college with no intention of seeking a doctoral degree felt similarly by their senior year. Yet again, liberals and those on the far left were far more likely to express a newfound

FIGURE 3-8

PLANS TO SEEK A DOCTORATE

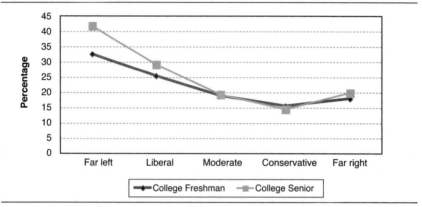

SOURCES: *HERI 2004 College Student Survey and HERI 1999 Survey Incoming Freshman.*

interest in a doctoral degree (22 percent) when compared to moderates (15 percent) and those right of center (11 percent). We cannot explain why students' educational goals change over time or why these shifts tend to benefit those on the left. However, if conservatives were abandoning their dreams of pursing a doctorate largely as a result of political persecution, we might expect to see a greater difference in the opt-out rate between the far right/conservatives (65 percent) and moderates (62 percent). The substantially lower opt-out rate among left-of-center students (47 percent) might indicate that liberal students are more likely to find faculty mentors who guide them toward graduate study.

Conclusion

A lack of ideological diversity within academia is arguably a serious problem, especially in the social sciences and the humanities, where philosophical orientations may affect teaching and research. Yet, since the underlying cause is rather complex, there is no simple solution to this imbalance.

The results in figure 3-7 confirm something that political scientists and social psychologists have long known: ideology represents far more than a collection of abstract political values. Liberalism is more closely associated with a desire for excitement, an interest in creative outlets, and an aversion to a structured work environment.[23] Conservatism is linked to a greater interest in financial success and a stronger desire to raise families. From this perspective, the ideological imbalance that permeates much of academia may be somewhat intractable. While there are steps that universities can take to narrow the ideological gap, it seems unlikely that any measures will achieve anything approaching ideological parity. Nevertheless, the results of our analysis do suggest two important ways (short of imposing ideological quotas) that universities may attract conservative students to doctoral programs.

First, in light of our prior research, which shows that students react negatively to overt partisanship, professors within the social sciences and the humanities should make a special effort to depoliticize their classrooms.[24] This does not suggest that political science or history courses should be bland or noncontroversial. Rather, if professors present both major ideological perspectives on contemporary issues and debates, they may help to reduce conservatives' relative dissatisfaction with their social science and humanities classes. If, in turn, conservatives enjoyed these courses more, they might be more likely to major in or get a doctorate in these disciplines.

Second, since conservatives place an especially high priority on financial security and raising a family, the academy needs to adopt policies that make academia a more family-friendly environment for their faculty. As it is, graduate school is not financially lucrative, and pretenure faculty careers often leave little time for family. In fact, a significant number of academics report that they delay marriage, delay having a family, or have fewer children than they desire because they worry that family life will interfere with their career goals. Those who have children report that they feel pressure to hide family obligations and put in extra "face time" on campus because they fear that children will be used against them in the tenure and promotion process.[25] The incompatibility of family life and academics is not imagined. One study shows that women who have babies early in their careers are less likely to receive tenure.[26] Given the demands of family life, the career of an academic is not especially appealing to individuals who place a priority on raising a family.[27]

Universities should adopt a more family-friendly approach to recruiting both prospective doctoral students and young faculty. For prospective graduate students, this might include subsidized housing for married couples,

TABLE 3-1

MAIN REGRESSION MODEL PREDICTING COLLEGE SENIORS SEEKING A PHD

Predictors (Listed in Order of Importance)	B	Standard Error	Std Beta
Statistically significant			
Wish to make theoretical contribution to science	0.081	0.005	0.169
Ideological orientation in 2003	0.044	0.005	0.095
Professional college major?	−0.077	0.008	−0.092
Wish to write original works	0.034	0.004	0.080
Average college grade	0.031	0.004	0.071
Opportunity to work in research project	0.036	0.005	0.068
Wish to be very well off financially	−0.026	0.004	−0.062
Self-confidence (intellectual)	0.022	0.005	0.044
Have been a guest in a professor's home	0.027	0.006	0.043
Wish to raise a family	−0.018	0.004	−0.041
Met with faculty outside class/office hours	0.022	0.007	0.035
Satisfied overall	−0.019	0.006	−0.034
Wish to develop meaningful philosophy of Life	0.010	0.004	0.027
Met with faculty during office hours	0.019	0.009	0.024
Not significant			
Satisfied with mentor	0.008	0.006	0.017
Opportunity to discuss coursework outside class	0.011	0.007	0.017
Wish to become a community leader	−0.007	0.004	−0.016
Opportunity to publish	−0.004	0.007	−0.006
Success in getting to know faculty	0.004	0.008	0.006
Satisfied with instruction	0.003	0.006	0.005
Emotional support and encouragement from faculty	0.002	0.007	0.004
Student's sex	0.003	0.008	0.003
(Constant)	−0.439	0.041	

SOURCE: Authors' calculations.

t-score	Sig	Average Independent Variable Scores by Ideology				Advantage for PhD
		Left	Middle	Right	All	
17.049	0.000	1.576	1.572	1.442	1.539	Liberal
9.680	0.000	n/a	n/a	n/a	n/a	Liberal
−9.118	0.000	0.206	0.367	0.381	0.320	Liberal
7.887	0.000	1.852	1.607	1.538	1.667	Liberal
7.136	0.000	4.793	4.639	4.777	4.725	Negligible
6.484	0.000	2.028	1.954	1.939	1.973	Liberal
−6.016	0.000	2.455	2.732	2.561	2.598	Liberal
4.295	0.000	3.896	3.766	3.863	3.834	Negligible
4.170	0.000	1.743	1.595	1.707	1.672	Liberal
−4.211	0.000	2.941	3.227	3.409	3.183	Liberal
3.037	0.002	2.357	2.276	2.265	2.299	Liberal
−2.998	0.003	3.213	3.200	3.291	3.228	Liberal
2.608	0.009	2.789	2.513	2.557	2.613	Liberal
2.216	0.027	2.357	2.276	2.265	2.299	Liberal
1.494	0.135					
1.525	0.127					
−1.601	0.109					
−0.598	0.550					
0.491	0.623					
0.425	0.671					
0.337	0.736					
0.342	0.732					
−10.656	0.000					

health insurance for spouses and young children, and an open commitment to work with young parents whose academic progress will inevitably be constrained by family considerations. For young faculty, the option of suspending the tenure clock to care for a newborn child would assure family-oriented conservatives that raising children will not jeopardize their academic career. Recently, several top universities have taken such measures. Princeton University increased support for graduate student parents to include paid maternity leave, child care benefits, and mortgage assistance.[28] Other schools have made serious efforts to accommodate the needs of junior faculty members by providing maternity leave and assistance for child care.[29] While these types of family-friendly policies are often designed to attract more women to academia, the data seem to suggest that they would also serve to make doctoral programs more attractive to conservative, family-oriented students. In fact, these programs would likely have the greatest effect on recruiting one of academia's least represented groups—conservative women.

Finally, although values and choice appear to provide the best explanation for why more conservatives do not get doctorates, it is important to note that our model explains only a portion of the difference between liberal and conservative career aspirations. Even accounting for grades, mentoring, personal choice, and a host of other factors, ideology remains the second best predictor of a student's intent to pursue a doctorate (see table 3-1). In fact, there remains a great deal that we do not understand about the relationship between ideology and the intention to pursue a PhD. For example, while a host of concrete indicators (overall satisfaction with college experience, grade point average, contact with faculty, etc.) do not tend to support the assertion that conservatives are frequently the victims of discrimination, academia may create an environment that *appears* hostile to young conservatives. Just as academic institutions have, in the pursuit of racial and ethnic diversity, taken great care to foster a climate of tolerance, so too should they consider how their doctoral programs might be made more inviting to ideological conservatives. Ultimately, the academy's relevance is dependent on its ability to recruit and retain scholars from diverse intellectual traditions.

Notes

1. See William E. Knox, Paul Lindsay, and Mary N. Kolb, "Higher Education, College Characteristics, and Student Experiences: Long-Term Effects on Educational Satisfactions and Perceptions," *Journal of Higher Education* 63 (1992): 303–28.

2. Students were asked to indicate their level of satisfaction with "courses in major field," "overall quality of instruction," "academic advising," "ability to find a faculty/staff mentor," "sense of community on campus," and "overall college experience." Each measure is based on a four-point scale, where 1 indicates the respondent was "dissatisfied," 2 indicates "neutral," 3 indicates "satisfied," and 4 indicates "very satisfied."

3. Rather unexpectedly, our research findings show that the decision to pursue a PhD is negatively correlated with overall satisfaction. Put simply, those who report a greater level of satisfaction with their college experience were less likely to express interest in earning a PhD. However, the difference in satisfaction between those who plan to attend graduate school and those who do not is relatively small.

4. Of the 2,945 respondents who indicated they were in a humanities-related major, 28 placed themselves on the far right of the ideological spectrum, scoring an average 4.54 with a standard deviation of 1.138 on the grade scale. In the natural sciences only 21 of 2,153 respondents placed themselves on the far right of the ideological spectrum. Together they scored an average of 5.10 with a standard deviation of 1.179 on the same grade scale.

5. Concerned that less-intelligent students might have self-identified as moderates simply because they did not comprehend the ideological classifications used in the survey question, we reclassified the respondents based on their answers to a battery of political questions included near the end of the student survey. We found that students who take objectively moderate positions on important political issues do earn lower grades than their ideological classmates do.

6. Samru Erkut and Janice R. Mokros, "Professors as Models and Mentors for College Students," *American Educational Research Journal* 21 (1984): 400.

7. Robert Huckfeldt and John Sprague, *Citizens, Politics, and Social Communication: Information and Influence in an Election Campaign* (New York: Cambridge University Press, 1995); see also Diana Mutz and Paul S. Martin, "Facilitating Communication across Lines of Political Difference: The Role of the Mass Media," *American Political Science Review* 95 (2001): 97–114.

8. Ernest Pascarella and Patrick Terenzini, "Patterns of Student-Faculty Informal Interaction beyond the Classroom and Voluntary Freshman Attrition," *Journal of Higher Education* 48 (1977): 540–52; Ernest Pascarella, Patrick Terenzini, and James Hibel, "Student-Faculty Interaction Settings and Their Relationship to Predicted Academic Performance," *Journal of Higher Education* 49 (1978): 450–63; Ernest Pascarella, "Student-Faculty Informal Contact and College Outcomes," *Review of Educational Research* 50 (1980): 545–95.

9. Students were asked, "How often have professors at your current (or most recent) college provided you with an opportunity to work on a research project," and "Since entering college, indicate how often you: (1) have been a guest in a professor's home, (2) met with a professor outside class or office hours." The values in figure 3-4 are all coded on a three-point scale, where 1 indicates "not at all," 2 indicates "occasionally," and 3 indicates "frequently."

10. T. W. Adorno, Else Frenkel-Brunswick, Daniel Levinson, and R. Nevitt Sanford, *The Authoritarian Personality* (New York: Harper, 1950).

11. R. A. Altemeyer, *Right-Wing Authoritarianism* (Winnipeg: University of Manitoba Press, 1981).

12. S. Robert Lichter and Stanley Rothman, "The Radical Personality: Social Psychological Correlates of New Left Ideology," *Political Behavior* 4 (1982): 207–35.

13. Pamela Johnston Conover and Stanley Feldman, "The Origins and Meaning of Liberal/Conservative Self-Identification," *American Journal of Political Science* 25 (1981): 617–45.

14. For a description of this personality assessment, see P. T. Costa Jr. and R. R. McCrae, "Normal Personality Assessment in Clinical Practice: The NEO Personality Inventory," *Psychological Assessment* 4 (1992): 5–13.

15. D. Carney, J. T. Jost, S. D. Gosling, K. Niederhoffer, and J. Potter, "The Secret Lives of Liberals and Conservatives: Personality Profiles, Interpersonal Styles, and the Things They Leave Behind" (manuscript, 2006), http://www.wjh.harvard.edu/~dcarney/Carney,%20Jost,%20Gosling.pdf.

16. Jennifer A. Lindholm, "Pathways to the Professoriate: The Role of Self, Others, and Environment in Shaping Academic Career Aspirations," *Journal of Higher Education* 75 (2002): 603–35.

17. D. Carney et. al., "Secret Lives of Liberals and Conservatives."

18. The question is based on a four-point scale, where 1 indicates the respondent was "dissatisfied," 2 indicates "neutral," 3 indicates "satisfied," and 4 indicates "very satisfied."

19. April Kelly-Woessner and Matthew Woessner, "My Professor Is a Partisan Hack: How Perceptions of a Professor's Political Views Affect Student Course Evaluations," *PS: Political Science and Politics* 39, no. 3 (2006): 495–501; April Kelly-Woessner and Matthew Woessner, "Conflict in the Classroom: Considering the Effects of Partisan Difference on Political Education," *Journal of Political Science Education* 4, no. 3 (July 2008): 265–85.

20. Each of the measures asks students to "indicate the importance to you personally of each of the following," including "raising a family," "being very well-off financially," "writing original works," and "developing a meaningful philosophy of life." All items are scored on a four-point scale, where 1 indicates the respondent rated the issue as "not important," 2 indicates "somewhat important," 3 indicates "very important," and 4 indicates "essential."

21. It is worth noting that moderates were consistently the least interested in developing a meaningful philosophy of life. While conservatives and the far right express

a greater interest in this life pursuit, they are ultimately outdone by the liberals and the far left. Nearly 22 percent of conservatives and 33 percent of the far right felt developing a meaningful philosophy of life was essential. By contrast, 27 percent of liberals and 40 percent of the far left felt it was essential.

22. Students were told, "Please indicate the highest degree you plan to complete eventually at any institution."

23. D. Carney et al.,"The Secret Lives of Liberals and Conservatives."

24. April Kelly-Woessner and Matthew Woessner, "My Professor Is a Partisan Hack." See also April Kelly-Woessner and Matthew Woessner, "Conflict in the Classroom."

25. Robert Drago, Carol Colbeck, Kai Dar Stauffer, Amy Pirretti, Kurt Burkum, Jennifer Fazioli, Gabriela Lazzaro, and Tara Habasevich, "The Avoidance of Bias against Caregiving," *American Behavioral Scientist* 49, no. 2 (2006): 1222–47. See also Joan Williams, "Singing the Grad-School Baby Blues," *Chronicle of Higher Education*, April 20, 2004, http://chronicle.com/jobs/news/2004/04/2004042001c.htm.

26. Mary Ann Mason, "Do Babies Matter? The Effect of Family Formation on the Lifelong Careers of Women," *Academe* 88, no. 6 (2002): 21–27.

27. Despite popular misconceptions about the lives of academics, most college professors actually maintain a rather rigorous work schedule, with the average full-time faculty member working in excess of fifty hours a week. See Robin Wilson, "Are Faculty Members Overworked?" *Chronicle of Higher Education*, November 5, 2004, 14.

28. Scott Jaschik, "Making Grad School 'Family Friendly,'" *Inside Higher Ed*, April 4, 2007, http://www.insidehighered.com/news/2007/04/04/family/.

29. Scott Jaschik, "The 'Family Friendly' Competition," *Inside Higher Ed*, April 25, 2007, http://www.insidehighered.com/news/2007/04/25/family/.

4

The Vanishing Conservative— Is There a Glass Ceiling?

Stanley Rothman and S. Robert Lichter

The politics of professors has emerged as one of the most contentious topics in political sociology. There are two major elements of this debate: What do professors believe, and what does it matter? Much of the evidence on these issues is dealt with in other chapters of this book. Here we deal with these issues insofar as they affect the academic profession, rather than faculty-student relations. Our question is this: Is academia heavily liberal and Democratic, and if so, does this affect advancement in the academic profession?

Our data are drawn primarily from the North American Academic Study Survey (NAASS), originally directed by S. M. Lipset, Everrett Ladd, and Stanley Rothman (a coauthor of this chapter), which is described in detail below. We also discuss a more recent survey, the Politics of the American Professoriate (PAP). In 2006, sociologists Neil Gross and Solon Simmons surveyed a stratified random sample of 1,417 faculty teaching in departments offering undergraduate degrees at 927 two-year, four-year, and graduate-degree-granting institutions. Among the numerous recent surveys on this topic, theirs is the best designed and executed for the purpose of studying the political attitudes and behavior of college professors. Nonetheless, we will take issue with the investigators' conclusion that there is less liberalism and more political moderation among faculty than other recent studies have claimed.[1]

North American Academic Study Survey (NAASS)

The NAASS represented a partnership between Rothman, as an extension of his numerous surveys of social leadership groups, and Lipset and Ladd, who had conducted surveys of academic groups going back three decades.[2]

Conducted in 1999 by the Angus Reid (now Ipsos-Reid) survey research firm, the NAASS sample encompassed students, faculty, and administrators at colleges and universities in the United States and Canada. The instrument included a wide range of items, among them demographic background variables; attitudes toward social, political, and academic issues; and (for faculty) academic background, activities, and accomplishments.

The United States sample included 1,643 faculty members drawn from 183 randomly selected universities and colleges. Full-time faculty were randomly chosen from each institution in numbers proportionate to its size. A response rate of 72 percent was obtained for the U.S. faculty sample.

Unfortunately, the deaths of two of the principals and illness of the third led to considerable delays in analyzing and reporting the findings. In 2005, communications scholar Robert Lichter (the other coauthor of this chapter) joined the project to edit a manuscript on the political attitudes and behavior of U.S. faculty, which appeared in the Berkeley Press online journal the *Forum* in spring 2005.[3]

Party Affiliation. The NAASS instrument included three separate measures of political identification: political party preference, ideological self-designation on a left-right scale, and a set of items on social and political attitudes. First, faculty were asked to identify their political party affiliation as Democrat, Republican, independent, or "other." Half (50 percent) identified themselves as Democrats, compared to 11 percent who identified themselves as Republicans, a ratio greater than 4 to 1. An additional 33 percent called themselves independent, and 5 percent specified some other party. At that time, 36 percent of the American public identified itself as Democrat and 29 percent as Republican.[4]

The largest spreads between the two parties were found in the humanities (62 percent D vs. 6 percent R) and the social sciences (55 percent D vs. 7 percent R). The least difference was found among business faculty, in which the two parties' representation was even (26 percent for both). This group also had the largest proportion of independents. The most heavily Democratic departments—English literature, sociology, history, psychology, linguistics, education, and the arts—contained at least eight self-described Democrats for every Republican.

Table 4-1 presents these results, as well as comparable findings from the PAP survey, for all fields and departments for which published data were available from both surveys. The PAP findings were remarkably similar to those of the NAASS, especially considering the differences in sampling and the seven-year gap between the two (2006 vs. 1999). Whereas the NAASS found 50 percent self-identified Democrats and 11 percent Republicans, the PAP found 50 percent Democrats and 14 percent Republicans. The similarities extend to numerous fields and departments, despite the rapid increase in confidence intervals as the number of cases diminishes.

Political/Social Attitudes. The NAASS also included numerous political attitude items, several of which were drawn from a 1995 survey of elite or "social leadership" groups in the United States.[5] A factor analysis produced two factors that accounted for much of the variance in political attitudes; these factors represented dimensions related to social and to political/economic liberalism. The items representing political liberalism asked about the government's responsibility for employment, income distribution, and environmental protection; the items representing social liberalism asked about gay rights, abortion, and extramarital sex.

The level of agreement with the liberal position ranged from a low of 66 percent who believed that the government should work to ensure full employment to a high of 88 percent who favored greater environmental protection, even at the cost of price increases or job losses. In addition, 84 percent agreed that it is a woman's right to decide whether to have an abortion, 77 percent regarded homosexuality as no less acceptable than heterosexuality, 75 percent endorsed cohabitation without marital intentions, and 72 percent favored government action to reduce income inequality.

Carnegie Survey Findings. Finally, the NAASS included a measure of ideological self-designation modeled on several national surveys of faculty conducted for the Carnegie Corporation from 1969 through 1997.[6] In 1969, 1975, and 1984, respondents were asked to identify their political

TABLE 4-1
PARTY IDENTIFICATION (D OR R) BY FIELD: NAASS VS. PAP

Field of Study	———NAASS———			———PAP———		
	D	R	Ratio	D	R	Ratio
All faculty	50%	11%	5-1	50%	14%	4-1
Social sciences	55	7	8-1	56	7	8-1
Humanities	62	6	10-1	54	11	5-1
Business	26	26	1-1	39	24	2-1
Engineering/computer science	37	15	2-1	28	23	1-1
Natural sciences	46	14	3-1	53	15	4-1
Selected departments						
Communications	47	11	4-1	49	13	4-1
Computer science	43	21	2-1	32	10	3-1
English	69	2	34-1	51	2	25-1
Biology	56	13	4-1	51	6	8-1
Psychology	63	7	9-1	78	7	11-1
Economics	36	17	2-1	34	29	1-1
Political science	58	8	7-1	50	6	6-1
Sociology	59	0	—	49	6	8-1
Nursing	32	26	1-1	60	22	3-1
History	70	4	18-1	79	4	20-1
Agriculture	24	31	1-1	NA	NA	

SOURCES: NAASS Survey, 1999; PAP Survey, 2006.

leanings as left, liberal, middle-of-the road, moderately conservative, or strongly conservative. In 1989 and 1997 the response categories changed slightly to liberal, moderately liberal, middle-of-the-road, moderately conservative, and conservative.

Figure 4-1 shows that an ideological shift among college faculty apparently began to occur sometime in the mid-to-late 1980s, as the difference between self-described liberals and conservatives began to widen. The liberal plurality of 45 percent vs. 27 percent in 1969 had narrowed to 40 percent vs.

34 percent by 1984. But by 1989, the gap had increased to 56 percent to 28 percent, a 2 to 1 ratio of liberals to conservatives. The 1997 survey found little change, with a slight drop in the proportion of conservatives. Of course, part of the shift beginning in 1989 may reflect the change in response categories. Since that year, however, the growing predominance of liberal over conservative faculty is clear. This is shown in figure 4-1, which also includes comparable data from the NAASS and PAP questionnaires, which are discussed below.

NAASS Findings. In 1999, the NAASS asked respondents to place themselves on a ten-point scale from "very right" to "very left." These were recoded into pairs matching the five Carnegie categories, i.e., responses of 1 and 2 were liberal, 3 and 4 were moderately liberal, etc. We reported in the *Forum* that the results indicated a strong tilt to the left among faculty, with the proportion placing themselves left of center (i.e., 1–4 on the scale) outnumbering those on the right (i.e., 7–10) by 72 to 15 percent, and the remaining 13 percent in the middle of the ideological spectrum (i.e., 5–6 on the scale).[7]

Following the publication of these data, however, we became aware of an error in the findings. When joining the project to revise the *Forum* manuscript, Lichter was unaware that the survey instrument contained the following screening question: "When it comes to political matters, do you ever think of yourself in terms of Left and Right?" Those who answered "no" were not asked to place themselves on the left-to-right scale. That turned out to be a substantial portion of the sample. So, the reported data applied only to the subsample of respondents who responded "yes" to this screening question. That amounted to 64 percent, leaving 36 percent who were not counted on this variable.

We regret the error, and we seek here to provide a better indicator of ideological self-placement that covers the full sample. In order to have some idea of how the ideological self-placement would look if the nonrespondents were included, we imputed scores for them on the political self-identification scale according to their responses on the attitude questions shown in table 4-2. When this was done, the proportion of left-of-center faculty fell from 72 percent for the original subsample of respondents to 62 percent for the full sample; the proportion of those to the right of center

FIGURE 4-1

PROPORTION OF LIBERAL AND CONSERVATIVE FACULTY

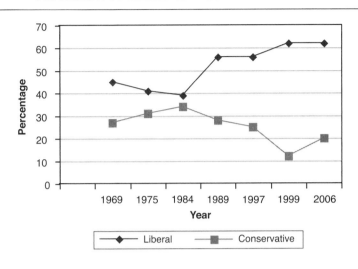

SOURCES: Data for 1969–1997 from Carnegie surveys; data for 1999 from North American Academic Study Survey (excludes two-year colleges); data for 2006 calculated from Politics of the American Professoriate survey, which includes "slightly" liberal and conservative categories.

dropped from 15 to 12 percent; and the proportion of middle-of-the-road respondents doubled, from 13 to 26 percent.

The overall findings and those for various fields and departments are shown in table 4-2. Notably, the revised NAASS findings more closely resemble the 1989 and 1997 Carnegie findings, as well as the 2006 PAP finding that 62 percent of faculty depicted themselves as left of center, 20 percent as right of center, and 18 percent as middle-of-the-road, following the item categories used by Gross and Simmons.[8] (Unfortunately their published data did not permit a department-by-department comparison.) However, that was not the conclusion reached by Gross and Simmons, as we discuss below.

The PAP Challenge. The PAP measure of political ideology asked faculty to characterize their political ideology as "extremely liberal, liberal, slightly liberal, moderate or middle-of-the-road, slightly conservative, conservative, or very conservative." In reporting the results, however, instead of combining

TABLE 4-2

POLITICAL IDENTIFICATION OF COLLEGE PROFESSORS
BY FIELD ON NAASS (%)

	Liberal	Conservative	N
All faculty	62	12	1,643
Social sciences	66	8	289
Humanities	77	8	449
Sciences	58	13	339
Selected departments			
English literature	85	3	87
Performing arts	79	11	31
Psychology	80	6	68
Fine arts	70	8	36
Theology/religion	67	14	26
Political science	79	2	67
Philosophy	79	4	26
History	79	7	62
Sociology	72	8	61
Biology	64	12	59
Communications	65	10	66
Music	63	9	53
Computer science	66	18	44
Mathematics	43	9	49
Physics	59	10	37
Linguistics	63	9	53
Chemistry	51	21	52
Education	57	21	88
Economics	43	27	44
Nursing	39	19	32
Engineering	42	15	90
Business	44	22	101

SOURCE: NAASS Survey.
NOTES: Scores for missing cases imputed by political attitude responses. This table includes all cases, with values imputed from responses to the political attitude items for respondents who declined to place themselves on a left-right spectrum.

the three response categories on either side of the moderate category to represent self-described liberals and conservatives, Gross and Simmons combined "slightly liberal" and "slightly conservative" with the middle-of-the-road category.

This recalculation produced 44 percent liberals, 44 percent moderates, and 9 percent conservatives. Gross and Simmons inferred from this that they had found "a moderate bloc . . . equal in size to the liberal bloc." Noting that this finding was similar to the 46 percent liberal/left group that the 1975 Carnegie survey found, they concluded that "the biggest change over the past 30 years" has not been growth on the left but decline on the right and "movement into moderate ranks."[9]

However, this conclusion derived entirely from the decision to recode the "slightly" liberal and conservative self-identifiers into an expanded moderate group, which automatically depleted the liberal and conservative groups. Was this justifiable? Gross and Simmons provided a testable argument: "We would not be justified in doing so if it turned out that the 'slightlys' were, in terms of their substantive attitudes, no different than their more liberal or conservative counterparts. But preliminary evidence indicates that they are different."[10]

The evidence came from political attitude items included in the PAP. Gross and Simmons computed the mean scores of each group on a scale derived from twelve Pew Values Survey questions, which dealt with attitudes toward the government's role in helping the poor, fighting terrorism with military force, etc. On these questions, the most liberal response was coded as 1, a middle-of-the-road response as 3, and the most conservative response as 5.

If the "slightlys" were really moderates, one would expect to find their average Pew Values scores hewing closer to those of the middle group than to the groups farther toward the ends of the ideological groups. But that isn't what happened. As figure 4-2 shows, the 1.7 mean score of the "slight" liberals was actually closer to the 1.4 mean score of the combined liberal and "extreme liberal" group than to the 2.2 mean score of the moderates. By contrast, the "slight" conservatives' 2.8 mean score was closer to the moderates' 2.2 than to the conservative and extreme conservatives' 3.7 score.

In addition, figure 4-2 shows visually how the entire spectrum of these responses was actually tilted to the left of center. The middle-of-the-road

FIGURE 4-2

SELF-IDENTIFICATION BY PEW VALUES SCALE SCORES (PAP)

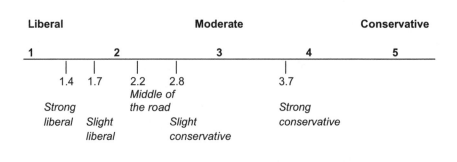

SOURCES: Gross and Simmons; PAP Survey.

position on the five-point Pew Values scale is represented by a score of 3. Yet four of the five groups of professors, including the "slight conservatives," had mean scores below 3, i.e., on the liberal side of the midpoint. The liberal/extreme liberal group was much closer to the left end of the spectrum than the conservative/extreme conservative group was to the right end.

Thus, it is difficult to understand how this statistical procedure could justify moving both slight conservative and slight liberals into the moderate camp. The slight liberals did *not* hold attitudes that placed them closer to the moderates than to the strong liberals. Moreover, the whole spectrum of faculty attitudes was skewed toward the liberal end. Thus, the "middle of the road" was actually well along the left fork of the road. Finally, the Pew Values items that were used to construct this opinion spectrum did not include the PAP's questions dealing with issues related to sex and gender, such as abortion and homosexuality, on which the faculty sample was tilted farthest toward the liberal position. So, these findings may underestimate the degree to which the overall tenor of even "moderate" faculty opinion is actually well to the left of center.

This tilt to the left is consistent with responses to other PAP items. For example, among PAP's faculty sample, the ratio of Democratic to Republican voters was about 2 to 1 in 1984 and 1988 and grew to 4 to 1 in 1992 and 5 to 1 in 1996, before receding to 3 to 1 in 2000. In addition, one out of four professors in the humanities and social sciences is by self-description a radical or activist, and one out of seven social scientists (including one out of four sociologists) a Marxist, again in accord with what Klein and Stern show in chapter 2 of this volume. These days, there are literally more Marxists in faculty lounges than in the Kremlin.

We do not question the PAP's methodology, only the researchers' interpretation of the results. In fact Gross and Simmons's own summary is more circumspect than media accounts might suggest: "Although we would not contest the claim that professors are one of the most liberal occupational groups in American society, or that the professoriate is a Democratic stronghold . . . there is a sizable, and often ignored, center/center-left contingent."[11] To which those who see a liberal hegemony in academe may well reply, "With enemies like these, who needs friends?"

Summary. When we combine the trends in ideological self-description with party affiliation and attitude data, it seems clear that American college and university faculty are heavily Democratic and liberal, especially among the social sciences and humanities, and that their ideological homogeneity has increased since the mid-1980s. On these points, our survey generally replicated the findings of other recent researchers.

Politics and Professional Status

The NAASS data confirm the predominance of liberal faculty on American college campuses. But it is harder to determine whether this predominance makes it more difficult for conservatives to advance in their profession. To show that conservatives have more difficulty advancing, we would need to show not only that conservatives are underrepresented on college faculties, but that any gap between their success and that of liberal colleagues is not simply due to a lack of merit on their part.

To address these issues, we examined the correlation between quality of academic affiliation and the three NAASS measures of political orientation—left-right self-identification, political party identification, and social and political attitudes. To determine whether any political differences could be explained by different achievement levels by right- and left-leaning faculty, we constructed an academic achievement index from items measuring the number of refereed journal articles, chapters in academic books, and books authored or coauthored, as well as service on editorial boards of academic journals, attendance at international meetings of one's discipline, and proportion of time spent on research. This index was highly correlated with a simple count of academic publications. However, such counts have been criticized as simplistic or unidimensional measures of achievement, so we included other factors.

There are various emblems of professional success in academia, ranging from salary to awards to chaired professorships. However, the most significant factor in the academic status hierarchy is the quality of the college or university with which one is affiliated. Therefore, we operationalized professional status in terms of institutional quality. We constructed an institutional quality index by combining the Carnegie Foundation for the Advancement of Teaching classification with the well-known *U.S. News & World Report* rankings of universities and colleges.

The widely used Carnegie classification divides schools into two levels each of research universities, doctorate-granting universities, comprehensive universities and colleges, and liberal arts colleges. Altogether these make up what are described as eight "tiers" of institutions. While controversial among some educators, the *U.S. News* rankings are widely used, and they are derived from a plausible and measurable set of variables, including peer ratings, test scores of incoming students, resources available to students, etc. Further, the most frequently heard criticism is that the rankings measure institutional reputation rather than quality of students' education; for our purposes, this is not necessarily a disadvantage.

U.S. News places the best colleges and universities in its national rankings. Institutions that do not make it into the national rankings are ranked regionally. We modified the *U.S. News* ratings by placing the national institutions in the top four Carnegie tiers and the regional institutions in the bottom four tiers, with the particular tier determined by the school's ranking.

To determine whether professional advancement is influenced by ideological orientation over and above the effects of scholastic achievement, we conducted a multiple regression analysis in which scholarly achievement and political orientation were the key independent variables of interest, and the dependent variable was the quality of one's institutional affiliation (operationally, the tier in which the institution is located). In addition to the political variables, we included several other factors that have been cited as sources of discrimination in other social contexts. Among them were race, religion, gender, sexual orientation, and marital status.

We entered each of our measures of ideological orientation individually into separate equations. This was done to provide a comparison of the statistical contribution of the various measures while avoiding problems of multicollinearity, since party affiliation, ideological self-description, and the attitude indices are all intercorrelated. Preliminary bivariate analysis also showed an interactive relationship between religion and institutional affiliation—quality of school was related to religion only among active practitioners (defined as those attending services "at least once or twice a month"). Therefore, we included "practicing Christians" and "practicing Jews" as dummy variables in the equation. (Other religions contained too few practitioners for statistically valid comparisons.)

The various equations we examined all showed that scholarly achievement—primarily but not entirely based on publications—counted by far for the most variance in professional status, as we would expect in a meritocracy. However, political orientation also played a role, with the amount dependent on the measure that was used. First, placement on the left-right scale did not contribute significantly to explaining variation in institutional affiliation for the subset of individuals who were willing to provide such a self-designation. When the imputed values were assigned to the missing cases, this variable did contribute significantly. However, since the political attitude items were used to create these variates, it makes more sense to simply use the attitude indices rather than this hybrid measure.

In the *Forum* article, we combined the social and political/economic ideology items into a single index. When we disaggregated this index into separate measures, however, it became clear that social ideology accounted for the relationship between professorial politics and professional advancement. This can be seen in table 4-3, which shows the unstandardized and standardized (beta) regression coefficients and amount of variation explained in two slightly different models. Model I includes both attitudes and party affiliation to predict the quality of institutional affiliation. This equation shows that the contributions of economic/political liberalism (beta = .04, ns) and party affiliation (beta = .04, ns, for Republican affiliation) were both artifacts of the role played by social liberalism (beta = .134, p .001).

Moreover, the significance of religiosity disappeared as well (beta = .041, ns, for practicing Christians), suggesting that its apparent significance was due to its intercorrelation with social conservatism. That is, the independent influence of religion, political party affiliation, and political/economic ideology (defined as attitudes toward the government's role in equalizing economic conditions and protecting the environment) all disappeared, revealing the underlying influence of social ideology (attitudes toward social or cultural issues such as abortion, homosexuality, and sexual morality). Of course, the most important factor in all the equations was scholarly achievement (beta = .375, p .001).

The more parsimonious Model II eliminated the party variable, which slightly raised the beta weight of the social ideology variable to .147, while the beta for the achievement index remained at .375. In Model II, however, social ideology explained about one-third as much variation in institutional affiliation as did achievement. In both models, the independent variables together accounted for 20 percent of the variation in level of institutional affiliation (R^2 = .202).

Both models also contained two other variables that contributed to explaining level of institution with achievement held constant. These were race (beta = −.053, p .05 for blacks) and gender (beta = .07, p .01 for women). Both relationships are statistically significant, accounting for about one-third and one-half as much variation, respectively, as did social ideology. We are still exploring the source of the latter relationships, both of which suggest a basis for concern in areas where many colleges have sought to add diversity to their faculties in recent years. However, we have already uncovered some pertinent evidence.

In the case of race, the relationship with institutional prestige disappeared when historically black colleges were deleted from the sample. This suggests that the presence of mainly black faculty at these schools, which tend to fall into the lower institutional tiers, may account for at least part of this relationship. The influence of gender seems to be more complicated. We found an interaction among gender, productivity, and institutional quality. High-achieving women were as likely as high-achieving men to be affiliated with more prestigious institutions. But women who were relatively

TABLE 4-3

REGRESSIONS PREDICTING QUALITY OF ACADEMIC AFFILIATION

	————Model I————		————Model II————	
	Unstandardized Coefficients	Standardized Coefficients	Unstandardized Coefficients	Standardized Coefficients
Social ideology index	0.145[c]	0.134	0.158[c]	0.147
Political ideology index	−0.040	−0.040	−0.028	−0.028
Republican	−1.211	−0.034		
Independent	−0.787	−0.033		
Female	−1.824[b]	−0.072	−1.764[b]	−0.070
Black	−2.974[a]	−0.058	−2.756[a]	−0.053
Asian	1.155	0.022	1.096	0.021
Gay or lesbian	1.041	0.019	1.105	0.020
Married	0.776	0.030	0.775	0.030
Practicing Jewish	1.275	0.023	1.249	0.023
Practicing Christian	−.920	−0.041	−0.878	−0.039
Faculty achievement index	0.423[c]	0.375	0.423[c]	0.375
Constant	43.921[c]		40.937[c]	
Adjusted R squared	0.202		0.202	
N	1625		1625	

SOURCE: Authors' calculations.
NOTES: a. Significant at the 0.05 level; b. significant at the 0.01 level; c. significant at the 0.001 level.

unproductive in their scholarly activities were less likely than similarly unproductive men to be affiliated with higher-tiered institutions. For example, among faculty who had published two or more books, 72 percent of females and 73 percent of males were affiliated with high-tiered institutions. By contrast, among those who had not published any books, 58 percent of male faculty were nonetheless located in high-tiered institutions, compared to only 44 percent of women.

Summary and Conclusion

The purpose of our study was to advance the now-contentious debate over the political culture of academia and its effects on the careers of faculty members with divergent political perspectives. In effect, we formulated the debate in terms of two testable hypotheses: first, most professors in American colleges and universities are left of center politically; second, this ideological homogeneity hinders the professional advancement of conservatives.

To test these hypotheses, we made use of the 1999 North American Academic Study Survey, which provided a systematic and comprehensive data set on the characteristics of American college faculty that permitted some time-series comparison with the Carnegie surveys conducted between 1969 and 1997. First, we examined the political party preferences of faculty members, their ideological self-descriptions on a left-right scale, and their views on controversial social and political issues, ranging from government intervention in the economy to environmental protection to abortion rights. We found that the political orientation of the professoriate at the turn of the millennium was tilted toward liberal attitudes and Democratic Party affiliation. Further, the predominance of liberal and Democratic perspectives was not limited to particular types of institutions or fields of study. A significant body of evidence points to the growing hegemony of the liberal-left. Furthermore, a comparison of the 1999 survey with previous surveys of American faculty indicates a substantial shift to the left in party identification and ideology since the mid-1980s, at a time when ideological and party identification among the general public has been relatively stable. We believe that more recent data from the PAP in large part replicated our findings, although Gross and Simmons argue that a "center/center left" group is unduly ignored by our conclusions.

Second, we performed a multiple regression analysis to test the effect of social and political/economic ideology on professional status. We found that even after taking into account the effects of academic achievement, along with many other individual characteristics, social (but not political/economic) conservatives taught at lower-quality schools than did liberals. That is, more liberal responses to the social attitude questions predicted a higher quality of institutional affiliation, after controlling for scholarly achievement.

This mode of inquiry, by its nature, cannot prove that ideology accounts for this difference in professional standing. There may be some other factor at work for which we failed to account, or we may have failed to eliminate some source of measurement error. It is important to note the limitations of our findings. They do not address the questions of whether or how self-selection may account for the political differences we observed. Nor do they deal with ways in which ideological factors may affect the behavior of faculty members in or out of the classroom.

But the results are consistent with the hypothesis that at least one form of conservatism confers a disadvantage in the competition for professional advancement. These results suggest that conservative complaints about the presence and effects of liberal homogeneity in academia deserve a hearing on their merits, despite their self-interested quality and the anecdotal nature of the evidence that is frequently presented. In conjunction with evidence from other studies, our findings suggest that a leftward shift began on college campuses sometime in the later 1980s, and has progressed to an extent that conservatives have nearly disappeared from some departments.

Our findings on the more controversial issue of discrimination against conservative faculty should be regarded as more preliminary. To our knowledge, this is the first time this sort of empirical analysis has been applied to this question, and there may be much more to learn from additional data analysis, as well as from newer data sets such as the PAP. Our goal was to draw attention to the application of rigorous methods to evaluate this controversy systematically, rather than letting the debate deteriorate into anecdotal charges and countercharges. Our statistical analysis provides prima facie evidence that conservative complaints are not frivolous, despite their connection with the broader "culture wars" of contemporary politics. The important thing is that such complaints be evaluated by methods that minimize the strong feelings such disputes bring out on both sides.

Notes

1. Neil Gross and Solon Simmons, "The Social and Political Views of American Professors" (paper presented at the Harvard University Symposium on Professors and Their Politics, Cambridge, MA, October 6, 2007).

2. See Robert Lerner, Althea Nagai, and Stanley Rothman, *American Elites* (New Haven, CT: Yale University Press, 1996); Everett Carll Ladd Jr. and Seymour Martin Lipset, *The Divided Academy: Professors and Politics* (New York: McGraw-Hill, 1975).

3. Stanley Rothman, S. Robert Lichter, and Neil Nevitte, "Politics and Professional Advancement among College Faculty," *Forum* 3, no. 1 (2005), http://www.bepress.com/forum/vol3/iss1/art2/; see also Stanley Rothman, S. Robert Lichter, and Neil Nevitte, "Fundamentals and Fundamentalists: A Reply to Ames et al.," *Forum* 3, no. 2 (2005), http://www.bepress.com/forum/vol3/iss2/art8/. The first of these articles contains the item wordings and scale constructions referred to below.

4. Harris Poll 1999, 2002, 2004, http://www.harrisinteractive.com/harris_poll.

5. Stanley Rothman and Amy Black, "Elites Revisited: American Social and Political Leadership in the 1990s," *International Journal of Public Opinion Research* 11, no. 2 (1999): 169–95.

6. See, for example, Carnegie Council on Policy Studies in Higher Education, *Carnegie Council National Surveys, 1975–1976: Faculty Marginals*, vol. 2 (San Francisco: Jossey-Bass, 1978); Carnegie Foundation for the Advancement of Teaching, *The Condition of the Professoriate: Attitudes and Trends* (Princeton, NJ: The Carnegie Foundation for the Advancement of Teaching, 1989).

7. Rothman, Licher, and Nevitte, "Politics and Professional Advancement."

8. Gross and Simmons, "Social and Political Views of American Professors." These data do not take into account possible differences resulting from the inclusion of two-year community colleges in the Carnegie and PAP surveys but not in the NAASS sample. Based on data appearing in Richard F. Hamilton and Lowell L. Hargens, "The Politics of the Professors: Self-Identifications, 1969–1984," *Social Forces* 71, no. 3 (1993): 603–27, the inclusion of two-year colleges in the sample lowered the overall proportion of liberals by two percentage points in the 1984 and 1989 surveys.

9. Gross and Simmons, "Social and Political Views of American Professors," 28.

10. Ibid., 26.

11. David Glynn, "Few Conservatives but Many Centrists Teach in Academe," *Chronicle of Higher Education*, October 19, 2007, A10.

PART II

"Diversity" in Higher Education

5

Groupthink in Academia: Majoritarian Departmental Politics and the Professional Pyramid

Daniel B. Klein and Charlotta Stern

Generally speaking, we can observe that the scientists in any particular institutional and political setting move as a flock, reserving their controversies and particular originalities for matters that do not call into question the fundamental system of biases they share.

—Gunnar Myrdal[1]

Perhaps we avoid studying our institutional lives because such work is not valued by our colleagues. The academy is, after all, a club, and members are expected to be discreet. Like any exclusive club, the academic world fears public scrutiny. Research is in the public domain. Outsiders might use what the research reveals against the academy.

—Richard Wisniewski[2]

The "thousand profound scholars" may have failed, first, because they were scholars, secondly, because they were profound, and thirdly, because they were a thousand.

—Edgar Allan Poe[3]

We thank Richard Redding, Robert Maranto, and Anne Himmelfarb for detailed feedback that significantly improved this chapter.

In baseball, fans of different teams can agree on general issues concerning rules, umpiring, and performance evaluation because such matters are separable from support for a specific team. In academia, however, we find that rules and standards for performance are not separable from support for specific beliefs. Ideological sensibilities and commitments in academia tend to be bound up with notions of the whole academic enterprise. That is, one's positions on how performance should be umpired or evaluated and one's support for a certain "team" *are not separable*.

We think discussion of ideology in academia is itself bound to be ideological, and that good scholarship calls on us to declare that what principally motivates the present investigation is our belief that, by and large, professors in the humanities and social sciences are weak in certain sensibilities that we ourselves hold. Specifically, there is little classical liberalism among academics. In policy terms, classical liberalism favors domestic reform generally in the directions of significantly decontrolling markets and personal choice, reducing the welfare state, and depoliticizing society. A further policy feature of classical liberalism, in our view, is a strong disposition against military entanglements abroad. "Libertarian" (with a small "l") is the current label closest to classical liberal, although the beliefs of the classical liberal are properly understood as somewhat looser and more pragmatic; we also prefer the label "classical liberal" because it reminds us of the historical arc of liberalism.

Ample evidence on the ideological profile of professors in the humanities and social sciences indicates that, though not monolithic, the dominant sensibilities combine social democratic leanings and support for (or acquiescence to) most domestic government interventions. (We identify modern American "liberalism" as social democracy, a political outlook that readily treads on voluntarist ethics, that sees the polity as an organization, and that therefore advocates the pursuit of collective endeavors, such as equalizing well-being and opportunity.)

Social democratic views do not always run against the grain of classical liberalism. But, in our view, such frictions as do exist indicate problems with the ideological profile of faculty. Also, even absent friction, the neglect of important classical liberal ideas itself often counts as a problem. Our analysis rests on the judgment that the relative absence of classical liberal views among humanities and social sciences professors is unfortunate. But that judgment is not argued here.

Our analysis may be adapted by other viewpoints that likewise see problems in the ideological profile of faculty and that find themselves systematically excluded and marginalized. In particular, conservatives, in a narrow sense that would clearly separate them from classical liberals, may use a version of our analysis as a conservative diagnosis of the problem. Our classical liberal viewpoint, then, is but one of two major viewpoints that may find the current account especially valuable.

Adapting Groupthink to the Academic Setting

We analyze academic ideology in terms of *groupthink*. Groupthink analysis examines decision making presupposed to be defective. In that sense, groupthink analysis is pejorative.

In the seminal work on groupthink, *Groupthink: Psychological Studies of Policy Decisions and Fiascoes*, Irving L. Janis begins by looking at a number of well-known fiascoes, including the Bay of Pigs, escalation in Vietnam, and Watergate[4]—episodes that came to be judged fiascoes even by those responsible for them. That is, he starts with defectiveness and seeks to explain the absence of correction. He defines groupthink as "members' strivings for unanimity overriding their motivation to realistically appraise alternative courses of action" and declares the term's "invidious connotation."[5]

Paul 't Hart, who developed the Janis tradition in *Groupthink in Government: A Study of Small Groups and Policy Failure*, calls groupthink "excessive concurrence-seeking,"[6] a behavior that explains "flaws in the operation of small, high-level groups at the helm of major projects or policies that become fiascoes," such as the Iran-Contra affair.[7] Diane Vaughan's discussion of the Space Shuttle Challenger disaster, which involves both bottom-up and top-down organizational errors, can be said to occupy an intermediate position between traditional Janis-Hart analysis and the analysis offered here.[8]

The groupthink theorist wants to gain standing as a social theorist and therefore wants to avoid unnecessary controversy. Accordingly, groupthink theorists—at least those like Janis and Hart—have focused on episodes where, in hindsight, the judgment of failure (or error) is uncontroversial. The need for uncontroversial judgment is one reason why the scope of groupthink applications has been quite limited.

In this essay, we apply groupthink theory to a setting where the pre-supposition of failure is anything but uncontroversial. Academe is quite different from the settings examined by groupthink theorists. We suggest, however, that, given the presupposition of failure, central mechanisms in academe make it possible to adapt groupthink theory to academe. We try to make plausible the idea that, if academic groups were caught up in defective thoughts, the defectiveness would be resistant to correction. We explain persistence, or the lack of correction. We do not address "how the problem got started," partly because of space limits, partly because there never was an Eden.

To be sure, we ought to be very cautious about using groupthink to interpret academic ideology in the humanities and social sciences. The groupthink literature in the tradition of Janis and Hart mostly examines the belief processes of policymaking groups. The cases usually have the following features: (1) The group is small. (2) The group is fairly neatly defined—a group of "insiders." (3) The group is chief-based with highly centralized decision making. (4) The group is concerned about security leaks or other constraints that lead it to put a premium on secrecy. (5) The group acts under great stress. (6) The group makes decisions that run great risks and huge possible dangers. (7) The group is dealing with an issue of great immediacy and exigency. (8) The group's bad beliefs are specific to the decision at hand. (9) The bad beliefs are shallow; they are not about issues of identity. (10) The potential for eventually admitting defectiveness usually exists.

In all these features, these groups differ quite significantly from academic groups. Academic groups—whether colleagues in a university department or the leadership at a prestigious journal or association—are larger, less well defined, much less chief-based, much less specific-action oriented, and much less subject to stress, urgency, risk, and danger. Their bad beliefs are much deeper, more complex, and more incorrigible. They are more of the nature of moral, political, and aesthetic values. These differences make the academic group more diffuse and variegated in purpose.

Despite all these differences, however, we see basic similarities between Janis-Hart groups and academic groups. Both types of groups hold defective beliefs. Both types tend toward concurrence seeking, self-validation, and exclusion of challenges to core beliefs. Finally, mechanisms in academe work to create an "in-group" that is insular, self-perpetuating, and self-reinforcing.

Departmental Majoritarianism

Let us imagine a university called XYU. It is natural to imagine the inner workings of XYU as being like those of other institutions, that is, hierarchical in purpose, structure, and authority. XYU is an organization led by the provost, deans, and so on. Beneath the administration come the academic departments.

Actors within an organization subdivide labor. In most nonacademic organizations, the bosses can scarcely tamper with tasks assigned to subunits; rather, they look for results that advance the organizational mission. In academe there is the same necessary subdivision and delegation, but the sense of organizational mission is much fuzzier. Furthermore, oversight is more problematic, since scholarship is inherently specialized and embedded in the scholarly community. Even Adam Smith, who criticized academia, emphasized that any "extraneous jurisdiction" over substantive issues of teaching "is liable to be exercised both ignorantly and capriciously."[9] The upshot is that administrators generally rubber-stamp departmental decisions. While the department may appear to be structurally "under" the administration, in practice the department is left to decide the important questions (about hiring, firing, promoting, teaching, research, graduate student training, and so on), nor is it guided in matters of an ideological nature.

The most important departmental decisions are tenure-track faculty hiring, firing, and promotion. Such decisions come down to majority vote. Yes, the chair exercises certain powers, committees control agendas, and so on. But the central and final procedure for rendering the most important decisions is democracy among the tenure-track professors—*departmental majoritarianism.*

Most intellectuals develop ideological sensibilities by the age of twenty-five or thirty.[10] They come, by this time, to basic outlooks and sensibilities, and rarely substantially revise them. Intellectual delight and existential comfort are had, not in going back and reexamining prior decisions, but in refining and developing ideas down the path already mastered.[11] Professors are likely to respect scholars who pursue questions similar to their own, who master similar paths. They are not likely to respect scholars who pursue questions predicated on beliefs at odds with their own. Indeed, a scholar engaged in a task that might threaten a colleague's sense of self can be a source of personal distress and create acrimony between colleagues. More publicly, one professor, call him Professor A, might lose standing and credibility with students if a colleague, Professor B, teaching the same students but in a different course, were to explode some of the premises of Professor A's course materials, lectures, and writings.

In the matter of hiring a new member of the department, the majority will tend to support candidates like them in the matter of fundamental beliefs, values, and commitments. Indeed, one of the prime responsibilities of scholars is to navigate their way through the big issues, to make judgments and commitments, and move on. These judgments are not apart from science or scholarship, and scholars rightly can say: "If Candidate A has judged differently on fundamentals, then Candidate A has exhibited bad scholarly/scientific judgment." This point of judgment universalizes and cannot be disposed of. There is no way for anyone to step outside of it. Discriminating on the basis of differences in fundamentals, therefore, cannot be condemned, in the abstract, as contrary to responsible scholarship. We all discriminate on the basis of ideology, and—again in the abstract— doing so is perfectly justifiable.

We noted that the academic setting differs from the settings examined by groupthink theorists. Yet some of those differences might compensate for each other. In academia, the focus of belief and action is not any crucial policy decision, such as invading Cuba. That means there is no corresponding secrecy and needful separation from regular channels of discourse. Another difference, however, has to do with the depth or personal significance of the beliefs in question. In academia, the beliefs are deepseated and connected to selfhood and identity. For that reason, their protection and preservation is often a matter of high personal stakes. The existential significance of ideological beliefs in some respects compensates for the fact that personnel and other decisions in academia are otherwise mundane and socially inconsequential.

In context, people know they must judge and act on deep sensibilities, and they know, if only tacitly, that there is no real scandal in doing so. Theories of group formation and social dynamics tell us that social groups tend to seek and attract newcomers like themselves,[12] tend to screen out and repel misfits,[13] and tend to mold the unformed in their own image.[14] This is merely human nature.

Suppose it is time to make a new hire, and 51 percent of the department shares a broadly similar ideology—say, progressivism/social democracy, conservatism, or classical liberalism/libertarianism—and, further, believes that, in order to be a good colleague and a good professor, one must broadly conform to that ideology. What happens? The members of the department hire one like themselves. The 51 percent becomes 55 percent. Then it becomes 60 percent, then 65 percent, then 70 percent, and so on. As noted by Stephen Balch and others, majoritarianism tends to produce ideological uniformity within the department.[15]

The syndrome does not depend on what the ideology happens to be. The George Mason University Economics Department is led by and dominated by classical liberals. Some would self-identify as conservative. Only a few would self-identify as liberal (in the current sense). A case of ideological discrimination? The classical liberals and conservatives think that being an interventionist in the manner of, say, Kenneth Arrow, Joseph Stiglitz, Paul Krugman, or Dani Rodrik reveals failings in economic judgment. Many GMU economists regard undue confidence in government and politics to be bad science, and consider arcane work a scientific failure to address the most important things.

We speak of tendency, not lockstep uniformity. Some degree of variation will be normal and acceptable—for example, there are ongoing internal tensions between the more radical left and the establishment left. In any case, the tendency toward uniformity is not the whole story. An ideological oddball might be well liked and considered unthreatening, perhaps because he is meek or does research in some arcane mode that makes him irrelevant to fundamental issues. Moreover, departments usually have an ethic of *consensus*. Colleagues are human beings, and they are stuck with each other. They usually seek to avoid acrimony and aggravation. The majority does not steamroll over minority interests. The consensus factor works toward a blandness in personnel matters—the majority advances a job candidate who is in their camp but not too strident or outspoken. The consensus factor moderates the majority but does not undo the tendency toward uniformity. Probably its main effect is to pull that uniform character toward blandness, that is, to a presumption in favor of the conventional policies and opinions of whatever major party the departmental majority favors.

Outsiders often think that the classical liberal or conservative professor needs only to get tenure in order to ensure his professional success and psychic well-being. But imagine building a career through graduate school and pretenure employment (about eleven years) before feeling able to be yourself. You find you are no longer yourself—not that your ideological views have changed much, but that any ideological *motivation* has likely receded. You "go native," as they say. Your twenties and early thirties are a crucial period of development and cannot be reversed. Moreover, even after tenure, you depend on department colleagues for pay raises, resources, teaching assignments, scheduling, promotions, recognition, and consideration. Tenure alone clearly is not a sanctum for the departmental miscreant.

Because of departmental majoritarianism, then, each department tends toward ideological uniformity, perhaps watered down. Some XYU students lament that the History Department lacks classical liberals or conservatives. But at least citizens at large can hope that the public conversation among prestigious academic historians includes such viewpoints. Perhaps they can hope to shop for a university that has a history department with an ideology more to their liking.

The Professional Pyramid

Let us imagine a college freshman named Sarah who comes from a family that admires thinkers like Adam Smith, F. A. Hayek, and Milton Friedman. She has gone off to XY University. After her first year she informs her parents that the humanities and social science departments seem to be dominated by social democrats. Her parents grumble, but what's done is done. However, they have another child looking forward to college to study history. This time, they shop more carefully and investigate the history departments at different schools. Everywhere they see signs of a social democratic bent, and wonder: Why is that?

The principal explanation for the uniformity across campuses lies in understanding what the individual history department is at an existential level. The XYU History Department, for example, is not so much a subunit of XYU as it is a village of the larger tribe, history *as a profession*. History, the profession, has a settlement at XYU, the XYU History Department. As

FIGURE 5-1

HISTORY RESIDES IN SETTLEMENTS THROUGHOUT ACADEME

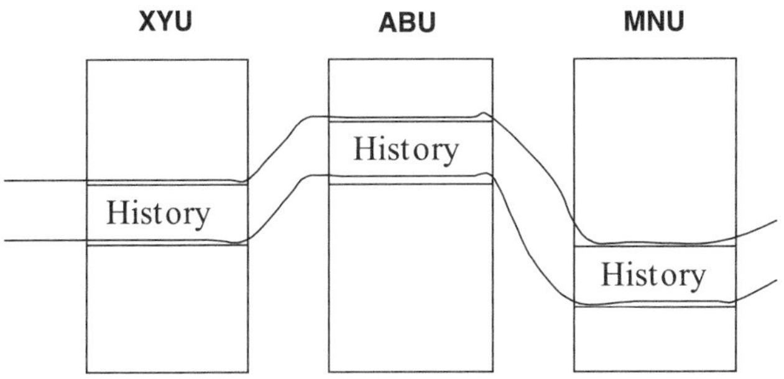

SOURCE: Authors' illustration.

professional researchers, members of that department find much of their meaning and validation in belonging to and serving the history profession. The historians at XYU might share a roof with philosophers, language professors, and so on. In fact, they almost never engage in scholarly discourse with those people. Rather, their scholarly life takes place within the tribe of History, which resides in settlements situated *laterally* across geography and physical institutions (see figure 5-1). History is the "invisible college" to which most historians really principally belong. The department is more a creature of history as a profession than of XYU.

Again, the XYU History Department has to make decisions on hiring, etc. Those are micro decisions. But to make decisions and justify the actions taken, they draw on the macro norms and values of the tribe. The micro and macro are intimately and thickly interconnected.

In structure, the tribe is pyramidal, with the elite at the apex and widening echelons at each step down (see figure 5-2). Position within the pyramid is based on focal, conventional rankings of key institutions, notably academic journals, departments, publishers, citations, grants, awards, and other markers of merit. Aside from playing specific roles (as teacher, writer, journal editor, etc.), individual scholars help to organize the tribe by performing activities that determine or affirm rank, such as writing letters, praising work, and citing research, and they, too, are subject to ranking. All the usual metrics are intertwined and mutually reinforcing.

Research is very specialized. The tribe is broken down into subfields. American history, for example, might be broken down by period, by aspect (social, cultural, economic, gender, political, legal, etc.), by mode of research, by theme or character. Prestige and eminence are really determined within the subfield, a kind of club within the tribe. The clubs constitute the tribe, just as agencies and branches constitute the government. Each club sorts people, with overt reference to pedigree, publication, citations, and letters of reference. The club controls these filters and then applies them to itself. It controls the graduate programs and journals. Spawning and hiring new PhDs, the club reproduces itself.

The academic job market is quite unlike the market for waiters or cab drivers. In all but the literal sense, one history department "sells" its newly minted PhDs to other history departments. The consumers (history departments), the producers (other history departments), and the products (newly minted history PhDs) *are all historians*. Waiters and cab drivers are accountable to their employers, who are accountable to consumers. Historians are accountable mainly only to other historians. Meanwhile, they are spending monies drawn from taxpayers, tuition payers, foundations, and charitable donors.

The pyramid of club and tribe is self-validating. But who else could possibly provide the validation? The pyramidal structure is, to a great extent, in the nature of the beast. A department's micro decisions are decisions about friends, colleagues, enemies, friends of friends, students of mentors, and so on. If it wants to look beyond itself to make and justify its decision, it looks to the higher echelons of the profession, as one looks to heritage.

This allegiance is partly a sincere faith in the tribe—and, after all, we would agree that the official rankings do express genuine quality in some important dimensions of scholarship. But partly it is a practical matter of needing ways of establishing standards and practices that are commonly understood. The tribe's standards are focal points around which expectations are mutually coordinated and consensus is tolerably achieved.[16] Without an encompassing standard, a discipline has no prospect of being a coherent enterprise. The precept *History is what historians do and historians are those with history degrees and appointments* may not be intellectually satisfying, but at least it keeps the wheels turning fairly smoothly.

FIGURE 5-2

THE PROFESSION PYRAMID OF HISTORY: STATUS RANKINGS
OF DEPARTMENTS, JOURNALS, ETC.

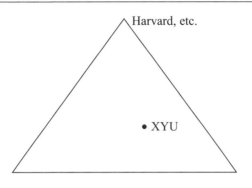

SOURCE: Authors' illustration.

The reliance on the tribe's standards to decide on jobs, pay, security, teaching loads, grants, RAs, etc. is so entrenched and ingrained that players come to value the standards for their own sake. Having an article accepted at a top journal brings concrete gains and prestige, regardless of the intrinsic value of the article or the journal. Functionality depends on internalizing the discipline's norms.

Now, suppose that the departments and journals at the apex of the pyramid adhere to ideology J. Then there is no internal conflict, and any dissent from below is safely ignored. Indeed, inferiors will be inclined to refrain from criticism, because they are dependent on superiors' acceptance and endorsement. Micro decisions throughout the pyramid will tend to follow the apex. And besides such concurrence mechanisms, there is propagation; that is, the apex produces PhDs and places them well.

Consider a conventional ranking of two hundred economics departments worldwide, where the top thirty-five are treated as the apex.[17] In these top thirty-five departments, more than 90 percent of faculty got their PhDs from the same thirty-five departments; the top is almost entirely self-regenerating. According to the regression line, the department ranked one hundredth would have about 65 percent of its faculty from the top thirty-five. Departments further down the pyramid are generally much smaller, so the top thirty-five departments train and mentor the people who populate most of the top two hundred departments. The profession, especially at the higher echelons, mostly consists of people directly indebted to and personally loyal to the apex.

Yet these results do not fully capture the domination by the top departments, which in fact have vastly disproportionate influence in journals, grants, second-generation degrees, and so on.[18] In sociology, for instance, Val Burris documents the extraordinary power exercised by the leading American departments:

> Graduates from the top 5 departments account for roughly one-third of all faculty hired in all 94 departments. The top 20 departments account for roughly 70 percent of the total. Boundaries to upward mobility are extremely rigid. Sociologists with degrees from non-top 20 departments are rarely hired at top 20 departments and almost never hired at top 5 departments.[19]
>
> The hiring of senior faculty by prestigious departments is even *more* incestuous than the hiring of new PhDs. . . . Of the 430 full-time faculty employed by the top 20 sociology departments . . . only 7 (less than 2 percent) received their PhD from a non-top 20 department, worked for three or more years in a non-top 20 department, and, after building their scholarly reputations, advanced to a faculty position in one of the top 20 departments.[20]

Because of the mechanisms that operate within disciplines—propagation, follow-the-apex, and freeze-out, if the apex goes ideology J, it will tend to sweep ideology J into positions in every department all the way down the pyramid. We are oversimplifying, but perhaps not much. There will be some dissent, but heterodoxies focus on criticizing the mainstream pyramid, because the pyramid remains the gravitational well of group practice and individual ambition. Like any central power, people fight over its exercise and distribution. If parallel pyramids get erected, they generally are either ignored or co-opted into the fringes of the official pyramid, altering its character somewhat. The professional pyramid and departmental majoritarianism function together to effectively exclude scholars opposed to ideology J, especially from the more highly ranked departments. This explains why in most fields of the humanities and social sciences, there is practically no institutional classical liberal presence with any significant professional standing.

Academic Groupthink

Although academia differs from the settings explored by groupthink theorists, it exhibits many of the same tendencies and failings. Irving Janis provides a summary table of antecedent conditions and symptoms of groupthink.[21] We list them below verbatim (in boldface), omitting a few items that do not fit the academic application (such as "Provocative Situation Context"). We add (in regular type) our comments suggesting how these conditions and symptoms operate in academia; we sketch a narrative of increasing social democratic groupthink from about 1972, when the ratio of Democrats to Republicans in the humanities and social sciences was about 4 to 1, to today, when it is about 8 to 1.[22]

ANTECEDENT CONDITIONS:

Decision-Makers Constitute a Cohesive Group—The professional pyramid and departmental autonomy tend toward group cohesiveness.

Structural Faults of the Organization

Insulation of the Group—No one outside the pyramid is qualified to judge the group. Insiders safely ignore outside opinion.

Homogeneity of Members' Social Background and Ideology— Sorting and molding mechanisms produce ideological homogeneity, both throughout the pyramid and within the individual department. In 1972, the social science/humanities faculty was preponderantly Democratic. Once the skew became too great, it tumbled into a self-reinforcing process. Among professors, the Democratic tent is significantly narrower in policy views than the Republican tent.[23]

OBSERVABLE CONSEQUENCES:

Symptoms of Groupthink

Type I: Overestimation of the Group

Illusion of Invulnerability—Academics feel that those outside the pyramid lack knowledge and credibility, and that those inside the pyramid would not dare become renegades.

Belief in Inherent Morality of the Group—Individuals choose to join an academic profession. Many say they do so to serve scholarship, learning, science, truth, society, etc. Belonging is infused with dedication and purpose. It is part of one's identity. Heightened uniformity makes the group overconfident. Members take their ideas to greater extremes. Facing less testing and challenge, the habits of thought become more foolhardy and close-minded.

Type II: Closed-Mindedness

Collective Rationalizations—Academic professions develop elaborate scholastic dogmas to justify the omission of challenging or intractable ideas. Discussions that go outside conventional boundaries and explore substantially different arrangements are dismissed as "ideological" or "advocacy." Classical liberal formulations of voluntary versus coercive action would be dismissed as illusory and ideological. In economics, where mathematical model building dominates the theoretical literature, important facets of knowledge and discovery, including the virtues of free markets, have little chance to be heard. As Janis writes: "When a group of people who respect each other's opinions arrive at a unanimous view, each member is likely to feel that the belief must be true. This reliance on consensual validation tends to replace individual critical thinking and reality-testing."[24]

Stereotypes of Out-Groups—Janis writes: "One of the symptoms of groupthink is the members' persistence in conveying to each other the cliché and oversimplified images of political enemies embodied in long-standing ideological stereotypes."[25] It is not uncommon for social democrat academics to lump their critics together as "conservatives" or "the right," and, as noted, for example, by Bauerlein,[26] to assume that these critics are represented by the likes of George W. Bush, Ann Coulter, Rush Limbaugh, Bill O'Reilly, and Sean Hannity. Few social democratic academics engage the classical liberal alternative offered by Adam Smith, F. A. Hayek, Milton Friedman, or Richard Epstein.

Self-Censorship—The pyramid functions much like a genteel society, in which criticism is muted. Particularly because of norms of consensus, it is impolitic to alienate colleagues. Going along to get along, dissidents and miscreants tend to suppress their disagreements with the dominant view, leading to what Timur Kuran calls "preference falsification."[27]

Direct Pressure on Dissenters—In Janis's work, an insider who dissents is pressured to toe the line. In academia, the dissenter is more likely frozen out. As the group's beliefs become more defective, the group becomes more sensitive to tension, more intolerant of would-be challengers and miscreants. This leads to tighter vetting and expulsion, more uniformity, more intellectual deterioration, and more intolerance. Rothman et al. provide evidence that conservative scholars hold less academically prestigious positions than their peers,[28] controlling for research accomplishment, and Klein and Stern show that Republican-voting scholars who are members of major academic associations are more likely than their peers to have landed outside of academia (particularly in sociology, history, and philosophy).[29]

Symptoms of Defective Decision-Making

Incomplete Survey of Alternatives

Incomplete Survey of Objectives

Failure to Reappraise Initially Rejected Alternatives

Poor Information Search, Selective Bias in Processing Information at Hand

All five of the foregoing items from Janis's figure can be applied to the way social democratic dominance in academia colors the perception of other beliefs. Classical liberal and conservative ideas are often ignored, dismissed by way of elaborate dogmas, or treated only in false caricature.

Some Examples

Perhaps the clearest way to illustrate how we see the problem of social democratic groupthink in the humanities and social sciences is to do a thought experiment. Imagine a doctoral student who unabashedly holds classical liberal ideas like those listed below. Ask yourself whether such a student would be able to find warm support in elite departments of political science, sociology, history, etc. Ask yourself whether the student, no matter how solid his research, would be likely to win grants, be published by the most respected journals, and succeed in the academic job market.

Consider some specific claims that a student's research might explore:

- FDR and the New Deal prolonged the Great Depression.

- American labor laws, such as union privileges, have never been justified and have hurt the poor.

- The K–12 school system in the United States is fruitfully analyzed as a socialist industry, and it exhibits most of the characteristic failings of socialism.

- Most mandated recycling programs are a waste.

In our view, such findings are more than merely plausible, and it would be easy to multiply the examples. Research of this type is not completely unheard of within the tribe of economics.[30] But, especially in other disciplines, a new PhD developing such claims, and substantiating them thoroughly, would fail in the job market and in the "good" journals. The lack of tribe credentials and seals of approval would justify micro decisions to freeze out such a scholar.

Consider some broader theses in philosophy, politics, sociology, anthropology, and history, many of which could be pursued empirically:

- "Social justice" makes no sense (as argued by Hayek).

- "Social justice" is an atavism (as argued by Hayek).

- Government intervention, such as the minimum-wage law, is coercive; the social democratic state is a society of wholesale coercions.

- The prime features of democratic processes include ignorance, superficiality, and systematic biases.

- Democracy often treads on liberty, decency, and prosperity.

- The rise of social democracy since the late nineteenth century may be fruitfully regarded as a subversion of liberalism, specifically in that it promotes a view of the polity as a kind of organization.

- Since 1880, intellectuals have altered the meaning of many key terms of the liberal lexicon—such as "freedom," "liberty," "liberalism," "justice," "rights," "property," "rule of law," "equity," and "equality"—so as to undermine their power in opposition to a social democratic worldview.

- Organizational integrity varies positively with the voluntary basis of participation and funding—that is, government organizations tend to lack organizational integrity because they do not face the threat of loss of support based on voluntary participation.

- The distinction between voluntary and coercive action (or laissez-faire versus interventionism) provides a better framework for analyzing political views and public opinion than liberal versus conservative.

These ideas are anathema to the tribes of sociology, history, political science, philosophy, etc. Groupthink keeps them out of the prestigious journals and course curricula. Some of these fields have alternative centers and associations that would pursue such ideas, but they generally remain peripheral to the professional pyramid. Classical liberal and conservative scholars know the score, and if they nonetheless try to get on in academia, they find themselves watering down their ideas and cloaking or misrepresenting who they really are.

Conclusion

The social democratic element is dominant in the humanities and social sciences, but the wider world of thought and opinion is more diverse. Public discourse is increasingly competitive and individuated. The social democratic professor can inspire commitment in attacking American militarism, but his domestic agenda smacks of paternalism and collectivism. Although collectivist appeals based on democracy and the political "we" are here to stay, the continual advancement of communications, wealth, and globalization would seem to ensure that those appeals will languish in a political culture of ever-increasing fragmentation.

Our hunch about the future is that the social democratic dominance within the humanities and social sciences will grow increasingly insipid. Over time, it will become less hostile to classical liberal and conservative ideas, and such scholars of a mild, strategic kind will have greater success in permeating these fields. Enlightenment has its own power and rewards, and, nowadays, even scholarly discourse is much too contestable to succeed in keeping classical liberalism down.

Notes

1. Gunnar Myrdal, *Objectivity in Social Research* (1969; Middletown, CT: Wesleyan University Press, 1983), 53.

2. Richard Wisniewski, "The Averted Gaze," *Anthropology and Education Quarterly* 31, no. 5 (2000): 8.

3. Edgar Allan Poe, "The Rationale of Verse," in *The Complete Works of Edgar Allan Poe*, vol. 14, *Essays and Miscellanies*, ed. J. A. Harrison (New York: Crowell, 1843), 210.

4. Irving L. Janis, *Groupthink: Psychological Studies of Policy Decisions and Fiascoes*, 2nd ed. (Boston: Houghton Mifflin, 1982).

5. Ibid., 9.

6. Paul 't Hart, *Groupthink in Government: A Study of Small Groups and Policy Failure* (1990; Baltimore: Johns Hopkins University Press, 1994), 7.

7. Ibid., 4. Hart reviews several applications of groupthink research; see ibid., 12–15.

8. Diane Vaughan, *The Challenger Launch Decision: Risky Technology, Culture, and Deviance at NASA* (Chicago: University of Chicago Press, 1996).

9. In treating the matter of extraneous jurisdiction, as by bishop, governor, or minister, Adam Smith continues: "In its nature it is arbitrary and discretionary, and the persons who exercise it, neither attending upon the lectures of the teacher themselves, nor perhaps understanding the sciences which it is his business to teach, are seldom capable of exercising it with judgment." See Adam Smith, *The Wealth of Nations* (1776; Indianapolis, IN: Liberty Fund, 1981), 761.

10. David O. Sears and Carolyn L. Funk, "Evidence of the Long-Term Persistence of Adults' Political Predispositions," *Journal of Politics* 61, no.1 (February 1999): 1–28.

11. P. H. Ditto and D. F. Lopez, "Motivated Skepticism: Use of Differential Decision Criteria for Preferred and Non-preferred Conclusions," *Journal of Personality and Social Psychology* 63 (1992): 568–84. R. S. Nickerson, "Confirmation Bias: A Ubiquitous Phenomenon in Many Guises," *Review of General Psychology* 2 (1998): 175–220.

12. Miller McPherson, Lynn Smith-Lovin, and James M. Cook, "Birds of a Feather: Homophily in Social Networks," *Annual Review of Sociology* 27 (2001): 415–44.

13. Gordon W. Allport, *The Nature of Prejudice* (Cambridge MA: Addison Wesley, 1954); Marilynn B. Brewer, "The Psychology of Prejudice: Ingroup Love or Outgroup Hate?" *Journal of Social Issues* 55, no. 3 (1999): 429–44.

14. E. Katz and P. F. Lazarsfeld, *Personal Influence. The Part Played by People in the Flow of Mass Communications* (New York: Free Press, 1955), 62–63; Serge Moscovici, "Social Influence and Conformity," *The Handbook of Social Psychology*, 3rd ed., vol. 2, ed. G Lindzey and E. Aronson (New York: Random House, 1985), 347–412; Daniel B. Klein, "If Government Is So Villainous, How Come Government Officials Don't Seem Like Villains?" in *3 Libertarian Essays* (Irvington, NY: Foundation for

Economic Education, 1998), 61–86. This piece by Klein treats self-sorting, screening, and belief plasticity in the tendency toward uniformity in the organizational culture of governmental agencies.

15. Stephen H. Balch, "Toward a Reconstitution of Academic Governance," *Academic Questions* 17, no. 1 (Winter 2003–2004): 67–72.

16. See Richard Whitley, *The Intellectual and Social Organization of the Sciences* (Oxford: Oxford University Press, 1984).

17. Daniel B. Klein, "The Ph.D. Circle in Academic Economics," *Econ Journal Watch* 2, no. 1 (2005): 133–48, www.econjournalwatch.org/pdf/KleinInvestigatingApril2005.pdf.

18. Ibid.

19. Val Burris, "The Academic Caste System: Prestige Hierarchies in PhD Exchange Networks," *American Sociological Review* 69 (April 2004): 247–49. Compare these findings about law schools by Richard Redding: "A third of all new teachers [hired in law schools between 1996 and 2000] graduated from either Harvard (18%) or Yale (15%); another third graduated from other top-12 schools, and 20 percent graduated from other top-25 law schools." R. E. Redding, "Where Did You Go to Law School? Gatekeeping by the Professoriate and Its Implications for Legal Education," *Journal of Legal Education* 53 (2003): 594–614.

20. Burris, "Academic Caste System," 251.

21. Janis, *Groupthink*, 244.

22. These figures exclude two-year colleges. See Daniel B. Klein and Charlotta Stern, "Professors and Their Politics: The Policy Views of Social Scientists," *Critical Review* 17, no. 3–4 (2005): 264.

23. Ibid., 272.

24. Janis, *Groupthink*, 37.

25. Ibid.

26. Mark Bauerlein, "Liberal Groupthink Is Anti-Intellectual," *Chronicle of Higher Education*, November 12, 2004, B6.

27. Timur Kuran, *Private Truths, Public Lies: The Social Consequences of Preference Falsification* (Cambridge, MA: Harvard University Press, 1995).

28. Stanley Rothman, S. Robert Lichter, Neil Nevitte, "Politics and Professional Advancement among College Faculty," *Forum* 3, no. 1 (2005), http://www.bepress.com/forum/vol3/iss1/art2/.

29. Klein and Stern, "Professors and Their Politics," 275.

30. It is conceivable that in economics a scholar would succeed in placing such an article in a reputable journal, but it is likely that she would nonetheless have no prospects at the leading economics departments.

6

The Psychology of Political Correctness in Higher Education

William O'Donohue and Richard E. Redding

Particularly because the term "political correctness" means different things to different people, it is difficult to define. Merriam-Webster's dictionary (eleventh edition) defines PC as "conforming to a belief that language and practices which could offend political sensibilities (as in matters of sex or race) should be eliminated." Though not an authoritative source, Wikipedia's definition reflects the common understanding of PC and its associated controversies:

> "Political correctness" . . . is a term used to describe language, ideas, policies, or behavior intended to provide a minimum of offense to racial, cultural, or other identity groups. Political correctness in a critical usage also suggests adherence to political or cultural orthodoxy, and particularly leftwing orthodoxy. Conversely, the term "politically incorrect" is used to refer to language or ideas that may cause offense to some identity groups, or, in a broader sense, that are unconstrained by orthodoxy.
>
> The term itself and its usage are hotly contested. The term "political correctness" is used almost exclusively in a pejorative sense. Those who use the term in a critical fashion often express a concern that public discourse, academia, and the sciences have been dominated by liberal, anti-religious viewpoints. . . . Some commentators, usually on the political left, have argued

that the term "political correctness" is a straw man invented by the New Right to discredit what they consider progressive social change, especially around issues of race and gender.[1]

In the previous chapter, Klein and Stern provide a social-psychological analysis, based on groupthink theory, of the mechanisms by which university faculties replicate themselves to produce increasingly liberal and less ideologically diverse faculties. In this chapter, we deconstruct the psychological goals and assumptions underlying the foundational principles of the politically correct university—principles that emphasize diversity in race, gender, ethnicity, and sexual orientation but not sociopolitical ideas, and that require "cultural sensitivity" (seen in policies such as speech codes) so that minority and disadvantaged groups do not suffer offense or harm.

Drawing on recent psychological research, we argue that sociopolitical diversity may be the most important form of diversity for achieving the educational benefits that diversity is supposed to produce. In addition, we challenge the assumption that certain viewpoints, research agendas, and speech should be prohibited or curtailed because they will offend and harm minority or disadvantaged groups. Finally, we explore the consequences of PC. Political correctness is a political orthodoxy that has a chilling effect on scholarly inquiry and debate. It institutionalizes costly remediation to correct perceived harms against protected groups, but helps some while hurting others (e.g., Lawrence Summers, former president of Harvard).[2] PC promotes a culture of alleged victimizers and victims rather than one of resilient individuals able to withstand the expected frictions associated with a free society.

"Diversity" in Today's Academy

In today's academy, diversity—a concept that originated in higher education—is the central, unifying ethical and pedagogical imperative. The breadth of its application—in faculty hiring, student admissions, scholarship and financial aid distribution, curricula and course design, residence life programs, and extracurricular programs—is remarkable. The diversity doctrine traces its origins to Justice Powell's opinion in *Regents of the University of California v. Bakke*, which provided what would later become the U.S. Supreme Court's constitutional rationale for racial preferences in university admissions. The rationale is that racial preferences are justified because of the educational benefits derived from having demographically diverse students (and therefore diverse ideas) in the classroom. Yet the most ardent proponents of diversity frequently dismiss calls for greater intellectual or sociopolitical diversity on campus, seemingly unaware that much of the diversity program was founded on the claim that intellectual diversity in the classroom is essential to good teaching and learning.

In practice, "diversity" in higher education has become a regime that approaches questions through the lens of race, class, and gender, and that tends, almost by definition, to very strongly favor particular political ideologies and to exclude groups that do not share these ideologies. As Klein and Stern document in chapter 2 of this volume, conservatives and libertarians are vastly underrepresented in the academy, especially in the social sciences, humanities, and education. There is less imbalance in fields that are inherently more conservative (e.g., economics, law, business), but there still are significantly more liberal than conservative faculty even in these disciplines. And, although liberals have always outnumbered conservatives in the academy, the trend has been accelerating in recent years—younger faculty are the most politically homogeneous.

The academy's definition and practice of diversity is too narrow and limited; racial, ethnic, and gender diversity are not the only kinds of diversity that we should be striving for. The politically correct university insists that we look beneath the surface of our institutions and social practices to uncover the "false consciousness," power structures, and hidden inequalities it conceals, yet it understands diversity as involving only the most readily apparent physical differences among people. We challenge the assumption that diversity applies only to race, ethnicity, gender, and sexual orientation, though we readily acknowledge the importance of these forms of diversity. We argue instead for a more inclusive definition of diversity that encompasses intellectual diversity, particularly a diversity of sociopolitical viewpoints in the classroom and in research (especially research on public policy).

The Rationale for Diversity

In higher education today, the most important differences among people are thought to be racial, ethnic, and gender differences. Three assumptions about human psychology are at the core of this belief:

1) *The Personal Identity Assumption:* People's race, ethnicity, gender, and sexual orientation are central to their personal identity (or "sense of self") and view of the world, and it is important to recognize and celebrate these identities in pedagogy and university programs.[3]

2) *The Discrimination Assumption:* People suffer discrimination due to their race, ethnicity, or gender, and this discrimination requires remedies (such as diversity training).[4]

3) *The Educational Benefits Assumption:* With racial, ethnic, and gender diversity comes a diversity of life experiences, values, and ideas; and exposing students to these various perspectives has educational benefits.

As we discuss below, each of these assumptions also applies—and perhaps applies even better—to sociopolitical diversity. Recent psychological research suggests that people's sociopolitical values are a core part of their self-identity, that people are discriminated against on the basis of their sociopolitical beliefs, and that sociopolitical diversity enhances education and scholarship.

The Personal Identity Assumption

Because they reflect morality-based differences in how we perceive the world, our sociopolitical values, just like our ethnicity and gender, are fundamental to who we are as individuals. Researchers have found that sociopolitical beliefs are linked to our personality traits and early childhood and family experiences,[5] and studies show that genetic factors account for about half of the variability in our political beliefs.[6] The link between genetic and personality factors and political beliefs suggests that such beliefs derive from, and are basic aspects of, the self. Rooted in our fundamental moral values, sociopolitical worldviews provide meaning and significance to life, and act as a kind of security blanket against life's uncertainties—even our own mortality. Experimental studies show, for example, that being reminded of death increases both our favorable attitudes toward those having similar political beliefs and our negative attitudes toward those having opposing beliefs.[7]

Thus, just as minority students may feel alienated in educational environments lacking minority professors or culturally sensitive course content, conservative students may feel alienated when few (often none) of their professors share or respect their views and when conservative perspectives are excluded from pedagogy. Such alienation decreases the likelihood of academic and vocational success. People often opt out of careers they discover to be inconsistent with, or unsupportive of, their self-identity and fundamental values,[8] and this may partly explain why there are so few conservatives on university faculties. Particularly in the humanities and social sciences (where conservative students report less satisfaction with their courses than their liberal peers), conservative students react negatively to the partisanship that they perceive in these disciplines. Indeed, conservative students have more distant relationships with their professors and apparently have fewer opportunities to conduct research with faculty, as Woessner and Kelly-Woessner show in a previous chapter.

The Discrimination Assumption

People may be discriminated against on the basis of their political beliefs, just as they may be on the basis of ethnicity and gender. People often negatively stereotype those with opposing beliefs and have unconscious biases against them, and these biases drive discriminatory behavior.[9] The aphorism that "opposites attract" could not be more inaccurate. A strong finding from psychological research is that people have greater affinity for those who share their attitudes and often dislike those whose attitudes differ too much from their own,[10] particularly when sociopolitical values are involved. Blood is thicker than water, but sociopolitical values are thicker still. Consider a recent study that examined how demographic and attitudinal characteristics of fraternity pledge candidates affect fraternity admissions decisions. The similarity in sociopolitical views between the candidate and fraternity members was more important in admissions decisions than almost any other factor, including race or ethnicity.[11] Other studies likewise suggest that sociopolitical bias may be stronger than racial or ethnic bias,[12] perhaps because an opposing sociopolitical worldview challenges our view of the world, our fundamental moral precepts, and ultimately, our own personal identity.

Moreover, research indicates that people make many of their political judgments more or less intuitively, on an emotional level.[13] Studies show that judgments on sociopolitical issues are better predicted by people's emotional reactions to the issues than by their perceptions of the actual effects of policy alternatives.[14] Because sociopolitical attitudes tend to be deep-seated, emotionally driven, linked to fundamental personality attributes and core values, and applied in decision making in a largely intuitive and automatic fashion,[15] there is a human tendency to be biased and prejudiced against the sociopolitical "other."[16]

Indeed, a certain closed-mindedness exists among many liberal academics who espouse tolerance as a metavalue but who are intolerant of conservatives and conservative views. To succeed in the academy, conservative students and young faculty members frequently feel that they must accommodate themselves to the views of the majority of the faculty. They feel that the academic culture is hostile to their politics, and they hesitate in expressing or exploring nonliberal viewpoints.[17] Rothman and Lichter's finding (see chapter 4) that conservative academics are underplaced in the academic meritocracy relative to their liberal peers also has implications here; the lack of political diversity among faculty may result in discrimination against conservative scholars in faculty hiring.[18]

The Educational Benefits Assumption

As the U.S. Supreme Court made clear in the 2003 *Grutter v. Bollinger* decision, affirmative action is legally justified only because of the educational benefits produced by diversity.[19]

That sociopolitical diversity enhances student learning as well as faculty scholarship has been documented; research demonstrates that exposure to multiple perspectives stimulates critical thinking and creativity, produces more complex reasoning styles and attitudes, improves understanding and decision-making quality, and facilitates values clarification and moral development.[20] In addition, research has shown that people who are part of sociopolitically diverse groups tend to be willing to consider ideas different from their own.[21]

Thus, the political imbalance in academic research on political or public policy issues, and in research in the social sciences and humanities, is unfortunate. Studies show that a scholar's values significantly affect the research questions asked, the way such questions are framed and defined, the interpretation of findings, and even seemingly objective matters like choice of methods for data collection and analysis.[22] If one approaches problems only from a liberal perspective, as the overwhelming majority of academics do, one is likely to get only liberal answers. The fact that the professoriate is overwhelmingly liberal is necessarily going to lead to a much narrower and more myopic research agenda than otherwise would be the case, thereby also narrowing the range of ideas to which students are exposed. Moreover, politically conservative students who wish to explore conservative research paradigms find that there are few, if any, mentors with whom they can work, since their professors are not engaged in, or receptive to, such research. Perhaps this is why conservative students have fewer opportunities to do research with their professors, as documented in an earlier chapter by Woessner and Kelly-Woessner.

The Importance of Sociopolitical Diversity

To be sure, differences in values and life experiences often accompany differences in race, ethnicity, and gender, but the same is true for sociopolitical differences. If we are sensitive to the former, we should be sensitive to the latter. In any event, the demographic or psychological variability *within* a particular group can be as great as or greater than the variability *among* groups. In addition, research shows that there is virtually no relationship between demographic diversity and attitudinal diversity.[23] Race, ethnicity, gender, or sexual orientation is not necessarily the most relevant influence on personal identity and worldview. Each is just one of several influences among a multitude, including the individual's sociopolitical values.[24]

To argue that sociopolitical differences cannot be equated with differences like race and gender—and therefore that sociopolitical diversity is not important in higher education—flies in the face of a sizeable and compelling body of research showing the powerful and pervasive effects of sociopolitical value differences on interpersonal relationships (including discriminatory practices) and human performance in school and workplace settings. If, as multiculturalists believe, human identity is culturally dependent, then sociopolitical values are an important part of that culture and identity. We also must recognize the inevitable discriminatory effects of liberal groupthink, which excludes or marginalizes conservatives and their views. The academy's multicultural project cannot succeed when *diversity* is defined to include every kind of difference except the one that may matter most.[25]

The PC University's Assumptions about Psychological Harm

PC is foundational to the identity politics that taxonomizes the world into oppressor and victim classes, and then defines the work that needs to be done to remediate the oppression. It is based on a revelatory epistemology associated with a liberal political ideology instead of a scientific ideology.[26] After PC "consciousness raising," one comes to see the world in terms of oppressors and victims. At the outset, we note that this taxonomy poses significant conceptual problems. There is uncertainty about how to parse cultures: the term "Native American" lumps together four hundred distinct Indian nations and tribes; the broad term "Asian-American" does injustice to all the variety of cultures encompassed under the rubric "Asian."[27] In turn, we are uncertain about which groups constitute the oppressor and victim classes; the two become fungible according to the beliefs and motivations of those in the academy charged with enforcing the PC ethic. (Why, for example, are Jews not typically included under higher education's PC umbrella, given historical and contemporary anti-Semitism?)

In viewing human interactions through a political lens (e.g., unequal power relations) and according to the psychological reactions of members of the victim classes, the PC university relies upon two core psychological assumptions:

1) *The Offense/Harm Assumption:* Certain viewpoints, activities (particularly speech), or policies offend or harm members of particular groups (usually minority or disadvantaged groups).

2) *The Intervention Assumption:* The psychological offense or harm is of such a magnitude or kind that preventing or prohibiting it—and in some cases, even punishing the alleged perpetrators—is justified.

Consider, for example, campus speech codes, such as that at Texas Tech, which bans any speech that can cause "reasonable apprehension" or "psychological harm," or that is "humiliating, demeaning or degrading to any member of the university community."[28] Or consider Texas A&M's code, which prohibits speech that fails to show "respect for personal feelings."[29] Until a lawsuit was brought challenging its constitutionality, the speech code of the State University of New York at Brockport contained a laundry list of prohibited conduct, including "calling someone an old bag" and telling "jokes making fun of any protected group."[30] As these speech codes and many other university programs and practices illustrate, First Amendment guarantees of free speech are not always available in academia, the very place free speech should be valued.

In addition, PC often implicitly (and sometimes explicitly) contains a third assumption:

3) *The Unconscious Assumption:* The PC transgressor may be unaware of his or her prejudices because such attitudes are often unconsciously held.[31] The alleged perpetrator's true report of having no intention to offend or harm is therefore insufficient and even irrelevant.

Thus, PC relies on the psychological assumptions that individuals will feel offended and/or be harmed psychologically by violations of PC, that often the offender is not conscious of possessing the prejudices that gave rise to the offense, and that interventions are necessary to prevent or correct the harm. But let us consider some alternative hypotheses:

1) The offense/harm claim is inaccurate (i.e., there is no harm).

2) The offense/harm claim is not objectively true but is the result of the psychological makeup of those claiming harm.

3) The offense/harm claims and interventions serve to satisfy other individual or group psychological needs; they serve as stalking horses for identity politics and a liberal political orthodoxy disguised as a psychological issue.

4) The intervention will fail to have a restorative effect or will perhaps have even a net harmful effect, on the alleged victims and/or perpetrators.

We explore these hypotheses in the following sections.

Evidence of Harm

Empirical research is needed to determine whether purported violations of PC actually do cause harm. We do not know what percentages of people are offended or harmed by these violations, the magnitude of offense or harm, or the contexts and boundaries of these regularities. In addition, there is no research on the awareness hypothesis: we do not know in how many cases harm was intended and in how many cases unintended. The thresholds for offense and harm should be explicated: Is the victim devastated or just mildly annoyed? Does the victim's self-esteem drop ten points on some scale for at least six months? Does the offense produce posttraumatic stress disorder? It may be the case that while there is offense or harm, it does not reach a significant bar. "I am uncomfortable with . . ." would be a low bar for offense but one that is often used in the world of PC. This bar makes false and dangerous assumptions about the psychological comfortableness of life, freedom, and human interaction. By contrast, "I am traumatized by . . ." would be a high bar, though we hypothesize that diagnosable full or partial posttraumatic stress disorder as a result of (even repeated) PC offenses would be exceedingly rare.

To be sure, a body of research on what is known as "stereotype threat" suggests that the academic and work performance of minorities is impaired by their exposure to negative societal stereotypes,[32] and this might be seen as an argument for prohibiting speech or scholarship that asserts these stereotypes.[33] (Under this theory, Lawrence Summers's suggestion that men and women might have different abilities in math and science had measurable effects on women's success in scientific careers because it reinforced gender stereotypes.[34]) But scholarly inquiry and debate cannot be constrained by attempts to protect people from the alleged harmful effects of scientific knowledge.[35] As Harvard psychology professor Stephen Pinker says, "It's hard to imagine any aspect of public life where ignorance or delusion is better than an awareness of the truth, even an unpleasant one." This is especially true in our colleges and universities, places whose very existence is predicated on the academic freedom to explore and debate *a diversity of ideas*. In any event, we do not know what kinds of speech and ideas actually are harmful, the type and degree of harm caused, or how the harm may vary across individuals and contexts. Most importantly, we do not know whether greater harm is caused by suppressing "offensive" ideas than by airing and debating them.

Or consider the common assumption in PC that offensive speech (or policies or practices deemed to be noninclusive) will lower the self-esteem of minority or disadvantaged groups. Not only is there a lack of direct empirical evidence to support this assumption, but recent psychological research has called into question the value of self-esteem. By causing people to overestimate their strengths and abilities, high self-esteem may have negative effects on academic and job performance and engender a narcissistic self-concept.[36] In any case, efforts to protect or improve the self-esteem only of certain groups may be a zero-sum game: self-esteem is "a scarce and contested resource, which individuals [can] gain at the expense of others. . . . Because individuals are, in part, the source of the self-esteem of others, not everyone can attain the highest [self esteem]."[37]

Problems with Self-Reports of Harm

Like many psychological experiences, the offense and harm claimed by members of protected groups as a result of particular speech or sociopolitical views is usually not objectively observable, but is based instead upon self-report by individuals or groups. Self-reports alone, however, cannot be regarded as authoritative. People have complex motivations that often make their self-reports suspect, even when they are making every effort to be truthful.[38] What, then, is the proper role of self-report in these offense and harm claims, and what other evidence should be probative?

First, we should consider who is making the claim of offense or harm. No doubt, some would argue that examining the person(s) or group(s) claiming harm is itself offensive, being nothing more than "victim-blaming."[39] But it is relevant, indeed necessary, to do so. Aristotle suggested that in any argument, three issues are relevant: 1) *logos*—the logic of the argument; 2) *pathos*—the emotion associated with the case; and 3) *ethos*—the character of the speaker.[40] In claims of psychological injury, ethos is always an issue. Because the offended person is making a claim about his or her internal states, that person's psychological makeup is relevant.

Typically, only some members of the relevant class of individuals report offense or harm. Why are these individuals offended while others in the group are not? Perhaps they have "raised consciousnesses," or are uniquely vulnerable because of past experiences, or are more sensitive or assertive. But some claimants also may be psychologically constituted in problematic ways that go beyond having heightened sensitivity. The *Diagnostic and Statistical Manual of Mental Disorders*, the taxonomy of mental disorders used by mental health professionals, includes a relatively common class of disorders known as "personality disorders." A few of these disorders may, in some cases, be implicated in the perception or reporting of offense or harm:

- People with *narcissistic personality disorder* have "a grandiose sense of self-importance," "require excessive admiration," have "a sense of entitlement," and are "interpersonally exploitive." They easily sustain "narcissistic injuries" and are readily offended by any comments or behaviors that they perceive to be critical.[41]

- People with *histrionic personality disorder* are "uncomfortable in situations in which they are not the center of attention," "show self-dramatization," are "suggestible," and "often act out a role (e.g., 'victim' or 'princess') in their relationships with others."[42]

They may be attracted to the drama of a PC injury for the attention that it provides them.

- People with *antisocial personality disorder* have a personality makeup characterized by "deceitfulness, irritability and aggressiveness," "a lack of remorse," and "consistent irresponsibility."[43] They may be attracted to the personal gain derived by claiming a PC injury.

- People with *borderline personality disorder* have an "unstable self-image," "affective instability due to marked reactivity of mood," "inappropriate intense anger," "transient stress-related paranoid ideation," and "a tendency to see offense where there is none."[44] Such characteristics may predispose these individuals to easily take offense and to (perhaps angrily) demand some sort of intervention.

To be clear, we are *not* suggesting that most PC injury claims are associated with these disorders—only that in *some* cases those claiming injury may be predisposed toward these disorders, which make them more likely to perceive offense or allege harm to achieve personal gain. Epidemiological studies indicate that about 5 to 10 percent of the population has at least one of these personality disorders, which often co-occur.[45]

Other Psychological Needs Served by PC

Other psychological needs may also be served by PC. Psychological theory and research in the social learning tradition suggest that some maladaptive interpersonal interactions (e.g., those between a parent and oppositional child) occur, in part, because the participants are using coercive control instead of more positive control techniques (e.g., positive reinforcement, communicating rationales).[46] The coercively oriented parent resorts to threats in order to get the oppositional child to obey. The child uses tantrums and other punishing behaviors in a reciprocal attempt to coerce the parent to terminate demands for obedience. This leads to a downward spiral, wherein a great deal of negative emotion is generated as both parties increase their attempts at coercive control.

Similarly, PC behavior may be generated by individuals or interest groups who have been reinforced to use coercive interactional behavior and assume the victim's mantle to gain power and advantage in the polity of the ivory tower. PC interest groups may, for example, coerce others to remain silent, to refrain from criticizing favored beliefs and practices, or steer clear of research on politically incorrect topics (e.g., group differences in IQ). Individuals claiming offense or harm threaten to use negative labels or sanctions against the offender; saying "I'm offended" allows the victim to terminate what he or she does not like. When offended parties successfully terminate what they find aversive, the law of effect suggests that they are more likely to engage in such behavior in the future (and thus may appear to become increasingly "sensitive"). This may have the harmful effect of making victims seem (even to themselves) more psychologically vulnerable and fragile, unable to cope with life's slings and arrows through positive assertive behaviors.

In the recent book *One Nation under Therapy*, philosopher Christina Hoff Sommers and psychiatrist Sally Satel argue that our "overhelping" therapeutic society sees people as fragile, rejects stoicism, and encourages people to share their discomforts.[47] The PC university also sees people as fragile and encourages an openness about feelings and possible injuries. The corrective measures for such injuries (e.g., disciplining alleged offenders, mandatory diversity or sensitivity training, providing counseling or therapy) all attempt to help, or perhaps to "overhelp." What might be the motivation for this? The African American scholar Shelby Steele argues that one legacy of slavery and historical white supremacy is "white guilt," which diminishes the moral authority of whites. To expiate this guilt and regain moral authority, the majority constructs politically correct movements and programs that serve to satisfy its psychological needs.[48] This raises provocative questions. Is the PC university a mechanism for assuaging guilt, thereby satisfying the in-group's psychological needs instead of solving the out-group's problems? Are PC rhetoric and dogma tropes to gain interpersonal power—for those individuals claiming offense and for the academy's liberal sociopolitical in-groups?

PC "Helps" Some by Hurting Others

Finally, PC is paradoxical and self-defeating: it seeks to decrease offensive acts toward certain groups through offensive acts toward other groups—that is, it helps some by hurting others. In another chapter in this volume, Wood refers to the "new kind of aristocracy" created by PC, with its hierarchy of privilege based on perceived victimization. This hierarchy also entails a class of victimizers who are accused, explicitly or implicitly, of a range of crimes.

Consider diversity training programs, which are a central feature of the freshman orientation and residence life programs (as well as many other programs) at colleges and universities today.[49] In 2007, for example, the University of Delaware implemented a sensitivity training program that was mandatory for all students living in the university dormitories. The highly ideological program (which had won awards from the American College Personnel Association) was discontinued after protests from students and alumni.[50] It included individual and group sessions with students, training for resident assistants in how to confront students resistant to culturally sensitive viewpoints, and a "zero-tolerance" policy toward any speech or behavior deemed to be insensitive (with incident reports written about students who expressed non-PC viewpoints or resisted the sensitivity training). Attitudinal questionnaires were periodically administered to students, and a file kept on each student's attitudes and progress toward achieving the program's educational objectives, which were to raise students' consciousness about racism, sexism, homophobia, and white oppression. To meet the educational objectives, students were required to recognize, for example, "that systemic oppression exists in our society" and that "white culture is a melting pot of greed, guys, guns, and god."[51] The training materials defined a racist as "one who is both privileged and socialized on the basis of race by a white supremacist (racist) system. *The term applies to all white people* (i.e., people of European descent) living in the United States, regardless of class, gender, religion, culture, or sexuality. *By this definition, people of color cannot be racists.*"[52]

The apparent goal, as one student seemed to suggest, was "to make us feel guilty about the privileges we have, and to convince us of our part in white supremacy. . . . I'm being told it's wrong to be a white male. The whole system being used seems to be trying to change the students into all holding the same views. . . . This is in no way diversity."[53] In the sessions, students were required to confess their privilege or oppression and were asked questions about their political views and sexual orientation. Students were strongly urged to participate in various liberal advocacy activities and to "examine [their] textbooks and course work to determine whether [they are] equitable, representative, and multicultural."[54]

Consider also the behavior of the professoriate in the Duke lacrosse case. For many Duke professors, "whose careers [had] been devoted toward imposing a race/class/gender worldview on the academy . . . the lacrosse case was too tempting not to exploit. White males who played a sport associated with the Eastern elite were accused of raping a poor, black, local woman."[55] Professors made public speeches and comments opining on the players' guilt and bad character. No fewer than eighty-eight Duke professors (including 80 percent of professors in African American studies, 72 percent in women's studies, 60 percent in cultural anthropology, and many professors in the English, foreign languages, history, and art departments) placed an advertisement in the Duke newspaper stating that the university was undergoing a "social disaster" because the students "know themselves to be objects of racism and sexism." English professor Houston Baker published a letter demanding that the university expel the entire lacrosse team, which he said had been given "license to rape, maraud, deploy hate speech, and feel proud of themselves in the bargain." His letter repeatedly disparaged the race of the players. But none of these professors retracted their comments or apologized after the players' innocence was proven, the charges dismissed, and prosecutor Mike Nifong indicted for prosecutorial misconduct. On the contrary, one prominent Duke professor accused the players of perjury and hate crimes. His evidence? They were embodiments of "the perfect white self."[56]

All of this leads us to conclude with an observation about the psychological world created by PC. There is an ongoing debate about whether psychological interventions should focus on people's weaknesses and attempt to shore those up or identify and build upon their strengths. The latter approach, so-called "positive psychology,"[57] has been in ascendance in the last few decades, partly in reaction to the older view of individuals as vulnerable and weak. Perhaps the proponents of PC should adopt such an approach. Instead of assuming that life's bumps require ameliorative interventions for victims and/or punitive interventions for offenders, the message could be—as research indeed demonstrates[58]—that individuals are often resilient and frequently do not require interventions to save them from life's slings and arrows.

Indeed, not only does PC help some by hurting others, but it may ultimately end up hurting the very people it tries to help.

Notes

1. Wikipedia, "Political Correctness," www.http://en.wikipedia.org/wiki/Political_correctness.

2. Lawrence Summers lost his job as president of Harvard University, due in large part to a speech in which he speculated that the "variability [between] the male and female population" in mathematical and scientific ability might partly explain the relatively small number of female scientists. Lawrence Summers, "Remarks at NBER Conference on Diversifying the Science and Engineering Workforce," January 14, 2005, http://www.president.harvard.edu/ speeches/2005 /nber.html. Female members of the Harvard faculty organized against Summers, resulting in a no-confidence vote at a meeting of the arts and sciences faculty. See James Atlas, "The Battle behind the Battle at Harvard," *New York Times*, February 27, 2005. Summers resigned soon thereafter. More recently, in 2007, the regents of University of California, Davis rescinded their invitation to Summers to speak at their board dinner after the female faculty circulated a petition opposing his presence.

3. See Richard E. Redding, *The Political Is the Personal: The Centrality of Political Self-Identity* (forthcoming); Richard E. Redding, *What's Politics Got to Do with It?: A New Way to Think about Diversity* (forthcoming).

4. Redding, *What's Politics Got to Do with It?*

5. John R. Alford, Carolyn L. Funk, and John R. Hibbing, "Are Political Orientations Genetically Transmitted?" *American Political Science Review* 99 (2005): 153–67; John T. Jost, Jack Glaser, Arie W. Kruglanski, and Frank J. Sulloway, "Political Conservatism as Motivated Social Cognition," *Psychological Bulletin* 129 (2003): 329–75; George Lakoff, *Moral Politics: How Liberals and Conservatives Think*, 2nd ed. (Chicago: University of Chicago Press, 2002).

6. Alford, Funk, and Hibbing, "Are Political Orientations Genetically Transmitted?" 164.

7. Jeff Greenberg, Sheldon Solomon, and Tom Pyszczynski, "Terror Management Theory of Self-Esteem and Cultural Worldviews: Empirical Assessments and Conceptual Refinements," in *Advances in Experimental Social Psychology* 29, ed. M. P. Zanna (New York: Academic Press, 1997), 61–139.

8. See Richard E. Redding. "Sociopolitical Diversity in Psychology: The Case for Pluralism." *American Psychologist* 56 (2001): 205–15.

9. Redding, "Sociopolitical Diversity in Psychology," 208–10; Redding, *The Political is the Personal*; Redding, *What's Politics Got to Do with It?*

10. See Elizabeth Mannix and Margaret A. Neale, "What Differences Make a Difference?: The Promise and Reality of Diverse Teams in Organizations," *Psychological Science in the Public Interest* 6, no. 2 (2005): 31–56; Milton E. Rosenbaum, "The Repulsion Hypothesis: On the Nondevelopment of Relationships," *Journal of Personality and Social Psychology* 51 (1986): 1156–66.

11. Jonathan Haidt, Evan Rosenberg, and Holly Hom, "Differentiating Diversities:

Moral Diversity Is Not Like Other Kinds," *Journal of Applied Social Psychology* 33 (2003): 1–36.

12. Ibid.; and Chester A. Insko, Rupert W. Nacoste, and Jeffrey L. Moe, "Belief Congruence and Racial Discrimination: Review of the Evidence and Critical Evaluation," *European Journal of Social Psychology* 13 (1983): 153–74.

13. Joshua Greene and J. Haidt, "How (and Where) Does Moral Judgment Work?" *Trends in Cognitive Sciences* 6 (2002): 517–23; Jonathan Haidt, "The Emotional Dog and Its Rational Tail: A Social Intuitionist Approach to Moral Judgment," *Psychological Review* 108 (2001): 814–34.

14. Jonathan Haidt and Matthew Hersh, "Sexual Morality: The Cultures and Emotions of Conservatives and Liberals," *Journal of Applied Social Psychology* 31 (2001): 191–221.

15. Greene and Haidt, "How (and Where) Does Moral Judgment Work?"; Haidt, "The Emotional Dog and Its Rational Tail."

16. Mannix and Neale, "What Differences Make a Difference?"; Redding, *The Political Is the Personal*; Redding, *What's Politics Got to Do with It?*

17. People are less likely to express their views when they perceive that others do not share them. See Carroll J. Glynn, Andrew F. Hayes, and James Shanahan, "Perceived Support for One's Opinions and Willingness to Speak Out: A Meta-Analysis of Survey Studies on the 'Spiral of Silence,'" *Public Opinion Quarterly* 61 (1997): 452–63.

18. Studies in organizational behavior show that employers (e.g., academic departments in universities) tend to hire those who share their values. See Redding, "Sociopolitical Diversity in Psychology," 210.

19. *Grutter v. Bollinger*, 539 U.S. 306 (2003).

20. Redding, "Sociopolitical Diversity in Psychology"; Scott E. Page, *The Difference: How the Value of Diversity Creates Better Groups, Firms, Schools, and Societies* (Princeton, NJ: Princeton University Press, 2007); Mannix and Neale, "What Differences Make a Difference?"

21. Penny S. Visser and Robert R. Mirabile, "Attitudes in the Social Context: The Impact of Social Network Composition on Individual-Level Attitude Strength," *Journal of Personality and Social Psychology* 87 (2004): 779–95.

22. Redding, "Sociopolitical Diversity in Psychology."

23. See Mannix and Neale, "What Differences Make a Difference?" 44.

24. Sally L. Satel and Richard E. Redding, "Sociopolitical Trends in Mental Health Care: The Consumer/Survivor Movement and Multiculturalism," in *Kaplan & Sadock's Comprehensive Textbook of Psychiatry 1*, ed. Benjamin J. Sadock and Virginia A. Sadock (Philadelphia: Lippincott Williams and Wilkins, 2005), 644–55.

25. At the same time, however, the boundary conditions of "diversity" require definition. Diversity for diversity's sake is problematic. It needs to be constrained by some criteria for assessing legitimacy and value, which is no easy task.

26. Kenneth Minogue, *Alien Powers: The Pure Theory of Ideology* (London: Transaction Press, 2006).

27. William T. O'Donohue, "Cultural Sensitivity: A Critical Examination," in *Destructive Trends in Mental Health*, ed. Richard Wright and Nicholas Cummings (New York: Taylor and Francis, 2005), 29–44.

28. Greg Lukianoff, "Campus Speech Codes: Absurd, Tenacious, and Everywhere," *Academic Questions* (forthcoming).

29. Ibid.

30. Ibid.

31. For a discussion and critique of social science research on unconscious prejudice, see Richard E. Redding, "Bias on Prejudice?: The Politics of Research on Racial Prejudice," *Psychological Inquiry* 15 (2004): 289–93.

32. Claude M. Steele, "A Threat in the Air: How Stereotypes Shape Intellectual Identity and Performance," *American Psychologist* 52 (1997): 613–29.

33. In recent years, psychologists have begun to investigate not just the process and negative effects of stereotyping but also the degree to which stereotypes may be accurate. See, for example, Redding, "Bias on Prejudice." This emerging research suggests that some stereotypes are accurate, that they do not necessarily exaggerate group differences, and that relying in part on stereotypes does not necessarily produce inaccurate judgments about individuals. See Lee J. Jussim and Clark R. McCauley, eds., *Stereotype Accuracy: Toward Appreciating Group Differences* (Washington, DC: American Psychological Association, 1995). Nonetheless, "it is difficult, even dangerous, to talk about group differences. . . . Such candor is bound to provoke accusations of insensitivity and even racism. . . . To evade the accusations and to be politically correct, social scientists avoid a frank discussion of significant cultural differences." Victor Ottati and Yueh-Ting Lee, "Accuracy: A Neglected Component of Stereotype Research," in ibid., 29–62.

34. See Amy K. Keifer and Denise Sekaquaptewa, "Implicit Stereotypes, Gender Identification, and Math-Related Outcomes: A Prospective Study of Female College Students," *Psychological Science* 18 (2007): 13–18.

35. There is a long list of politically incorrect topics in science, including questions such as these: Do men and woman differ in aptitudes and emotions? Are suicide bombers mentally healthy and morally motivated? Was the decrease in the crime rate during the 1990s due in part to the legalization of abortion? Is the average IQ of Western populations declining because less intelligent people are having more children than smarter people? Although these topics are highly controversial, there is sufficient scientific evidence supporting each of these hypothesis to merit further scientific investigation, and any findings could have potentially significant scientific and policy implications. Stephen Pinker, "In Defense of Dangerous Ideas," *Chicago Sun-Times*, July 15, 2007.

36. Roy F. Baumeister, J. D. Campbell, Joachim I. Krueger, and Kathleen D. Vohs, "Does High Self-Esteem Cause Better Performance, Interpersonal Success, Happiness, or Healthier Lifestyles?" *Psychological Science in the Public Interest* 4 (2003): 1–44.

37. Joachim I. Krueger, Kathleen D. Vohs, and Roy F. Baumeister, "Is the Allure of Self-Esteem a Mirage after All?" *American Psychologist* 64 (2008): 64.

38. See Richard Nisbett and Timothy Wilson, "On Saying More Than We Can Know: Verbal Reports on Mental Processes," *Psychological Review* 84 (1977): 231–59.

39. See William Ryan, *Blaming the Victim* (New York: Pantheon Books, 1971).

40. See *On Rhetoric*.

41. American Psychiatric Association, *Diagnostic and Statistical Manual of Mental Disorders*, 4th ed. (Washington, DC: American Psychiatric Association, 2000), 714–17.

42. Ibid., 711–14.

43. Ibid., 701–6.

44. Ibid., 706–10.

45. William T. O'Donohue, K. Fowler, and Scott Lilienfeld, *Handbook of Personality Disorders: Toward the DSM-V* (Boston: Allyn and Bacon, 2007).

46. Gerald R. Patterson and L. Bank, "Some Amplifying Mechanisms for Pathologic Processes in Families," *The Minnesota Symposia on Child Psychology: Systems and Development* 22, ed. Megan R. Gunnar and Esther Thelen (Hillsdale, NJ: Erlbaum, 1989).

47. Christina Hoff Sommers and Sally Satel, *One Nation under Therapy* (New York: Simon and Schuster, 2006).

48. Shelby Steele, *White Guilt: How Blacks and Whites Together Destroyed the Promise of the Civil Rights Era* (New York: Harper, 2007).

49. See Wood's chapter in this volume; see also Thomas Wood, "Residence Life, the Shoha Troupe, and Social Justice Education at U Mass Amherst," December 28, 2007, http://www.nas.org/aa/ExecDir_Comments/Archives/Tracking/tracking_001.htm; Alan Charles Kors and Harvey A. Silvergate, *The Shadow University: The Betrayal of Liberty on America's Campuses* (New York: Free Press, 1998).

50. See Adam Kissel, "Habits of Mind?: The Brainwashing Curriculum at the University of Delaware" (paper presented at the 19th Educational Policy Conference, the Constitutional Coalition, St. Louis, MO, January 25, 2008); Stuart Taylor Jr., "Academia's Pervasive PC Rot," *National Journal*, November 12, 2007.

51. Quoted in Taylor, "Academia's Pervasive PC Rot."

52. Quoted in Kissel, "Habits of Mind" (emphasis added).

53. Quoted in ibid.

54. Ibid.

55. Taylor, "Academia's Pervasive PC Rot."

56. This account of the Duke case is from Stuart Taylor and K. C. Johnson, *Until Proven Innocent: Political Correctness and the Shameful Injustices of the Duke Lacrosse Rape Case* (New York: St. Martin's Press, 2007), 85. For the text of Baker's letter, see "Provost Responds to Faculty Letter Regarding Lacrosse," Duke News and Communications, April 3, 2006, http://www.dukenews.duke.edu/mmedia/features/lacrosse_incident/lange_baker.html.

57. Martin Seligman, P. A. Linley, and S. Joseph, *Positive Psychology in Practice* (Washington, DC: American Psychological Association, 2004).

58. Meyer D. Glantz and Jeannette L. Johnson, eds., *Resilience and Development: Positive Life Adaptations* (New York: Springer, 1999); Hoff Sommers and Satel, *One Nation under Therapy*.

7

College Conformity 101:
Where the Diversity of Ideas
Meets the Idea of Diversity

Peter Wood

Some words or concepts exercise power over our minds and our feelings through their impressive generality. We know what it is to be free, even if we lack a constitutional lawyer's capacity to detail particular freedoms guaranteed by law. The man or woman who once lived under an oppressive government may have a vivid sense of freedom without being able to abstract from that sense to the political theory of freedom. The same applies to many of the key concepts that shape our culture and civilization. Equality, fairness, honesty, ownership, family, and friendship, among others, are large ideas rooted in common experience. We can assign such words precise meanings—often for legal purposes we *must* assign them precise meanings—but such precision is an afterthought. To a large extent, the *poetry* of the idea comes first. There is little point in trying to pin down freedom in a book or a legal decision, unless some substantial number of people are already moved by the idea. And so on with equality and fairness and the other terms I mentioned.

So where does the term "diversity" come into this picture? Is it primarily a legal formalism, launched on its current career by Justice Powell in 1978, in his opinion in *Regents of the University of California v. Bakke*,[1] and from there taken up by university activists looking to put racial preferences in college admissions on a more secure basis? Or is "diversity" one of these root ideas, like freedom, or like equality, that speaks to our moral intuitions first and that has its own poesis, long before it is reduced to the precision of the law?

It is not a question with a simple answer. I wrestled with it in my 2003 book, *Diversity: The Invention of a Concept*, and came up with a divided answer, which I can do no better than repeat.[2] Diversity is really two quite different ideas, one old and one quite recent, that have been muddled together in current usage. The older of these two ideas is the sense that we have been bundled into a world full of unforeseeable human differences. Those differences make up a good portion of the real world, and, according to this idea, we had best learn to recognize them and negotiate with them. The differences of which I speak are not intrinsically good or bad; they are not to be automatically celebrated, or automatically shunned. Rather they call for intelligent discernment and good judgment. This form of diversity, as far as I can tell, was never actually called by the word "diversity," but it was a major theme in nineteenth- and early twentieth-century American thought. One of our best literary evocations of it is in the opening pages of Herman Melville's *Moby Dick*, set in the cosmopolitan capital of the whaling industry, New Bedford, where the self-proclaimed wanderer Ishmael meets all manner of men, including the tattooed South Sea cannibal, Queequeg.

The other idea of diversity—the more recent one—is, in several respects, a negation of the first. Instead of pointing to a world of unforeseeable human differences, it posits a world in which the important human differences are already specified and not just known but also morally calibrated with exactitude.[3] A person growing up with this kind of diversity must be taught to see that important differences are the ones connected to a history of social oppression—the greater the history of collective oppression, the greater the current value to be attached to the difference.

Diversity, in this newer sense, is to be *celebrated*, but that is to say, only those human differences that are symbolically invested with a history of oppression are to be celebrated. Other differences may in some technical sense contribute to diversity, too, but they are morally insignificant, and celebrating *them* would amount to morally awkward insensitivity to the differences that actually matter. The moral stance called for by this new diversity is not tolerance or even curiosity, but deference. If we look for a literary evocation of this new diversity, the harvest is thin. That is because the muse of new diversity mainly visits the artists of identity-group tribulation. The true diversity novel is a novel about how *my* ancestors, *my* group, and *I* as part of *my* group have suffered unjustly at the hands of a society that has insufficiently appreciated diversity.[4]

Back to the question: is diversity, like equality and freedom, one of those root ideas that speaks first to our moral intuitions? My answer is that the older idea of diversity was and still is just that kind of idea. The newer idea of diversity, however, has a completely different moral standing.

When I say that the older idea of diversity appealed to moral intuition, I do not mean to elevate it artificially to the status of equality and freedom. Those ideas appear in our Declaration of Independence and in our Constitution. Diversity does not; and if we hunt assiduously for kindred ideas, the closest we come is the fear of factions laid out in Federalist Number 10.[5] If diversity in the sense of prompt and prudent awareness of human differences was part of our young nation's moral intuitions, that awareness did not summon legal form for itself.

The newer idea of diversity, by contrast, seemed to spring full-grown from the brow of Justice Powell.[6] He may have been seizing something that was in the air; the diversity rationale was mentioned in the amicus brief in the *Bakke* case filed by the ACLU and written by a young lawyer named Ruth Bader Ginsberg. But in 1978, to pronounce on diversity as Powell did was an act of intellectual legerdemain that failed to touch any widespread moral intuitions about diversity. Powell declared that the University of California–Davis medical school might have justified its racial preferences had it thought to emphasize the *educational* benefits of having in its classrooms the diverse *ideas* that Powell assumed would automatically flow from black students *admitted with lower qualifications* than other students.

The subsequent development of the concept was as much a response to the fractures in this idea as it was to the idea itself. There are three fractures. The first is that Powell took no account of actual classroom dynamics. "Diversity" of students, he said, would enhance the exchange of ideas in the classroom. But the medical school classes in question were mostly lectures, in which the diversity of opinion among students was irrelevant. This original flaw in the Powellian concept of diversity has put subsequent diversiphiles in the position of having to discover or to create a mechanism whereby the supposed intellectual enrichment of diversity actually takes place. One result has been the emergence of a diversiphile pedagogy that reduces the amount of time college courses spend teaching the subject at hand, in favor of encouraging students to speak and write about their personal experiences.[7]

The second fracture in Powell's concept of diversity was the failure to show that the university would actually enhance diversity of ideas by categorizing and preferentially admitting students by race. He simply assumed that racial difference equated to intellectual difference. So, right at the beginning of the diversity doctrine, we find radical racial stereotyping.

The third fracture in Powell's concept of diversity is that if we do make diversity of ideas a key educational objective, surely there were and are more expeditious ways to determine what people think than by examining the color of their skin—or by asking them to divulge their ethnic identity.

Powell gave supporters of racial preferences in college admissions a new concept to consider—a concept that seemed to have the imprimatur of the Supreme Court, even though no other justice had joined that part of Powell's opinion. But to put Powellian diversity to work, advocates of racial preferences had to fill in the three blanks that Powell left. What educational benefit could come from racial preferences? How could classifying students by race be made to yield even a suppositious connection with diversity of ideas? What ideas reliably match up with dark skin tone?

The campus advocates of racial preferences did not answer these questions overnight. But by 1982, we had the beginnings of a new "diversity" doctrine on some campuses. Rather than recount this history—which I have done elsewhere—it is perhaps best to jump to the complete diversity doctrine as we now have it. What educational benefit comes from diversity? The University of Michigan crisply gave the answer in its briefs in the *Grutter* and *Gratz* cases, decided in 2003.[8] Diversity improves "critical thinking" and enhances students' readiness for civic participation. And how does classifying students by race yield diversity of ideas? It does so because even students who have never themselves suffered outright racial discrimination bear the distinctive wounds of a heritage of group discrimination. Their suffering, even if remote from their actual experience, endows them with a distinct point of view that translates into a contribution to the intellectual diversity of the classroom.

The reasoning in these answers strikes many as strained, including many who support racial preferences in college admissions. A critique of "diversity" has emerged on the left to the effect that the diversity doctrine is a nuisance standing in the way of a more forthright policy that upholds racial preferences for the sake of "social justice" and not as a tool for creating more intellectually enlivened classrooms.[9] According to these critics, diversity requires us to pretend that the reason we want more blacks, Hispanics, and Native Americans in the classroom is so that the white kids can get the benefits of "diversity." It was a ruse, they confess, that grew up because the Left mistakenly built on Powell's opinion rather than develop a more compelling justification for racial preferences.

But at this point, even if it wanted to, the multicultural Left cannot very easily extract itself from the diversity doctrine. That is because diversity now is a rationale not only for preferences in admissions but also for racial and ethnic favoritism in faculty appointments, academic programs and centers,[10] curricula,[11] course design,[12] and policies governing new-student orientation and residence halls. Diversity is behind separate graduation ceremonies; board appointments and the recruitment of deans, provosts, and presidents;[13] library acquisitions policies; the distribution of financial aid;[14] student activities;[15] and alumni events. I do not know of a single area of campus life that is not put through the diversity regimen.

How did it happen that a speculative rumination on medical school admissions by Justice Powell in 1978 mutated in a quarter of a century into American higher education's single most important concept? Diversity is now promoted as central by vastly more colleges and universities than the idea of civilization or the importance of free institutions. If we take college viewbooks and promotional literature as a measure, diversity is often emphasized far more emphatically than even the pursuit of knowledge.

The ideology of diversity has now been, to a large extent, institutionalized by its advocates. All those deans and college presidents who competed for their positions when they were advertised with the tag line "proven commitment to diversity a must" owe their careers to this concept, and have gone on to create a permanent diversity infrastructure, including deans or even provosts of diversity.

As colleges and universities wend their way through their ten-year cycle of regional reaccreditation, many name diversity as an institutional priority. Regional accreditors were driven out of the diversity-promotion business in the early 1990s, after the Middle States Association of Colleges and Schools attempted to impose a diversity standard on two colleges that did not want it. When Secretary of Education Lamar Alexander told the association to withdraw the rule or forfeit its Department of Education license to accredit, the association backed down.[16] But nowadays, the regional accreditors are back in the game of enforcing diversity because colleges and universities themselves ask them to.[17]

Diversity is far more than a *pretext* for bending admissions standards. Many if not all its advocates sincerely support what they suppose are its intellectual benefits. Beginning around 1988, diversity also spread beyond the campus to become a justification for practices in business, entertainment, sports, the arts, and the military. This wider diffusion of the idea means that universities can count on public support for their ideology. The motives behind that public support, of course, vary. The jostling of the crowd and the fear of being singled out are factors, but so is the appeal of the older kind of diversity—the Ishmael-and-Queequeg-in-New-Bedford kind of diversity. Only now, the older idea has been submerged in the new one. To feel pleasure in the actual and surprising wealth of human difference around us gets confused with assent to the deadening contemporary doctrine that each of us is the sum of his race-class-gender social coordinates, and that group grievances flow down through the well-engineered compensatory channels to group entitlements.

Diversity ideology is regnant. In its fully developed form, it has many friends, real or coerced, and few campus foes, or even open critics. So is there any well-founded reason to think that diversity may, at some point, cease to dominate the campus? Reforming the politically correct university seems an unlikely prospect unless we can see a way past the supremacy of the diversity doctrine. Diversity is *not* the only idea sustaining the Left's dominance of American higher education, but it is the only idea with popular support outside the precincts of faculty lounges or Modern Language Association meetings.

So let me turn from measured awe at the success of the diversity doctrine to a consideration of its vulnerabilities. I will start with the Pledge of Allegiance. As you must know, it goes like this:

> I pledge allegiance to the flag and my constitutional rights with which it comes. And to the diversity in which our nation stands.

> One nation, part of one planet, with liberty, freedom, choice, and justice for all.

That is the version cobbled together by some students at Boulder High School, who recited it in a protest on September 27, 2007. They were objecting to the phrase "one nation, under God" in the more familiar version of the text. About one hundred students walked out of their first class to recite their alternative.[18]

This juvenile protest is one small indication that the diversity doctrine is in trouble. By swapping out "and to the Republic for which it stands" and substituting "and to the diversity in which our nation stands," the kids innocently followed the logic of diversity to its terminal conclusion. "Diversity" evokes a conceptual and a political order that has no need of a "republic" and is in some ways opposed to representative self-government. How so? If we leave to one side the constitutional standing that Justice O'Connor granted diversity in *Grutter* and focus on diversity as it is taught in schools, promulgated in universities, and experienced in American life, we see that it specifies a system of group rights and privileges that subordinate virtually all claims of the common good. Within this system of group rights and privileges, some groups have superior claims by virtue of a hereditary entitlement. This regime is not a republic; it is an aristocracy.

To be sure, it is a new kind of aristocracy. Old-style aristocracies founded their claims on conquest or the innate superiority of the favored groups. Nouveau diversity instead presents a hierarchy of privilege based on the extremity of past injustice. It offers a hierarchy of victimization. Status within this hierarchy can be contested. Who has suffered more, the African American descendants of slaves or the Hispanic descendants of an immiserated peasantry? Gays and lesbians or the physically handicapped? Asian refugees or illegal Mexican immigrants?

Questions of this sort are far from the minds of the teachers and textbook publishers who have made "celebrating diversity" seem like an exercise in the wholesome inclusion of those who were formally excluded from the benefits of full participation in American life.[19] When we speak of diversity, we must always keep this double-sidedness in mind. Diversity presents itself, on one side, as the completion of a centuries-old quest for equality of rights. And in this guise, its tone is bright and welcoming. On the other side, diversity is a hard-edged destruction of the ideal of individual equality and its replacement by a doctrine in which an individual's true identity is rooted in social division. And in this guise, its tone is angry and aggressive.

Grievance-based diversity claims are now well-established in American life, but they are politically vulnerable. In 1996, California voters passed Proposition 209, which outlawed racial preferences in public institutions. Voters in Washington State in 1998 and in Michigan in 2006 passed similar propositions. These are liberal states, and surely if a ballot question had been formulated along the lines of "Do you favor the pursuit of diversity in public institutions?" the result would have been a ringing affirmation of the diversity concept. Ward Connerly and the American Civil Rights Institute, prime movers behind the California, Washington, and Michigan initiatives, in 2008 attempted to put Proposition 209–style questions on the ballot in Colorado, Missouri, Arizona, Nebraska, and Oklahoma. They were blocked in all but Colorado and Nebraska by the legal maneuvers race-preference supporters who have learned to fear popular referenda. The Colorado proposition narrowly lost. The Nebraska one passed by a significant margin.

So here we have a major fissure in the diversity movement. The public remains enthralled with the beautiful image of diversity—the image of men and women of every ethnic background, religion, and persuasion cheerfully working together and peacefully contributing to a shared society—but the public has also developed a sharp distaste for the practical methods of diversity planners, who wish to make collective identity the organizing principle for distributing the social and economic goods of our society.

The university sits in the middle of this. Diversity is a university idea—created to advance and sustain racial preferences in admissions; elaborated to include faculty hiring, the curriculum, etc.; expanded to include additional victim groups; inculcated into K–12 teachers though university schools of education; and spread to university graduates who carried it into almost every other American institution.

In that light, if the public turns against the practical methods of the diversity advocates, the university could face significant complications. High on the list of these complications is its moral credibility. In California, some public college and university campuses have flouted Proposition 209 and continued to employ racial preferences in admissions.[20] For example, a grand jury in Sonoma County recently issued a report finding that Santa

Rosa Junior College had illegally used racial preferences in admissions and had attempted to disguise its lawbreaking by invoking the pursuit of diversity. The college officials told the grand jury that diversity "had nothing to do with ethnicity or any other immutable characteristic and was therefore not illegal to use as a goal."[21] The grand jury did not buy Santa Rosa Junior College's explanation and concluded that

> a strong effort was being made at SRJC to achieve affirmative action goals by the creative use of a vaguely defined term, "diversity". . . . Giving preference to job applicants for certain faculty positions to those with somewhat exclusive life experiences may, in fact, lead to a stronger ranking for members of certain races and ethnicities. Proposition 209 specifically forbids any preferential treatment to any individual or group on the basis of race or ethnicity or national origin.[22]

Other California colleges and universities likewise exercise both bad faith and ingenuity to subvert the letter and the spirit of Proposition 209, but legal authorities shy away from the matter. The whistle-blower in the Santa Rosa case, Sylvia Wasson, tells me that the Sonoma County district attorney has expressed no interest in prosecuting the college. This, too, I take to be consistent with the social dynamics of "diversity." Members of the public, not professional elites, grow weary with the diversity excuse for racial preferences.

Santa Rosa Junior College points to a possibility. What if Americans decided: "Well, yes, we like the sunny side of diversity. But we can distinguish between the pleasure we take in human variety and the attempts by universities to *classify* people by race and ethnicity and grant special treatment to some classes." If this were to happen, higher education's tower of obfuscation would collapse. We would be back to recognizing that diversity really means two things: the old diversity of Melville's New Bedford, Queequeg and all; and the new diversity of Justice Powell's decision, in which racial categorization becomes a proxy for intellectual differences.

The Santa Rosa case is not the only crack in the diversity edifice. While looking at the record in that case, I came across a kind of lawbreakers' manual titled *We Could Do That: A Users' Guide to Diversity Practices in California Community Colleges.*[23] This manual, assembled by the Promoting Diversity

Practices Project at City College of San Francisco, documents projects at dozens of institutions that appear to skirt California law. *We Could Do That* shows how the pursuit of diversity increasingly entails lawlessness.

Some observers, like Claude Raines in *Casablanca*, who was "shocked! shocked!" to discover gambling in Rick's Place, may shrug at the "by any means necessary" approach of some diversiphiles. But Americans have limited tolerance for situations in which elites put themselves above popular laws, especially when they sense that the scofflaw elites are hurting the public good. Higher education is now faced with the public perception that a college degree awarded under a system of group preferences has been tainted—or at the very least, watered down and devalued.

This possibility feeds on several sources, including the growing recognition that some stalwarts of the diversity ideology do not believe their own words. We may not know how many diversiphiles profess to love diversity but married her only for her racial preference inheritance; the number is less relevant than the embarrassment that comes when the imposture is exposed. That is the significance of the call made by David Horowitz and other conservatives for "intellectual diversity" on campus. Powell's own pitch for racial preferences in his *Bakke* opinion was based on the importance of intellectual diversity in higher education, which leaves today's nouveau diversiphiles in an awkward spot. They cannot repudiate the value of intellectual diversity without kicking the traces out from under their own doctrine. Meanwhile advocates of "intellectual diversity" are essentially saying that Powell was right, at least in regard to the importance for students of finding in the university a robust representation of different intellectual views. The trouble, say these critics, is that the university increasingly presents, at least in the humanities and the social sciences, views almost exclusively on the political left. It would befit the institution if its intellectual diversity extended to conservative scholarship.

There is a small paradox here and a large one. The small paradox is that advocacy of diversity has sped the way to intellectual conformity on campus. That is because "diversity" is actually an aggressive ideology that stigmatizes and attempts to drive out anyone who does not actively support it. The larger paradox is that a battle over core principles is being conducted in the rhetoric of relativism. That is because some of those who have suffered most grievously under the diversity doctrine think they can now gain ground by appropriating it.

Of course the supporters of the diversity doctrine, who overwhelmingly dominate the contemporary university, have nothing but scorn for "intellectual diversity." They have been spending time lately devising reasons why the intellectual diversity argument should be dismissed. Stanley Fish, for example, rejects the call for intellectual diversity because he thinks it would divert the university into the improper task of "citizen building."[24] More orthodox supporters of diversity insist that the university is indeed involved in citizen building, and that exposure to diversity itself builds better citizens. Another tactic deployed against the intellectual diversity argument is to claim that the university, contrary to popular perception, already fosters wide-ranging intellectual views. This is one of the themes in a report, *Freedom in the Classroom*, issued by the American Association of University Professors in September 2007, and it appears again in a paper by Neil Gross and Solon Simmons, "The Social and Political Views of American Professors," delivered in October 2007.[25]

So has the intellectual diversity argument forced a new debate about the nature of diversity on campus? I do not think so. Fish's point and the claims by the AAUP and Gross and Simmons do reflect a growing anxiety on the part of leftist intellectuals over the success of conservatives in reframing the public perception of American higher education. But the intellectual diversity argument itself has so far made little headway in the academy. That is not to say that the diversity doctrine sits unperturbed.

I have one more suggestive piece of evidence that the diversity regime is in trouble, and that is the testimony of the diversiphiles themselves. Gary Orfield, for many years the head of Harvard University's Civil Rights Project, last year moved the project to UCLA. Recently, Professor Orfield began issuing a new stream of reports warning that "race-conscious action to diversify" higher education is under attack by "conservative legal action groups." As a result, warns Orfield, colleges and universities may be overly cautious in their commitments to diversity. He writes: "It is very important that our university faculties and leaders not give up on what has been a notable success but find the best ways to preserve it in a time of polarization."[26] Those words do not sound very confident. The titles of Orfield's two most recent reports likewise are admonitory. He issued *Charting the Future of College Affirmative Action: Legal Victories, Continuing Attacks, and New Research* in July 2007, and in August 2007, *Historic Reversals, Accelerating Resegregation, and the Need for New Integration Strategies.* The latter is mainly a lament over the Supreme Court's decisions in the Seattle and Louisville cases, in which the magic word "diversity" was not allowed to authorize racial classifications in public schools.

Orfield's displeasure is heartening. We are a nation, of course, in no danger of "resegregation." Today, it has become ever clearer that the nation wants to move beyond racial classifications and systems that grant privilege, or supposed privilege, according to identity group. But we have institutionalized elites who are panicked at this prospect and determined to fight very hard to maintain their own powers of deciding who gets what share of the social benefits they control.

That is a prediction that Powellian diversity will die hard—but it will die. As broad as our seeming enthusiasm for diversity now is, and as entrenched as it has become in the universities, it remains at odds with our deepest moral intuitions. We remain a republic founded on ideas of freedom and equality. In subtle but profound ways, Powellian diversity contradicts both those principles. Many Americans cannot quite express the contradiction, but they sense it. And in the end, this intuition will be diversity's undoing.

Notes

1. *Regents of the University of California v. Bakke*, 438 U.S. 265 (1978).

2. Peter W. Wood, *Diversity: The Invention of a Concept* (San Francisco: Encounter Books, 2003).

3. Writings on this kind of diversity are numerous beyond reckoning, but for the sake of benchmarking this assertion see Edison J. Tricket, Roderick J. Watts, and Dina Birman, eds., *Human Diversity: Perspectives on People in Context* (San Francisco: Jossey-Bass, 1994); Frederick R. Lynch, *The Diversity Machine: The Drive to Change the "White Male Workplace"* (New York: The Free Press, 1997); Mickey R. Dansby, James B. Stewart, and Schuyler C. Webb, eds., *Managing Diversity in the Military* (New Brunswick, NJ: Transactions Publishers, 2001); Martha C. Nussbaum, *Cultivating Humanity: A Classical Defense of Reform in Liberal Education* (Cambridge, MA: Harvard University Press, 1997); William G. Bowen and Derek Bok, *The Shape of the River: Long-Term Consequences of Considering Race in College and University Admissions* (Princeton, NJ: Princeton University Press, 1998).

4. The term "diversity novels" is not wholly my invention. It is used by some schools to designate a desired category of reading materials. The public schools of Independence, Missouri, for example, in 2006–7 set as a goal for "language arts" in the sixth grade, "Students will analyze diversity novels for literary elements and to explore diversity issues," http://64.233.169.104/search?q=cache:8rZviH6H2k0J:www.independence.k12.ia.us/public/LA%2520Brochure%25206-8.doc+%22diversity+novels%22&hl=en&ct=clnk&cd=2&gl=us. Some schools have courses titled "Diversity Novels." I have also found "diversity novels" as a term of art in college syllabi, such as Social Work 500.005, "Human Differences, Social Relationships, Well-Being & Change Through the Life Course," by Professor David Martineau at the University of Michigan, who promises his students "a selected list of diversity novels" on which to base one of their papers. Some "diversity novels" in my sense of the term are: Jhumpa Lahiri, *The Namesake* (Bengali immigrants in Boston); Amy Tan, *The Joy Luck Club* (Four immigrant Chinese women face difficulties in America); Sandra Cisneros, *The House on Mango Street* (Hispanic girl in Chicago reflects on oppression); Louise Erdrich, *Love Medicine* (Chippewa Indians in North Dakota overcome despair). Of course, the undisputed master of the diversity novel is Toni Morrison.

5. James Madison, "The Federalist No. 10," November 22, 1787, in *The Federalist*, ed. Jacob E. Cooke (Middletown, CT: Wesleyan University Press, 1967), 58–59, 64.

6. Contemporary observers are surprised that the diversity ideology had such a recent and modest beginning. While researching *Diversity: The Invention of a Concept*, I spent two years looking for uses of "diversity" in its current sense before Powell's opinion in *Bakke*. I found none that had commanded public attention, and this observation has not been successfully challenged.

7. Diversiphiles debate whether "diversity" produces its educational benefits primarily outside the classroom or primarily inside the classroom. See Christopher Mac-Gregor Scribner, "Racial Diversity Matters within the Classroom, Too," *Chronicle of Higher Education*, May 24, 1996, http://chronicle.com/che-data/articles.dir/art-42.dir/issue-37.dir/37b00301.htm. This move toward first-person reflection in the humanities and social sciences has historical origins apart from the diversity movement, but it has proved congenial to diversiphiles since it encourages students to emphasize race and other diversity-favored definitions of the self. Scribner, for example, writes of teaching a class on the history of the United States before 1865, in which he engaged students on the topic of the O. J. Simpson trial and what they thought "about having a white teacher lecture them about slavery." The felt need to document diversity's educational benefits also fostered a new genre of what might be called "diversity testimonials," i.e., collections of statements by students avowing that their exposure to campus diversity was educationally useful. The testimonials were often buttressed by survey questions sent to alumni. For an example of diversity testimonials, see Ruth Sidel, *Battling Bias: The Struggle for Identity and Community on Campus* (New York: Penguin Books, 1994), 203–23.

8. *Grutter v. Bollinger*, 539 U.S. 306 (2003); *Gratz v. Bollinger*, 539 U.S. 244 (2003).

9. See Randall Kennedy, "Affirmative Reaction," *American Prospect*, March 1, 2003, http://www.prospect.org/cs/articles?article=affirmative_reaction. Kennedy writes: "Many who defend affirmative action for the sake of 'diversity' are actually motivated by a concern that is considerably more compelling. They are not so much animated by a commitment to what is, after all, only a contingent pedagogical hypothesis. Rather they are animated by a commitment to social justice. They would rightly defend affirmative action even if social science demonstrated uncontrovertibly that diversity (or its absence) has no effect (or even a negative effect) on the learning environment."

10. Henry Louis Gates Jr., writing in 1989, evoked "diversity" as the chief justification for black studies centers. Henry Louis Gates Jr., "Academe Must Give Black-Studies Their Due," *Chronicle of Higher Education*, September 20, 1989, http://chronicle.com/che-data/articles.dir/art-42.dir/issue-37.dir/37b00301.htm. In 1991, the University of California–Davis and California State University at Fresno created a joint doctoral degree program to prepare school administrators to become expert in dealing with "ethnic diversity of students." "Cal Program Helps School Officials Cope with Diversity," *Chronicle of Higher Education*, February 6, 1991, http://chronicle.com/che-data/articles.dir/art-42.dir/issue-37.dir/37b00301.htm.

11. The transformation of the curriculum to foreground diversity began around 1988. That year, President Shaw of the University of Wisconsin system issued a report, *Design for Diversity*. The "design included a six credit requirement of diversity courses for all students." See "U. of Wis. to Require Multicultural Courses," *Chronicle of Higher Education*, December 13, 1989, http://chronicle.com/che-data/articles.dir/

art-42.dir/issue-37.dir/37b00301.htm; Scott Heller, "Colleges Told to Stress Tradition and Shared Views Even as They Bring More Diversity into Curricula," *Chronicle of Higher Education*, October 4, 1989, http://chronicle.com/che-data/articles.dir/art-42.dir/issue-37.dir/37b00301.htm.

12. English composition courses were an early target. Following a campus racial confrontation in October 1986, the University of Massachusetts at Amherst formed a Writing Program Diversity Committee and revised the Basic Writing class for 18,500 undergraduate students to emphasize writings by members of minority groups. The common thread, according to an instructor, was that "characters routinely experience some kind of discrimination." See Beverly T. Watkins, "Revamped Freshman Writing Courses at U. of Mass. Focuses on Issues of Racial and Social Diversity," *Chronicle of Higher Education,* December 19, 1990, http://chronicle.com/che-data/articles.dir/art-42.dir/issue-37.dir/37b00301.htm. Another way "diversity" entered course design was through claims that members of various groups have different "learning profiles." See Annette Kolodny, "Colleges Must Recognize Students' Cognitive Styles and Cultural Backgrounds," *Chronicle of Higher Education*, February 6, 1991, http://chronicle.com/che-data/articles.dir/art-42.dir/issue-37.dir/37b00301.htm. Today, the promotion of diversity as a major factor in course design has become even more ambitious. The American Association of Colleges and Universities, for example, sponsors a program to help colleges transform every course they offer into a vehicle that promotes diversity. See "A Sustainable Campus-Wide Program for Diversity Curriculum Infusion," *Diversity Digest* 10, no. 2 (2007): 14.

13. Peter Wood, "Dogfish: Why College Presidents Won't Save Higher Education," *Academic Questions* 12, no. 3 (1999): 50–64; Peter Wood, "Proven Commitment to Diversity," *National Review Online*, January 30, 2003, http://www.nationalreview.com/comment/comment-wood013003.asp; Courtney Leatherman, "Universities Choose Presidents from Once-Excluded Groups," *Chronicle of Higher Education*, July 24, 1991, http://chronicle.com/che-data/articles.dir/art-42.dir/issue-37.dir/37b00301.htm.

14. Scott Jaschik, "Secretary Seeks Ban on Grants Reserved for Specific Groups," *Chronicle of Higher Education*, December 11, 1991, http://chronicle.com/che-data/articles.dir/art-42.dir/issue-37.dir/37b00301.htm; Scott Jaschik, "Debate Continues on Minority Aid," *Chronicle of Higher Education*, December 18, 1992, http://chronicle.com/che-data/articles.dir/art-42.dir/issue-37.dir/37b00301.htm; Liz McMillen, "Foundations Struggle to Diversify Programs to Cope with Changing Society and Continuing Social Ills," *Chronicle of Higher Education*, April 11, 1990, http://chronicle.com/che-data/articles.dir/art-42.dir/issue-37.dir/37b00301.htm.

15. Too numerous to count, but for example: "At Golden West College [in Huntington Beach, California], more than 300 students and professors banged drums and shook maracas and tambourines in the finale of a weeklong festival celebrating the college's ethnic diversity." "Students Hold 'Drumming' Festival to Celebrate Diversity," *Chronicle of Higher Education*, March 31, 1993, http://chronicle.com/che-data/articles.dir/art-42.dir/issue-37.dir/37b00301.htm.

16. Scott Jaschik, "Delay in Recognition of Accrediting Agency by Education Department Draws Mixed Reaction," *Chronicle of Higher Education*, April 24, 1991, http://chronicle.com/che-data/articles.dir/art-42.dir/issue-37.dir/37b00301.htm; Jim Sleeper, "The Policemen of Diversity," *Washington Post*, June 30, 1991; Scott Jaschik, "Hundreds Weigh in on Issue of Accrediting Group's 'Diversity Standard,'" *Chronicle of Higher Education*, August 14, 1991, http://chronicle.com/che-data/articles.dir/art-42. dir/issue-37.dir/37b00301.htm.

17. The Western Association of Schools and Colleges also attempted to impose a diversity standard in 1991 but settled for a weakened version. Courtney Leatherman, "All Quiet on Western Front," *Chronicle of Higher Education*, March 2, 1994, http:// chronicle.com/che-data/articles.dir/art-42.dir/issue-37.dir/37b00301.htm. Specialized accreditors have also ventured into creating diversity standards. In February 2006, the American Bar Association's accrediting body approved an "Equal Opportunity and Diversity" standard requiring law schools to use racial preferences in admitting students. Katherine S. Mangan, "Foes of Affirmative Action Seek Revocation of ABA's Accrediting Power," *Chronicle of Higher Education*, March 17, 2006, http://chronicle.com/che-data/articles.dir/art-42.dir/issue-37.dir/37b00301.htm. The Council on Social Work Education likewise requires that each school's "curriculum model understanding of and respect for diversity." Council on Social Work Education, *Standard 6.0, Educational Policy and Accreditation Standards* (Washington, DC: 2004). See also National Association of Scholars, *The Scandal of Social Work Education* (Princeton, NJ: National Association of Scholars, 2007).

18. Mike McPhee, "Boulder Students Protest 'God' in Pledge," *Denver Post*, September 27, 2007.

19. This ideology is examined in detail by Diane Ravitch, *The Language Police: How Pressure Groups Restrict What Students Learn* (New York: Knopf, 2003).

20. David Leonhardt, "The New Affirmative Action," *New York Times Magazine*, September 30, 2007.

21. "SRJC's Commitment to Diversity: Post Proposition 209," *Sonoma County Grand Jury Final Report 2006–2007*, 46, http://www.sonomasuperiorcourt.com/ download/GrandJury/GJuryReport2006-2007/srjc8.pdf.

22. Ibid., 53.

23. Gail Waldron, Eva Schiorring, and Robert Gabriner, *We Could Do That: A Users' Guide to Diversity Practices in California Community Colleges* (San Francisco: City College of San Francisco, 2002).

24. Stanley Fish, "'Intellectual Diversity': The Trojan Horse of a Dark Design," *Chronicle of Higher Education*, February 13, 2004, http://chronicle.com/che-data/ articles.dir/art-42.dir/issue-37.dir/37b00301.htm.

25. American Association of University Professors, *Freedom in the Classroom*, September 11, 2007, http://www.aaup.org/AAUP/comm/rep/A/class.htm; Neil Gross and Solon Simmons, "The Social and Political Views of American Professors" (paper presented at the Harvard University Symposium on Professors and Their Politics,

Cambridge, MA, October 6, 2007). For responses to the AAUP, see Peter W. Wood, "Truths R Us: The AAUP Redefines Reality," *Inside Higher Ed*, September 21, 2007, http://www.insidehighered.com/views/2007/09/21/wood; Peter W. Wood and Stephen H. Balch, "A Response to the AAUP's Report, 'Freedom in the Classroom,'" National Association of Scholars, September 21, 2007, http://www.nas.org/polArticles. cfm?doc_id=32. For critiques of the AAUP report and Gross and Simmons's study in other chapters of this volume, see especially chapter 2 by Klein and Stern and chapter 4 by Rothman and Lichter.

26. Gary Orfield, foreword to *Charting the Future of College Affirmative Action: Legal Victories, Continuing Attacks, and New Research*, ed. Gary Orfield, Patricia Marin, Stella M. Flores, and Liliana M. Garces (Los Angeles: The Civil Rights Project, 2007), 1, 4.

8

The American University:
Yesterday, Today, and Tomorrow

James Piereson

There are today nearly eighteen million students enrolled in the more than four thousand colleges and universities currently operating in the United States. Over the next few years, enrollments will continue to increase because the high school graduating class of 2008 was the largest ever. In a few years, enrollments will approach twenty million students, at which point they are expected to level off and perhaps even to decline.[1] Today nearly 70 percent of the age cohort (eighteen to twenty-four) attends college in one form or another, and more than 80 percent of recent high school graduates do so. College attendance is now a near-universal rite of passage for youngsters in our society, primarily because a college degree has become an essential requirement for entry into the world of professional employment. Parents make sacrifices, financial and otherwise, to send their children to college primarily because they wish them to succeed in the competitive job market. Of course, they wish them to be educated as well, but they have little clear sense of what that actually means.

In 2009, another two million or so eighteen- and nineteen-year-olds will enter the academic world as college freshmen at institutions ranging from small liberal arts colleges with perhaps two thousand students to large public universities with as many as fifty thousand students. A small fraction of these students will attend institutions that are highly selective, admitting only between 10 and 20 percent of applicants, while the vast majority will enroll in institutions that, for all practical purposes, offer open admission.

More than 40 percent of undergraduate students (or 6.7 million) attend two-year community colleges, a rapidly growing segment of the college market. A few students who are either fortunate or enterprising will, over the course of four years, acquire a superb education in the liberal arts, while many others will acquire little of lasting value, aside from their degrees. The educational experience for college students in the United States today is thus widely diverse—and in many more ways than are referred to here.

Amidst all this variation, there exists a curious conformity among our institutions of higher learning. With but few exceptions, our colleges and universities define their mission in terms of a political ideology that most Americans find more than a little strange. This, of course, is the doctrine of diversity, which originated in the laudable goal of enrolling more minority students in academic institutions, but which gradually metastasized into something else entirely—the assertion (usually without demonstration) that the history of the United States is marked by exclusion and oppression of minorities, the result in large part of the nation's commitment to property, individual rights, and the free market. Academic leaders believe that it is the job of the university to expose this oppression in all of its forms and to make up for it by providing representation in the faculty, the student body, and the curriculum for the various groups that have been its victims. This doctrine is appealed to repeatedly in academic publications and promotional brochures put out by colleges and universities. Judging by these publications, this point of view is especially influential in the most prestigious and selective institutions. Indeed, few academics who seek advancement in their profession dare to criticize or even to question this doctrine. Yet one wonders why such a tendentious doctrine has been thought necessary to ensure equal treatment for all when this goal is perfectly consistent with the traditional tenets of liberalism. In an enterprise—higher education—devoted to challenging just about every received idea, it is strange indeed that this one is exempted from questioning and criticism.[2]

Many of the highly publicized controversies that have occurred on campuses throughout the country can be traced back to the diversity ideology, including the dismissal of Lawrence Summers as president of Harvard University, the elimination of ROTC from most leading institutions, the statement by University of Colorado professor Ward Churchill that the victims of the World Trade Center attacks were "little Eichmanns" who had it coming, the tragic fiasco at Duke University where eighty-eight faculty members declared members of the lacrosse team guilty of sexual assault before any facts were known, a dispute a few years ago at Columbia University over the (alleged) anti-Israel bias of faculty members teaching courses on the Middle East, and the now routine protests and disruptions when conservative speakers show up on campus. When academic institutions are in the news (leaving aside their athletic teams), the story is usually related to some transgression or extreme expression of the diversity ideology.

Many who are distressed by the politicization of the academy and by the quality of education now offered there see the diversity doctrine as a key source of these troubling developments. The critique of American society as racist, sexist, and materialistic obviously extends to Western civilization in general, and leads in turn to deemphasizing this vital subject in the curriculum, its place taken by new courses in feminism, environmentalism, and sexuality. Whole areas of study once thought to be essential to the education of the young—such as military, constitutional, and diplomatic history—have largely disappeared from the curriculum. Faculty hiring has been compromised by the imposition of diversity criteria in the recruitment process. Standards for admission and graduation have been weakened.

In keeping with the ideological thrust of the doctrine, faculty opinion on political issues has moved steadily leftward (see both chapters by Klein and Stern and the chapter by Rothman and Lichter in this volume).[3] Students at many prominent colleges report that they are subjected to a steady drumbeat of political propaganda in their courses, especially those in the humanities and the social sciences.[4]

What is the source of this conformity among institutions that in other ways are so varied and diverse? Are there trends in process or reforms that can be implemented that might weaken or displace the diversity orthodoxy and produce thereby some genuine intellectual pluralism both within and among our colleges and universities? Is there any likelihood that the universities of the future—the universities of 2030 or 2050—will look substantially different from those that we see around us today? After all, the college graduate of 1940 or 1950 must have some difficulty recognizing his alma mater in reports from the campus that he reads today. Will the college graduates of 2000 look similarly upon their institutions thirty or fifty years from now?

One of the reasons for the ideological conformity that we see on the campus is that the major colleges and universities in the nation today operate as never before within a single market for top students and faculty. It is very common today, as it was not in 1900 or 1950, for students to travel long distances from home to attend college. As a consequence, they tend to assess their college choices from a national point of view, in contrast to the local or regional perspective that probably guided their parents and grandparents.

There is a tendency in such markets for competitors to conform in important ways, which is accentuated in an industry where standards of excellence are established by a few prestigious institutions. Moreover, and perhaps more importantly, colleges tend to recruit their new faculty from a small number of graduate institutions who train and socialize their students in common disciplinary practices, a point documented by Klein and Stern in their essay in this volume on academic "groupthink." As Paul Cantor points out in another essay in this volume, the increasing standardization and uniformity of academic departments has mimicked the globalizing process that has been under way in recent decades in the corporate world, even as academics attack the standardizing logic of globalization.

These trends toward nationalization and conformity have been under way for many decades but surprisingly picked up momentum following the academic upheavals of the 1960s. They have been encouraged and reinforced by national membership associations, such as the American Political Science Association or the Modern Language Association (to name a few), which publish journals and hold annual meetings where new research is presented. These associations, through their publications and conferences, establish the terms and substance of legitimate research in their respective areas of study. The various fields have by now been standardized to the point that professors expect to be able to move from one institution to another without changing their approaches to teaching and research. Institutions that vary too widely from the expected standard will be marked by a badge of academic inferiority or, in extreme cases, blacklisted by faculty organizations like the American Association of University Professors.

Colleges and universities must follow the tenure model in hiring and promotion or risk condemnation by national faculty organizations. They must hew to commonly accepted standards in personnel and admissions policies and in the programs they offer in order to qualify for federal grants or to win certification from accrediting bodies. The rankings of institutions put out annually by a few national publications, such as *U.S. News and World Report*, further reinforce these tendencies toward a national market of institutions that conform to an established standard. Institutions that reject the diversity ideology as a guide to practice do so at the risk of being viewed as outside the mainstream.

A further reason why colleges and universities have been able to indulge in so much apparently self-defeating conduct is that, up until the recent stock market crash, they have been prospering financially as never before. The competition for entry into our leading institutions is keener than ever, owing to a recent population boom among college-age youngsters. Parents are now willing to pay extravagant tuition to send their sons and daughters to institutions that they believe will give them a leg up in the competition for good jobs. Tuition has been rising at leading institutions for the past quarter century at rates far ahead of inflation, reflecting the rising prosperity of the top 5 or 10 percent of the wealth distribution. Philanthropists continue to lavish large donations on prestigious institutions. College and university endowments, fueled by the stock market boom of the past quarter century, have reached levels never dreamed of before. In 1981, only one institution (Harvard) had an endowment exceeding $1 billion; as of 2007, more than sixty institutions had endowments in excess of $1 billion. Harvard's endowment reached $29 billion in 2006, Yale's $18 billion, Stanford's and Princeton's $14 and $13 billion, respectively. Princeton's endowment is nearly $2 million per student, which effectively yields about $100,000 per student annually—a sum that is more than double the annual tuition. Many state universities, such as Michigan, Virginia, and Texas, have accumulated large endowments even though they receive annual subventions from the public treasury.[5]

Even so, elite private institutions have fared far better in recent decades than their counterparts in the public sector. In recent rankings of national universities published by *U.S. News and World Report*, the top twenty positions were held by private institutions. Among the top thirty institutions, only five were public universities, the rest private.[6] This is a significant change from rankings taken during the 1960s, when several public institutions (including California-Berkeley, Michigan, Wisconsin, and Minnesota) were ranked among the top ten national universities, and several others were ranked in the top twenty.

The swollen endowments, besides providing a financial cushion, have also provided colleges and universities with a measure of independence from public opinion and protection from critics, who are wont to catalog their failures and excesses. It is always difficult to bring reform to institutions that are prospering from current practices. No transgression against common sense or propriety, however serious, seems to inflict any real pain on these institutions. Indeed, academic leaders often find in public embarrassments new opportunities to raise funds. After the controversies surrounding its Middle Eastern studies programs, Columbia University sought funds to encourage interreligious understanding on its campus.

It is not clear how these institutions, long accustomed to abundance and prosperity, will adapt to a new climate of austerity that is now clearly on the horizon. The *Chronicle of Higher Education* estimates that college and university endowments fell by about 23 percent between July and November 2008, on top of a 3 percent decline in the fiscal year ending June 30, 2008. Losses are expected to be even greater by the time the financial crisis eventually runs its course. Harvard University, for example, is forecasting a 30 percent decline in its endowment for the 2009 fiscal year which, given the size of the endowment, will result in a decline of about $500 million in annual operating income. As a consequence of the financial downturn, many colleges and universities across the country have announced salary and hiring freezes and suspended ambitious building projects. Some may have to revisit their generous financial aid practices, such as need-blind admissions policies and awarding grants to students in lieu of loans, which typically have been funded out of rising endowments. It is likely that the advantages in wealth and prestige that have accrued to private institutions in recent decades will begin to wither along with their endowments. Thus, we may be entering an era in which public institutions will begin to regain some of the ground they have lost to private colleges and universities. It is certainly possible that the diversity orthodoxy is itself a by-product of prosperity and expansion, an indulgence that cannot be sustained in a climate of austerity and real competition for resources among institutions.[7]

The growth in recent years of online universities, such as the University of Phoenix, American Intercontinental University, and Capella University, among many others, is taken by some as an emerging source of competition for established institutions. The University of Phoenix (the largest of the online institutions) has more than two hundred thousand students enrolled in its programs and is enjoying rapid growth. Thus far, however, the online universities have appealed mainly to the adult education market, with an emphasis on courses in business and professional training. There is as yet no strong evidence that such programs can compete with residential colleges for the patronage of the young, for whom higher education is tied up with separation from parents and day-to-day association with peers. Some (such as former Boston University president John Silber) doubt that online courses can ever replace the dedicated teacher in the classroom, but it is still far too early to tell whether these online programs will eventually pose a serious competitive challenge to established four-year institutions.[8]

At the same time, these institutions have only scratched the surface of the enormous educational potential of online technologies. In a society in which youngsters are far more adept than their elders at using these technologies, it seems safe to predict that innovative educational products will be developed to appeal to the rising generation. There is no inherent reason why online technologies cannot be put to use by residential institutions of all kinds. In the future, we may see eminent professors at prestigious institutions contracting with private companies to produce high-level courses that are taken for credit by students enrolled at institutions throughout the country. Universities may begin to market online courses developed by their own professors. As these products expand, administrators will find that they do not need to hire as many faculty members as before. In this way, students in the future will not be limited to taking courses from professors on their own campuses but will be able to select courses in a national market while studying in a residential institution. Students will thereby be given the opportunity to "vote with their feet" in the selection of courses—and will be able to render an up or down verdict on the curriculum to which they have been subjected in recent decades. This represents the next stage in the nationalization—indeed, the internationalization—of the academic marketplace.

Critics of the contemporary academy suggest various steps that might be taken to blunt the influence of the diversity ideology, to restore rigor and coherence to the traditional liberal arts curriculum, and to open up the campus to intellectual approaches that are widely held in the society at large but are not much found on today's campus. Most agree that colleges and universities cannot be ignored because, like it or not, they play an important role in shaping the minds of students; in addition, the ideas that have currency on the campus eventually find their way into socially influential professions, such as law, business, journalism, and public service. Conservatives who are not well represented on the campus have been able to develop and circulate ideas by means of influential think tanks, such as the American Enterprise Institute, which are able to speak more effectively and directly to government officials, journalists, and public policy experts. Yet, over the long run, conservatives will find that this tactic is difficult to sustain without augmenting it with a foothold in the academy.

There are some encouraging signs that the diversity crusade that has preoccupied activists and administrators over the past generation has begun to run its course. After several decades of intense effort, recruitment of minority students has reached a level where, from this time forward, only modest marginal gains are likely to be realized. There is also a growing sense among academic leaders, especially in the aftermath of the sensational events at Duke and Colorado, that the diversity movement on campus may have grown to a point where it is more trouble than it is worth. Judging by their conduct at these institutions and elsewhere, diversity activists on campus are bound neither by any sense of loyalty to their institutions nor by the canons of civil conduct that make academic life possible. Even the attacks on Western civilization, which once at least seemed bold, new, and exciting, are beginning to take on a weary and boring countenance. Calls for renewal of the traditional humanities curriculum are beginning to come from unlikely sources.[9] If the rage for diversity is indeed waning, opportunities will gradually open up at many institutions to restore some semblance of the traditional liberal arts curriculum and to recruit faculty who are competent to teach it.

Some have suggested that new colleges, universities, or graduate schools should be founded so that they might be established from the beginning on sound principles. Others advocate the restoration of a core curriculum in the liberal arts and humanities based upon the great books of Western civilization. Some wish to influence philanthropists so that they fund sound programs instead of adding to already swollen endowments.[10] Still others (such as Stephen Balch; see his essay in this volume) urge the creation of new academic centers based in one way or another on the ideals of American political institutions or on the works of Western civilization, an incremental strategy of first gaining entry into the academy and then, once in, building support among students and sympathetic faculty. All of these have merit, though a few strategies seem more promising than others. Conservative reformers understand that to change the university they must follow a course of thoughtful incremental action; they cannot employ the tactics of demand and confrontation that leftists employed in the 1960s to turn their institutions inside out.

The creation of new institutions is a particularly challenging enterprise today in view of the costs involved (especially the cost of scientific equipment) and the great difficulty of overcoming the reputational advantages of established institutions.[11] These were not issues for the institutions created in the nineteenth century and even in the first decades of the twentieth. The early half of the nineteenth century was a particularly fertile period for the creation of new religious colleges. The evangelical revivals of the period, combined with the westward movement of the population, contributed to the creation of countless religious colleges across the Midwestern and Plains states. Following the Civil War and into the 1920s, wealthy philanthropists like John D. Rockefeller, Leland Stanford, and Cornelius Vanderbilt created a host of now-prominent institutions such as the University of Chicago, Vanderbilt University, Stanford University, Johns Hopkins University, Clark University, Rice Institute, and many others. Most of these were research institutions with generally secular (rather than religious) orientations. Rockefeller contributed $80 million to establish the University of Chicago in 1892 and Stanford around $20 million (plus a grant of land) to establish Stanford University in 1891. In short order, both became nationally prominent universities, as did Johns Hopkins, Clark, and Vanderbilt.

By far the great proportion of new institutions created since 1950 have been public universities in states with rapid population growth. It is difficult to name many private institutions that have been created since 1950 that are competitive with the leading institutions established in earlier periods or, indeed, with many public institutions created in the modern era. Brandeis University (established in 1948) comes to mind, but few others. Liberty University, a fundamentalist college established in 1971 by the late Rev. Jerry Falwell, has made great strides in this direction, as has Patrick Henry University in just a few years, but neither has yet been able to pose a significant challenge to the long-established elite institutions.[12] On the other hand, the list of public institutions that have been established since 1950 is a very long one.

The private colleges that have been established in our era have, by and large, been created to appeal to narrowly defined segments of the population, usually according to religious principles, or are based on new online technologies. The fact is that few private donors can afford the near-prohibitive costs of establishing a private college or university that might compete with the well-established institutions created in earlier periods. Only a few people—Bill Gates or Warren Buffett, for example,—could afford to consider it and they are not inclined to do so. In this day and age, private philanthropists (even the minority who happen to be conservative) seem more inclined to make gifts to already existing institutions, thus taking advantage of their established programs, reputations, and physical plants.

The effort to restore a core curriculum based on Western civilization or on the great books runs into equally imposing difficulties. There is most certainly a strong case to be made for a required core curriculum, studied by all students as a condition of graduation, on the great works of Western civilization. The late Allan Bloom wrote a best-selling book two decades ago making just this case.[13] While many people bought his book, few seem to have endorsed Bloom's conclusions. Most of the prestigious colleges and universities around the country have long since adopted (following the lead of Harvard University) undergraduate curricula that are based on very loose distributional requirements under which students must take a certain number of courses in their academic majors and then a couple of courses each in other broad areas of study. Many colleges, such as Amherst and Brown, have no requirements at all beyond that of accumulating a certain number of credits for graduation. With few exceptions, there is no longer any required core curriculum in place at the leading undergraduate institutions and thus no coherent body of knowledge that students are expected to master before graduation.

The intellectual consensus that once supported the core curriculum has long since been shattered. There are, consequently, few professors at our leading institutions who would be competent to teach courses in a core curriculum in Western civilization and perhaps even fewer who would be sympathetic to the enterprise in the first place. After all, these are the faculty members who dismantled the old curriculum or who have been trained under the new dispensation put in place following the upheavals of the 1960s. In order to establish a core curriculum worth having, it would first be necessary to replace the faculties at most institutions—certainly an unlikely prospect. There is finally the question of where new professors competent to teach such a curriculum would be trained in view of the intellectual foci of most graduate programs in the humanities.

An alternative to these approaches is the strategy pursued successfully by Robert George at Princeton, Charles Kesler and his colleagues at Claremont McKenna College, and John Tomasi at Brown University, under which academic centers are created on the campus to promote the study of some aspect of Western civilization. These centers are established with the permission of deans, provosts, and departmental chairmen, and funded by modest grants from foundations and alumni. They cannot be introduced everywhere because they require for their success a faculty member on the inside (preferably tenured) who is willing and able to devote time and energy to making them work. Yet there are many advantages to proceeding along these lines. The directors of such programs do not require elaborate faculty approvals in order to proceed, as they would if they sought to make changes in the curriculum. They can be launched with modest contributions which may then be augmented from year to year as the programs gain strength. In some cases, the directors can recruit postdoctoral fellows who may be given approval to offer courses to undergraduates. This is already happening at several institutions, including Princeton and Brown. When these courses are popular and draw significant followings among undergraduates, they send signals to administrators about the kinds of courses students wish to take. These initiatives also bring speakers to campus who would otherwise not be invited and organize conferences and symposia on subjects not in favor among the majority of professors. In time, if done well, these programs encourage a wider dialogue on campus and make students aware of alternative ways of studying politics, economics, history, and related subjects. There are now philanthropic efforts, such as the Veritas Fund at the Manhattan Institute, willing to invest in such enterprises.

As we look into the future, then, we are not likely to see the academic landscape altered very much by new private institutions called into being by frustration with current colleges. Nor are we likely to see any time soon the reintroduction of traditional core curricula at our leading colleges and universities. Desirable as these instruments of change may be, they face financial and political obstacles that are, for now, insurmountable. We are, however, very likely to see the creation of undergraduate programs in the liberal arts that look very much like traditional departments in that they recruit their own faculties, offer a roster of courses, and allow students to enroll in them as a major area of study. In this way, the liberal arts curriculum will return to the campus as a field of elective study.

The incremental nature of this process is likely to frustrate those who look for large and immediate changes in the academy. Many ask why, if such changes can be introduced from the left, they cannot also be brought into the academy from a conservative direction. This question invites speculation about the inner character of the American university and where, given the momentum provided from the past, it is likely to move in the future.

In *The Soul of the American University*, George M. Marsden suggests that the American college and university have evolved according to the unwinding assumptions of liberal thought beginning with the founding of the first institution of higher learning on North American soil in Cambridge, Massachusetts, in 1636.[14] Marsden's particular concern is with the question of how colleges and universities founded by Christians for religious purposes evolved into the entirely secular institutions that we see today. However, since in this context "secular" and "liberal" are more or less interchangeable terms, Marsden implicitly raises the question of how the academy became home to orthodox liberalism. From the beginning, the ideals of diversity, inclusion, and universalism were central to the evolution of our institutions of higher learning.

Nearly all of the colleges established in the colonial era, from the founding of Harvard College down to the Revolution, were of a Protestant character and were created to train ministers in one or another of the denominational faiths. At the time of the Revolution, there were nine colonial colleges, all (save for one) with denominational affiliations. Harvard, Yale, and Dartmouth were of Puritan (or Congregational) origins; Kings College (later renamed Columbia) and William and Mary were Anglican; the College of New Jersey (later Princeton) was Presbyterian; Brown was founded by Baptists, and Queens College (later Rutgers) by Dutch reformers. Among these early institutions, only the University of Pennsylvania was secular in origin. By the time of the Revolution, these institutions faced a

challenge of absorbing into their educational programs students representing different denominational faiths. One solution, tried at Kings College, was
to appoint Presbyterian or Puritan professors to teach theology to students
of those faiths; but this strategy proved unworkable in institutions seeking
to define their missions in terms of broad or inclusive principles. A solution
was found in the teaching of an inclusive form of Christianity that embraced
the various denominational faiths, which left the more specific doctrinal
issues to be expounded from the pulpits of the particular churches.

As Marsden shows, this approach gave way in the late eighteenth and
early nineteenth centuries to an even more inclusive point of view in the
form of moral science. This was a secular, even a scientific, version of human
morals that developed out of the Scottish Enlightenment and located the
sense of right and wrong in inborn human sentiments; the idea was that
moral principles could be discovered by the exercise of reason through the
study of man. These principles of human sociability did not conflict with
Christian doctrine, though the new moral science pointed to a new way of
discovering established truths. Thus, as American colleges evolved during
the colonial and early republican periods, Christian inclusion replaced
denominational exclusion and moral science replaced theology as the basis
for moral teaching.[15]

The reformation of American universities according to the German
research model following the Civil War extended these secular and scientific trends still further.[16] The German model, which Johns Hopkins University was founded on in 1876 and which was applied to other major
institutions in the decades that followed, was based on the independent
professor's search for truth through the methods of scientific inquiry. This
approach pushed theology and religion even further into the background of
academic teaching and research, though Christian leaders remained convinced that the fruits of science would reveal, rather than displace, the laws
of God. It further established research as a central activity of the university,
implying thereby that the university would henceforth be organized around
the discovery of new truths rather than by the teaching of old ones. The
new model revolutionized the academy, leading in a short period of time to
institutional governance by the faculty, academic freedom as a basic right of
professors, the tenure system, and a revamped curriculum that stressed
secular and scientific studies.

The German influence, shaped as it was by the historical approach to scholarly inquiry, was strongly at odds with the assumptions of the Scottish and British Enlightenments, which had played such an important role in the founding of the Republic and the earlier efforts to bring scientific knowledge into the academy. That earlier school of thought, represented most clearly in the ideas of Locke, Hume, and Adam Smith, and later in *The Federalist*, was judged by modern scholars to be too reliant on the doctrine of natural rights and also far too abstract, formalistic, and unhistorical to be of use in a society undergoing rapid industrial change. In their view, this older doctrine would have to yield to modern historical scholarship and to a view that rights are created by society rather than by nature. In this way, ideas in tension with those that shaped the formative institutions of the United States were introduced into the American academy.[17]

The student upheavals of the 1960s led to further organizational and intellectual changes in the university that pushed the trends toward scientism and secularism about as far as they could be taken.[18] The concepts of diversity and inclusion, deployed as ideals to promote the recruitment of women and minorities on to the campus, had something in common with earlier attempts in the eighteenth century to broaden the definition of Protestant Christianity so as to encompass different denominational interests. The modern academic dogma, however, is not nearly as coherent as that earlier synthesis, because in our era the effort to accommodate new groups was undertaken by creating special places for them on the faculty and in the curriculum. This has been accompanied by a historical doctrine that claims that these exceptions and exemptions are required as means of redressing the abuses of the past.

In this way, contemporary academic doctrine, such as it is, incorporates the same tensions between the abstract ideal of equality and the narrower interests of groups that we see in liberal thought in general. The great difference in our era is that the markers between the life of the academy and that of the democratic polity surrounding it have been blurred to the point where they are barely detectable. What we see in the contemporary academy, therefore, represents not only an accommodation to new groups on the campus, but also an accommodation to the influence of those same groups in the wider polity. American colleges and universities, which were created and driven forward in their early years by religious preoccupations, have today been captured by secular political interests. The same diversity doctrine that defines the contemporary campus also defines the contemporary Democratic Party. The groups most active on the campus (feminists, minority activists, environmentalists) are also key constituent groups of the Democratic Party; contemporary liberal doctrine, reshaped in recent decades by the concept of diversity, animates activists both on the campus and within the Democratic Party.

The momentum for change in the American academy, then, has come mainly from one direction—that is, a secular and democratic direction. Such momentum is not of recent vintage but stretches back to the origins of American colleges and universities. Those who would change the academy from other directions must do so in the face of strong historical headwinds. This is not a reason to abandon these efforts, but rather a cause for assessing which tactics are most likely to bring improvement.

Given this enduring pattern in the evolution of the American university, it is possible to anticipate the outlines of some of the controversies on the horizon in the ongoing struggle to shape our institutions of higher learning. As the diversity thrust loses steam, liberal and far-left groups on the campus will not be at a loss for new causes to absorb their attention and energy. The next iteration of liberal reform in the universities is likely to involve further steps to detach these institutions from the American polity in which they are embedded. We have already noted that the intellectual foundations of the modern research university are somewhat at odds with the philosophy of natural rights that shaped our national institutions.

The logic of liberalism points toward the internationalization of the American university. We can already see fragments of this emerging trend at work in the elimination of ROTC from nearly all leading colleges and universities and in efforts to ban military recruiters from college campuses in order to disassociate the academy from American national policies. The enrollment of international students will receive greater emphasis in the coming decades, which will further reinforce this trend toward internationalization. Academic programs in American government or in American studies will be increasingly deemphasized on the grounds that they are parochial, in much the same way that programs in Western civilization were deemphasized in the past. If colleges and universities continue to augment their financial strength, or if they recover quickly from the recent financial meltdown, some may reach a point where they are no longer in need of government grants and other kinds of governmental support, which will further reinforce their sense of independence from the American polity.

It seems strange, and perhaps even impossible, to think that universities can detach themselves from the nation that funds, protects, and encourages them—yet it would have seemed just as strange a century ago to have asserted that within a few generations these same institutions would divest themselves of any religious affiliation. It is thus wise for reformers to remind themselves that in seeking to bring change to the academy, they are aiming at a target that is never at rest. Such is the nature of the university in a competitive and dynamic society—that is, in a liberal society. As they gear up to contest the battles of today to restore liberal studies to the campus or to eliminate quotas and preferential hiring, they should also be prepared to engage in new ones already apparent on the horizon.

Notes

1. These figures are taken from *Chronicle of Higher Education*, August 31, 2007, 16.

2. For a cogent discussion of the diversity doctrine and its origins, along with the ways in which it conflicts with the traditional ideals of liberalism, see Peter Wood, *Diversity: The Invention of a Concept* (San Francisco: Encounter Books, 2003). On a related theme, see Roger Kimball, *Tenured Radicals: How Politics Has Corrupted Our Higher Education* (New York: Harper and Row, 1990), especially chapter 1, "The Assault on the Canon." It is interesting that when quotas and preferences in student admissions and faculty hiring were first proposed, no eminent social scientists suggested that these policies be studied carefully before they were implemented. This was, after all, the promise of academic social science—that policies and proposals could be evaluated for their likely effects. Yet academics never thought to apply to themselves the research ideal that was central to their enterprise.

3. See also Stanley Rothman, S. Robert Lichter, and Neil Nevitte, "Politics and Professional Advancement among College Faculty," *Forum* 3, no. 1 (2005), http://www.bepress.com/forum/vol3/iss1/art2/; Christopher F. Cardiff and Daniel B. Klein, "Faculty Partisan Affiliations in All Disciplines," *Critical Review* 17, no. 3–4 (2005): 237–55; Daniel B. Klein and Charlotta Stern, "Professors and Their Politics: The Policy Views of Social Scientists," *Critical Review* 17, no. 3–4 (2005): 257–303; Gary A. Tobin and Aryeh K. Weinberg, *Profiles of the American University*, vol. 1, *Political Beliefs and Behavior of College Faculty* (San Francisco: Institute for Jewish and Community Research, 2006).

4. See American Council of Trustees and Alumni, *Politics in the Classroom: A Survey of Students at the Top 50 Universities* (Washington, DC: ACTA, 2004).

5. The college and university endowment figures for 2006 can be found in *Chronicle of Higher Education*, August 31, 2007, 32.

6. See *U.S. News and World Report*, "America's Best Colleges 2008," www.colleges.usnews.rankingsandreviews.com.

7. For information on the effects of the market downturn on college endowments, see Goldie Blumenstyk, "Market Collapse Weighs Heavily on College Endowments," *Chronicle of Higher Education*, February 6, 2009; Katie Zezima, "Data Show College Endowments Loss Is Worst Drop since '70s," *New York Times*, January 27, 2009; John Hechinger and Craig Karmin, "Harvard Hit by Loss as Crisis Spreads to Colleges," *Wall Street Journal*, December 4, 2008. On admissions and financial aid policies, see Kate Zernike, "Hard Pressed Colleges Accept More Applicants Who Can Pay Full Cost," *New York Times*, March 31, 2009.

8. See John Silber, "The Cost of Ignorance," *Claremont Review of Books* (Fall 2005), http://www.claremont.org/publications/crb/id.1366/article_detail.asp. At least one online program, the University of Phoenix, has been criticized for offering courses that do not meet minimum academic standards and for employing itinerant faculty members who come and go from semester to semester. It has also been embroiled in lawsuits with the federal government for alleged misuse of public funds. Sam

Dillon, "Troubles Grow for a University Built on Profits," *New York Times*, February 11, 2007, 1.

9. For a recent call for renewal of the humanities, see Anthony Kronman, *Education's End: Why Our Colleges and Universities Have Given Up on the Meaning of Life* (New Haven, CT: Yale University Press, 2007).

10. The debate over the core curriculum and liberal arts education is an old one. The most compelling recent statement for the case can be found in Allan Bloom, *The Closing of the American Mind* (New York: Simon and Schuster, 1987). Kronman, *Education's End*, also points in this direction. See also Barry Latzer, "The Hollow Core: Failure of the General Education Curriculum" (Washington, DC: American Council of Trustees and Alumni, 2004). On a new effort to influence and instruct donors to higher education, which is being led by the Center for Higher Education Reform, see Naomi Schaeffer Riley, "Alms for the Alma Mater," *Wall Street Journal*, October 13, 2007, and John Hechinger, "Big Money Donors Move to Curb Colleges' Discretion to Spend Gifts," *Wall Street Journal*, September 18, 2007.

11. On the rise of the modern research university, see Lawrence Veysey, *The Emergence of the American University* (Chicago: University of Chicago Press, 1965). On the formation of the University of Chicago and Johns Hopkins University, see George M. Marsden, *The Soul of the American University: From Protestant Establishment to Established Nonbelief* (New York: Oxford University Press), chapters 9 and 14.

12. On Patrick Henry University, see Hanna Rosen, *God's Harvard: A Christian College on a Mission to Save America* (Orlando, FL: Harcourt Books, 2007). On religious colleges in general, see Naomi Schaefer Riley, *God on the Quad: How Religious Colleges and the Missionary Generation Are Changing America* (Chicago: St. Martin's Press, 2005).

13. Bloom, *Closing of the American Mind*, sets forth a broad argument in favor of a great books curriculum. Bloom, however, criticized what he called the "cult of the great books," or the idea that simply reading great books is a sign of cultivation or sophistication.

14. See Marsden, *Soul of the American University*.

15. Ibid., chapter 2. See also Douglas Sloan, *The Scottish Enlightenment and the American College Ideal* (New York: Teachers College Press, 1971), chapters 3 and 4.

16. Veysey, *Emergence of the American University*, is still the best source for the transformation of the American university along the lines of the German academic model.

17. On the conflict between the German influences and the ideals of the Scottish Enlightenment, see Morton White, *Social Thought in America: The Revolt against Formalism* (Boston: Beacon Press, 1957). White's study takes up several prominent figures in the history of Progressivism, including Oliver Wendell Holmes, John Dewey, Charles Beard, and Thorsein Veblen.

18. On the legacy of the 1960s in higher education, see Roger Kimball, *The Long March: How the Cultural Revolution of the 1960s Changed America* (New York:

Encounter Books, 2000) and Stephen Macedo, *Reassessing the Sixties: Debating the Political and Cultural Legacy* (Kingston, MA: R. S. Means Company, 1997). As Kimball in particular shows, the upheavals of the 1960s challenged many of the well-established traditions of higher education, including a structured curriculum, the idea that students should be grounded in the great ideas of Western civilization, and dispassionate research and study.

PART III

Different Disciplines, Same Problem

9

When Is Diversity Not Diversity: A Brief History of the English Department

Paul A. Cantor

At the risk of shocking—and offending—my colleagues in English departments around the country, I will come right out and say that there is less diversity in our profession today than there was fifty years ago. I am, of course, talking about *intellectual* diversity, not the diversity of race, gender, and ethnicity that most English professors today proudly point to in their departments and curricula. The past few decades have indeed witnessed a massive diversification of English departments, in terms of both who teaches in them and what they teach. Perhaps the most famous—and controversial—aspect of this development has been the expansion of the canon, especially the inclusion of works outside the European literary tradition.[1] This diversification has been in itself laudable in my view. I have publicly defended the study of what is called postcolonial literature,[2] as well as teaching regularly in the area myself, and publishing studies of postcolonial authors, such as Salman Rushdie and J. M. Coetzee.[3]

But unfortunately the broadening of *what* is taught in English departments has often been accompanied by a narrowing of *how* it is taught. To oversimplify an admittedly complex situation: literature on our college and university campuses today is predominantly analyzed in terms of the categories of race, class, and gender.[4] Authors are viewed as participating in the exploitation of various minorities and subordinate groups, or rebelling against it. Works of literature are generally read not as expressions of genuine insights, but as reflections of the racial, social, and sexual prejudices of their authors, their countries, and their times—unless, of course, the authors can be shown to be challenging these prejudices, in which case they are said to be still capable of genuine insights. This is how literature departments have found a way of participating in the overall political agenda of the contemporary academy—to advance the cause of social justice and in particular the goal of racial, social, and sexual equality.

The result of this reorientation of English departments has been a strange combination of diversity and uniformity in the scholarship they are producing. If you look, for example, at the PhD dissertations graduate students are writing today, you will be struck by the wide range of authors they cover. But you will also notice that they are coming to roughly the same conclusions about this diverse material—it all somehow illustrates the oppressive character of Western civilization. A dissertation may be on medieval English dream visions, it may be on Dickens's novels, it may be on Chicano folk ballads—but it will likely end up showing the evils of the market economy, whether under protocapitalism, fully developed capitalism, or postindustrial global capitalism. I am, of course, exaggerating for rhetorical effect, but I would challenge anybody to find a graduate student in an American English department who is analyzing literature in a way that presents the free market in a favorable light. There may well be a handful of graduate students doing this kind of work—I think I know all five of them personally. But this is still not what one would expect if the study of literature were truly characterized by intellectual diversity.

Among economists, a genuine variety of opinions concerning the free market prevails—all the way from those, like the Austrian school, who champion it adamantly, to those, like the Neo-Marxists, who completely reject it in the name of various forms of reconstituted socialism. Somehow, when literary critics come to apply economics to literature, this wide range of views among economists gets narrowed down to an almost uniformly anticapitalist position, quite often explicitly Marxist or quasi-Marxist.[5] Reading today's literary critics, who typically feel obligated and, what is more, qualified to raise economic issues, one would conclude that capitalism is the worst thing that ever happened to humanity. And yet, the majority of scholarly work in economics has demonstrated the failure of all alternatives to capitalism, and history shows that capitalism has increased the material prosperity, health, life expectancy, social and cultural opportunities, and political freedom of people wherever it has prevailed. Why, then, is procapitalism never represented in literature departments today, even though they now pride themselves on focusing on economic issues?[6]

I want to concentrate on the institutional aspects of this and other developments in literary studies. Despite all the talk of diversity today, English departments have come to look much more like each other than they did fifty years ago—and largely, as I will argue, for institutional reasons. The standard charge against the English departments of the 1950s and '60s is that they all taught the same narrow range of books—the canon—consisting almost entirely of works by the infamous Dead White European Males. This may or may not be true—in fact, I think the canon was never as narrowly defined or as firmly established as its detractors today claim—but in any case, this uniformity of subject matter was counterbalanced by a diversity of approaches to it. Perhaps because critics were largely talking about the same works, they ended up arguing about them and indeed had a common ground for their disputes. The diversity of subject matter in today's English departments has paradoxically worked toward producing a uniformity of approach, perhaps because with fewer books in common, critics have less to argue about. With everyone safely ensconced in a subspecialty, a little realm of study on which nobody else can encroach, they end up largely talking past each other. To make another rhetorical overgeneralization: a half-century ago, the way to make a reputation in literary studies was to say something new about the same old works; today, the way is to say the same old thing about new works.

The diversity of critical approaches a half century ago was reflected in the divergent profiles of the major English departments in the United States and Canada. In the 1950s and '60s, one really could speak of meaningful differences among English departments, whereas today the differences are largely cosmetic and mostly a matter of what amounts to marketing. People who disparage the earlier era tend to think that it was simply and uniformly dominated by the movement known as the New Criticism, with its method of close reading, its rejection of historical and biographical contexts, and its championing of modernist values such as irony and ambiguity.[7] But the New Criticism was still "new" in the 1950s, fighting to establish itself throughout the academy and encountering considerable resistance. As an undergraduate at Harvard in the early 1960s, I heard disparaging comments about the New Criticism from several of my professors, and its chief representative within the English Department at that time, Reuben Brower, felt embattled.[8]

The Harvard English Department in those days was associated with two different movements in literary studies—the Old Philology and the New Humanism—both of which were hostile to the New Criticism. The Old Philology, whose patron saints at Harvard were Francis James Child and George Lyman Kittredge, grew largely out of nineteenth-century German universities, where the study of literature was conceived in the spirit of positivism as a science and chiefly involved the systematic study of languages (the older and more obscure the language the better; hence the focus on Gothic, Anglo-Saxon, Old Icelandic, Old Welsh, and so on).[9] Unlike the New Critics, the Old Philologists were deeply concerned with historical matters, and they had little interest in offering interpretations of literary works. They looked upon the elaborate interpretive readings of the New Critics as fanciful, and, what is worse, beside the point.[10]

The New Humanists at Harvard went all the way back to figures earlier in the century like Irving Babbitt, and, as the name indicates, they looked to chart broadly humanistic themes in literature.[11] Accordingly, they regarded the New Critics as too formalist in their aspirations. In contrast to the New Criticism, the New Humanism embraced intellectual history and also biography.[12] The chief representative of the movement when I was an undergraduate was Walter Jackson Bate, who wrote prize-winning biographies of Samuel Johnson and John Keats.[13] In New Critical terms, he wrote too much about the poet, rather than the poem. As for the Old Philologists, the New Critics looked upon them as dinosaurs, hopelessly out-of-date and impossibly pedantic.

Far from simply dominating the study of English in North America, the New Criticism in fact began as a regional phenomenon, with its roots, strangely enough, in the Southern Agrarian movement. Its original bastions in the 1930s and 1940s were at southern universities like Louisiana State University and Vanderbilt, and it began to penetrate the rest of the country from its foothold at Kenyon College in Ohio, with its influential journal, *The Kenyon Review*. The fact that Yale became the flagship of the New Criticism in the 1950s did signal its emergence as probably the single most influential movement in literary studies in its day, but even at Yale it did not go unchallenged. In the late 1950s, the Yale English Department turned out two of the greatest mavericks of the profession—Harold Bloom and E. D. Hirsch. Each in his own way reacted against the formalism of the New Criticism, with Bloom drawing upon religious thinking and Hirsch upon German philosophy to open up new vistas on the literature they studied.[14] In general, the formalism of the New Critics at Yale generated its antithesis in a variety of antiformalist movements. In the 1960s, Yale, together with Johns Hopkins, became the center of applying continental philosophy, especially French theory, to literary studies—first structuralism, and then poststructuralism.[15] It was no accident that the revolutionary movement known as deconstruction was headquartered at Yale in the late 1960s and throughout the '70s. The way the New Critics insisted on organic perfection of literary form—their demonstration of how beautifully poems, novels, and plays hang together—provoked a powerful reaction. The deconstructive method focused on reading against the grain and showing how literary works fall apart under critical scrutiny, which reveals them to be riddled with internal contradictions and incoherence of form.

While Harvard had its New Historicism and Yale had its New Criticism, a neo-Aristotelianism was flourishing at the University of Chicago in the 1950s.[16] With the university's president, Robert Maynard Hutchins, committed to the Great Books movement and especially to the study of classical thought, the Chicago English Department applied Aristotle's *Poetics* to the study of modern literature, including genres the Greek philosopher had never encountered, like the novel. The neo-Aristotelians at Chicago concentrated on questions of genre, structure, and rhetoric in studies that may have looked old-fashioned to their contemporaries but in fact demonstrated the continuing relevance of categories the ancient Greeks first developed. Chicago critics like Richard McKeon, R. S. Crane, and Wayne Booth drew inspiration from Aristotle to demonstrate that attention to form is compatible with a philosophical approach to literature.[17]

Meanwhile, in the same period, the Princeton English Department was renowned for its historical studies and its historicist philosophy, particularly a movement that was known as Robertsonianism, named after the influential medievalist D. W. Robertson Jr.[18] Robertsonianism stressed the need to study literature on its own historical terms, particularly when dealing with the Middle Ages. In contrast to the broadly humanistic approaches at Harvard, which looked for continuities in ideas over the centuries, or the

Chicago approach, which applied ancient categories to modern texts, Robertsonianism emphasized the radical discontinuities in literary history. Students of Chaucer and other medieval authors were constantly warned not to apply modern concepts of irony and ambiguity anachronistically, but instead to employ the exegetical method, modeled on medieval modes of interpretation themselves. In this view, a historical period is to be analyzed only in terms of its own categories, as if every age were hermetically sealed off intellectually and culturally from the others.

In the period we are talking about, the University of Toronto was dominated by the giant figure of Northrop Frye, one of the greatest literary critics of the twentieth century.[19] Developing a kind of mythic or archetypal criticism, Frye promised to found literary study on a new scientific foundation, and offered a new and universal theory of literature. The scope of his work was impressive: he developed new theories of genre (tragedy, comedy, and, above all, romance), and he constructed a system of literary cycles in which virtually every great work in the Western literary tradition could fit. For many would-be graduate students, the University of Toronto in the 1950s and 1960s *was* Northrop Frye, and they flocked to study with him.

The presiding spirit of the University of Virginia English Department in the 1950s and 1960s was Fredson Bowers. He was a leader of a movement known as the New Bibliography, which championed a particular method of analyzing the problems of textual history that are involved in editing—a method that stressed the importance of taking an author's intentions into account when producing scholarly editions.[20] Under Bowers's leadership, Virginia became a center of scholarly editing and bibliography at a time when much of the profession had become focused on the theory and practice of interpreting texts, rather than the process of how their exact wording should be determined. But Bowers was a pluralist and a pragmatist, and in trying to build the best English department he could, he brought in professors of all stripes. One of his key hires in the 1960s was E. D. Hirsch, who was worlds apart from Bowers in many respects, but whose hermeneutic theories also emphasized the importance of authorial intention (in contrast to the New Criticism, which rejected what it called the "intentional fallacy").[21] Informed by Hirsch's common sense and empiricist spirit, Virginia became known as a bastion of resistance to the abstractness of French literary theory.[22]

The distinctive profiles of English departments in the 1950s and '60s meant that the study of literature, far from being characterized by a bland uniformity, was remarkably diversified and intellectually exciting, and that it involved a number of high-profile institutions in competition with each other. Prospective graduate students in English had real choices to make about where to study, and not just the inevitable worries about fellowship support, living conditions, and job prospects. To be sure, I have emphasized the differences among these departments, and I will admit that they were never uniform in their approaches. New Critics could be found at Harvard at this time, historicists at Yale, and so on. Nevertheless, with all the necessary qualifications, there can be no question that, during this roughly two-decade period, people thought in terms of a distinctive Chicago school of criticism, a Yale school, a Princeton school—and in general had a sense that each department stood for something different.

I do not mean to idealize this period; I am by no means claiming that the 1950s and 1960s represented some kind of golden age of literary study. As a graduate student at Harvard in the late 1960s, I was often frustrated by what I was presented with in my classes. I have always been interested in political criticism, and the cultivated apolitical character of the Harvard English Department's rarefied humanism was almost as alien to me at the time as it was to the left-wing radicals among my fellow graduate students. I have always been put off by formalism of any kind, and, if any movement set the tone during this period, it was the formalist New Criticism. Thus, I am not calling for a return to the good old days of literary studies when I myself was a student. But I am making a historical observation: whatever the deficiencies of this era in literary studies—and I believe there were many—it was a time of genuine diversity of approaches, and each was roughly associated with a different English department.

That situation no longer prevails. In terms of their distinctive profiles, English departments today are a shadow of their former selves. Old reputations die slowly, and thus some sense of differentiation among the major departments lingers on. To take my own department as an example, I believe that Virginia is still thought of as a haven from the excesses of literary theory and as relatively traditional in its approach, with a focus on the older historical periods. I suppose that, by comparison with other English departments, like Duke's, this may be true. But Hirsch and his generation have almost all ceased teaching by now, and in the wake of their retirement, Virginia has done everything possible to make itself look just like every other English Department in the country. It has worked hard to hire professors in all the fashionable new fields, from women's studies to ethnic studies to cultural studies to media studies. Here we see the institutional imperative at work in today's English departments. Forget about ideology—the bottom line is at stake. In a standard marketing ploy, every department wants to be all things to all people, to reach as broad a range of customers as possible. Every department is desperately afraid of being thought of as behind the times and left out of the picture of contemporary literary studies. Departments have become larger and more diverse for the same reason that superstores have come to dominate the retail business.

English departments have thus become the Wal-Marts of the academy, offering one-stop shopping for anyone interested in any phase or mode of literary studies. Trapped in a perpetual game of catch-up, English departments increasingly resemble each other. In particular, driven by the need to attract the best graduate students, departments are constantly attentive to what their rivals are doing, and would generally rather imitate the competition than offer genuine alternatives to it. The proliferation of department Web sites has made it easy to monitor one's competition, but, if a department is not vigilant on its own, its graduate students will be quick to point out when it fails to follow the trends of the profession.

The capitalism underlying all this is, of course, the profound irony of the current state of the profession. In their theories, professors of literature may attack capitalism, but in practice, in their own careers, they seem to be participating in the very money-oriented society they loudly condemn.[23] As their own ideological views would suggest, English professors, like everyone else, are driven by economic motives, chiefly the need to maintain enrollments in their departments at both the undergraduate and graduate levels, and thereby to maintain their salaries, perquisites, and reputations. For decades, members of English departments in their professional lives have been participating in a process they generally condemn in their lectures—globalization. Globalization, as English professors will be the first to tell you, is the imposition of the rationalized homogeneity of modernity on a hitherto culturally heterogeneous world. That is to say, globalization wipes out local and regional differences in the name of a more efficient, because uniform, market system. That is a perfect description of what has happened to English departments—and higher education in general—during the past half century. In what amounts to a market competition, the local and regional differences among colleges and universities have gradually disappeared—to produce an increasingly national, and even to some extent international, system of higher education, in which both students and professors are free to circulate among different institutions. Interchangeable course credits among both domestic and foreign institutions are the (often debased) currency of this international trade in academics.

The homogenization of the academy has simply mirrored the larger homogenization of the United States. I remember a time when you used to have to go to the South for a bottle of Dr. Pepper or to Colorado for a six-pack of Coors. I remember a time when you used to have to go to Chicago for a dose of Aristotelianism. But today, in a world of national markets and the Internet, just about anything is available locally throughout the United States. Technological developments from e-mail to cell phones have made professors, like all Americans, more mobile in every sense of the term, and they no longer feel a need to reside in the same place, to congregate physically, in order to form schools.[24] In their personnel, English departments are no more stable these days than professional sports teams. Professors are much less attached and committed to their home institutions, and have come to think of themselves as intellectual citizens of the world.[25] In short, they have been globalized.

The economic benefits of these developments for all concerned are obvious and genuine. Indeed, contrary to what most English professors believe, markets do operate efficiently to maximize welfare. And what I am calling the globalization of literary studies has clearly had significant intellectual benefits as well. The degree of choice among different English departments has been greatly reduced, but at the same time, the choices available within each department have in some ways genuinely increased. Many of the approaches that were once available chiefly in specific departments are now practiced widely throughout the profession. As the economist Tyler Cowen has argued, this is what happens more broadly in economic globalization.[26] On the negative side, different countries begin to look more like each other, but, on the positive, people within each country have a wider range of options precisely because of the introduction of foreign influences into their daily lives. To an American, the opening of a McDonald's in the middle of the Sahara desert may look like the last stage of the complete homogenization of the world; to a Bedouin, it adds something exotic to his menu and actually makes his local world more heterogeneous.

In short, globalization offers a choice between different kinds of diversity, and English professors, of all people, should be aware that any such choice will involve losses as well as gains. The increasingly uniform nature of English departments across the country has made the system as a whole more efficient, but the elimination of local and regional differences has had many negative consequences. There is much to be said for having a variety of different schools of thought actually headquartered at different institutions. Morris Zapp to the contrary notwithstanding, like-minded thinkers concentrated together may well be able to develop their ideas more fully and powerfully.[27] A sense of distinct and competitive departmental identities in the 1950s and '60s helped fuel the explosion of intellectual movements in literary studies during that period.

I came across an interesting illustration of the issue of intellectual regionalism appropriately enough in *The Southern Register*, the bulletin of the Center for the Study of Southern Culture. The article discusses the plans of the new chairman of the University of Mississippi's English Department, Patrick Quinn. Although not exactly earthshaking news, the headline caught my eye: "New English Chair Proposes More Diversity in Literature." And in today's academy, the watchword of this new regime is indeed diversity:

> Another priority for Quinn is a celebration of the diversification in literature. He said he knows the graduate and undergraduate offerings are especially strong in the field of Southern literature and cultural history, which make the English department distinct from others in the country. "Certainly, Ole Miss has a great history in Southern literature," said Quinn. "However, I feel that expertise can be made richer when it is supplemented with offerings from African American, British, Caribbean, and other world literatures."[28]

As someone who regularly teaches a survey course in World Literature in English, which includes African, Asian, and Caribbean authors—from Achebe to Rushdie to Walcott—I sympathize with what Quinn is saying. Nevertheless, this passage epitomizes everything that troubles me in today's English departments. Quinn's way of increasing "diversification" at Ole Miss is to dilute what makes it "distinct" from other English departments in the country.

Is it really so terrible that a Southern university should specialize in Southern literature? Does it not actually increase our range of choices to have one institution concentrate its efforts in this area? There is a certain logic to drawing upon local traditions, resources, and expertise when studying literature—to make use of one's particular strengths and advantages to differentiate what one is doing and establish a distinct niche for oneself. Even in the age of superstores, specialty shops have managed to compete by developing their own niche markets. The real world still offers a variety of business models. Perhaps English departments chose the wrong one when they decided to follow the strategy of Wal-Mart. Do we really want Ole Miss to end up looking just like every other university in the United States? When English professors see this happening in economic globalization, they lament the loss of local difference in the name of a uniform modernity. But what they bitterly condemn in corporations, they eagerly embrace in their professional lives. Like the corporate juggernauts of globalization, they seem to be intent on wiping out all pockets of local resistance to the homogenization of literary studies—and, remarkably, all in the name of diversity.

I cannot offer any simple solutions to the difficult problems I have raised. I am certainly not advocating turning the clock in literary studies back to 1955. I readily grant that the kind of diversity celebrated in English departments today has an intellectual component, and that broadening the canon has helped to broaden minds. But we have seen that there are many different kinds of diversity—diversity of identity, diversity of ideas, diversity within English departments, diversity between English departments, and so on. Encouraging one form of diversity may involve discouraging others. The current obsession with identity studies in English departments has in many respects involved a contraction of their intellectual horizons, a blotting out of a whole range of issues they used to explore. And each department used to explore them differently, often taking pride in the idea that it alone was on the right track, while all other departments were misguided. This kind of competition encouraged exploration and innovation. I can assure my readers that I never, ever wish that I were back in graduate school. But when I look back at the 1960s, I cannot help thinking that it was a more intellectually exciting and vibrant time for studying literature. English departments may have lacked what is today called diversity, but they were considerably more different from each other than they are now. And it was a productive difference. I believe the situation was healthier and more stimulating when English departments were struggling to be different rather than to be the same.

Notes

1. For an account of this issue, see Harold Bloom, *The Western Canon: The Books and School of the Ages* (New York: Harcourt Brace, 1994), especially 15–41.

2. See Paul A. Cantor, "The Fixed Canon: The Maginot Line of the College Curriculum," *American Enterprise*, September/October 1991, 14–20; and "A Welcome to Postcolonial Literature," *Academic Questions* 12 (1998–99): 22–29.

3. See Paul A. Cantor, "Tales of the Alhambra: Rushdie's Use of Spanish History in *The Moor's Last Sigh*," *Studies in the Novel* 29 (1997): 323–41; and "Happy Days in the Veld: Beckett and Coetzee's *In the Heart of the Country*," *South Atlantic Quarterly* 93 (1994): 83–110.

4. For a thorough and wide-ranging analysis of this phenomenon, see John M. Ellis, *Literature Lost: Social Agendas and the Corruption of the Humanities* (New Haven, CT: Yale University Press, 1997).

5. On the prevalence of Marxism in the contemporary academy and especially in the humanities, see Darío Fernández-Morera, *American Academia and the Survival of Marxist Ideas* (Westport, CT: Praeger, 1996) and Frederick Crews, "Dialectical Immaterialism," *Skeptical Engagements* (New York: Oxford University Press, 1986), 137–58.

6. Incredible as it may sound, I know of only one book of literary criticism that is openly procapitalist: Frederick Turner, *Shakespeare's Twenty-First Century Economics: The Morality of Love and Money* (New York: Oxford University Press, 1999). When left-wing commentators speak of the procapitalism among literature professors, all they are arguing is that, in its expository writing program, a typical English department *inadvertently* serves the interests of capitalism by developing skills that will be useful in the corporate world. See Richard Ohmann, *English in America: A Radical View of the Profession* (New York: Oxford University Press, 1976).

7. For two of the classics of the New Criticism, see Cleanth Brooks, *The Well Wrought Urn: Studies in the Structure of Poetry* (1947; rpt. New York: Harcourt, Brace and World, 1975) and W. K. Wimsatt, *The Verbal Icon: Studies in the Meaning of Poetry* (Lexington: University Press of Kentucky, 1954). For analyses of this mode of criticism, see Gerald Graff, *Poetic Statement and Critical Dogma* (Chicago: University of Chicago Press, 1970), 87–111, and Gerald Graff, *Literature against Itself: Literary Ideas in Modern Society* (Chicago: University of Chicago Press, 1979), 129–49.

8. For Brower as a representative of the New Criticism, see his *The Fields of Light: An Experiment in Critical Reading* (New York: Oxford University Press, 1951).

9. For the influence of German models on the development of American universities, see Gerald Graff, *Professing Literature: An Institutional History* (Chicago: University of Chicago Press, 1987), 55–64. For the development of philology in English departments, see ibid., 65–76. In general, Graff provides here the best book-length coverage of the history of the American English department and treats matters discussed in this essay in much greater detail and depth. See also Gerald Graff and

Reginald Gibbons, eds., *Criticism in the University* (Evanston, IL: Northwestern University Press, 1985) for many interesting essays on the variety of schools of literary criticism in twentieth-century America. Another useful resource for readers looking for more background on the history of criticism is Elmer Borklund, *Contemporary Literary Critics* (London: St. James, 1977), which contains extensive encyclopedia-type entries on many of the critics mentioned in this essay: Walter Jackson Bate, Harold Bloom, Wayne C. Booth, Cleanth Brooks, R. S. Crane, Frederick Crews, Northrop Frye, Geoffrey Hartman, E. D. Hirsch, David Lodge, J. Hillis Miller, and W. K. Wimsatt.

10. To get a feel for the philologists' reaction to the New Critics, read "Prolegomenon to Any Future Study of *Winnie-the-Pooh*," allegedly by "Smedley Force," in Frederick Crews, *The Pooh Perplex* (New York: E. P. Dutton, 1965), 139–50. This marvelous collection of parodies of different styles of literary criticism is perhaps the most convenient—and certainly the most entertaining—way to sample the diversity of critical approaches in the period I discuss in this essay. The parody of the Chicago school of critics is particularly devastating (87–99).

11. For a representative work by Babbitt, see his *Rousseau and Romanticism* (1919; rpt. Cleveland: Meridian, 1955). Alfred North Whitehead was also a great influence on the humanists in the Harvard English Department; see especially his *Science and the Modern World* (1925; rpt. New York: Free Press, 1967).

12. For representative works of the humanist school at Harvard, see Douglas Bush, *Mythology and the Renaissance Tradition in English Poetry* (New York: W. W. Norton, 1963) and Herschel Baker, *The Image of Man* (New York: Harper and Brothers, 1961).

13. See W. Jackson Bate, *Samuel Johnson* (New York: Harcourt Brace Jovanovich, 1975) and *John Keats* (Cambridge, MA: Harvard University Press, 1963).

14. Bloom's first book, *Shelley's Mythmaking* (New Haven, CT: Yale University Press, 1959), begins with a quotation from the Jewish theologian Martin Buber—rather shocking for a work coming out of the Yale English Department in those days. Hirsch's first book, *Wordsworth and Schelling: A Typological Study of Romanticism* (New Haven, CT: Yale University Press, 1960), begins with a German philosopher and was thus in its own way equally shocking in the context of Yale. For a critical account of Bloom, see Frank Lentricchia, *After the New Criticism* (Chicago: University of Chicago Press, 1980), 318–46; for Hirsch, see 256–80.

15. The book generally credited with inaugurating the fascination with French theory in American literature departments is Richard Macksey and Eugenio Donato, eds., *The Structuralist Controversy: The Languages of Criticism and the Sciences of Man* (Baltimore: Johns Hopkins Press, 1970). The book grew out of an international conference held at Johns Hopkins in 1966.

16. For the manifesto of the Chicago school, see R. S. Crane, ed., *Critics and Criticism, Ancient and Modern* (Chicago: University of Chicago Press, 1952). For a critical account of the Chicago school from the perspective of the New Criticism, see Wimsatt, "The Chicago Critics: The Fallacy of the Neoclassic Species," in *Verbal Icon*, 41–65.

17. Booth's best-known work is *The Rhetoric of Fiction* (Chicago: University of Chicago Press, 1961). The Chicago school of literary criticism was unrelated to the work being done at roughly the same time at the university by Leo Strauss, who in retrospect appears to have made the more lasting contribution to theories of the interpretation of texts. See especially his *Persecution and the Art of Writing* (Glencoe, IL: Free Press, 1952).

18. See especially D. W. Robertson Jr., *A Preface to Chaucer* (Princeton, NJ: Princeton University Press, 1962). For a critical account of Robertson's work, see Lee Patterson, *Negotiating the Past: The Historical Understanding of Medieval Literature* (Madison: University of Wisconsin Press, 1987), 26–39.

19. For Frye's most synoptic work, see his *Anatomy of Criticism: Four Essays* (Princeton, NJ: Princeton University Press, 1957). For critical accounts of Frye's work, see Graff, *Poetic Statement*, 73–78; Lentricchia, *After the New Criticism*, 2–26; and Geoffrey H. Hartman, *Beyond Formalism: Literary Essays 1958–1970* (New Haven, CT: Yale University Press, 1970), 24–41.

20. For a statement of Bowers's position, see his *Textual and Literary Criticism* (Cambridge: Cambridge University Press, 1966). Bowers's influence can be seen in the journal he edited for many years, *Studies in Bibliography*.

21. For Hirsch's most important work in literary theory, see *Validity in Interpretation* (New Haven, CT: Yale University Press, 1967). For a contrary view from the New Criticism, see W. K. Wimsatt and Monroe Beardsley, "The Intentional Fallacy," in *Verbal Icon*, 3–18.

22. For a trenchant critique of the role of theory in the humanities, see Crews, "The Grand Academy of Theory," in *Skeptical Engagements*, 159–78.

23. Many observers have noted this paradox. See, for example, Harold Fromm, *Academic Capitalism and Literary Value* (Athens: University of Georgia Press, 1991), especially 210–26. The classic essay that makes this argument is Camille Paglia, "Junk Bonds and Corporate Raiders: Academe in the Hour of the Wolf," in *Sex, Art, and American Culture* (New York: Vintage, 1992), 170–248. Paglia writes: "The facile industry of high-tech criticism is as busily all-American as the Detroit auto trade. New! Improved! See next year's model today! A false progressivism has goaded the profession into a frantic tarantella. Hurry up; get on the ball; you must 'keep up with,' must stay in front. . . . French theory, with its empty word-play, produces sophists, experts in getting ahead, getting worldly rewards. . . . French theory is brand-name consumerism: Lacan, Derrida, and Foucault are the academic equivalents of BMW, Rolex, and Cuisinart, the yuppie trophies. . . . The McDonaldization of the profession means standardized, interchangeable outlets, briskly efficient academics who think alike and sound alike" (220).

24. This point was made brilliantly in David Lodge's academic novel, *Small World* (New York: Warner, 1984). Lodge's exuberant hero, Morris Zapp (said to be modeled on real-life academic entrepreneur Stanley Fish), explains his professional mobility this way: "There's no point in moving from one university to another these days.

There was a time when that was how you got on. . . . The assumption was that all the most interesting people were concentrated into a few institutions, like Harvard, Yale, Princeton, and suchlike. . . . That isn't true any more. . . . The day of the individual campus has passed. It belongs to an obsolete technology—railways and the printing press. . . . Information is much more portable in the modern world than it used to be. So are people. *Ergo*, it's no longer necessary. . . . to keep your top scholars corralled in one campus. There are three things which have revolutionized academic life in the last twenty years . . . : jet travel, direct-dialling telephones and the Xerox machine. Scholars don't have to work in the same institution to interact, nowadays: they call each other up, or they meet at international conferences. . . . As long as you have access to a telephone, a Xerox machine, and a conference grant fund, you're OK, you're plugged into the only university that really matters—the global campus" (49–51). These claims were already true when Lodge wrote this passage in the early 1980s; they are obviously even more valid in the age of the cell phone and e-mail.

25. See Paglia, "Junk Bonds," 221: "The conferences teach corporate raiding: academics become lone wolves without loyalty to their own disciplines or institutions; they're always on the trail and on the lookout, ears up for the better job and bigger salary, the next golden fleece or golden parachute. The conferences are all about insider trading and racketeering, jockeying for power by fast-track travelling salesmen pushing their shrink-wrapped product and tooting fancy new commercial slogans."

26. See Tyler Cowen, *Creative Destruction: How Globalization Is Changing the World's Cultures* (Princeton, NJ: Princeton University Press, 2002). See especially 14–15: "It is misleading to speak of diversity as a single concept, as societies exhibit many kinds of diversity. For instance, diversity *within* society refers to the richness of the menu of choice in that society. Many critics of globalization, however, focus on diversity *across* societies. This concept refers to whether each society offers the same menu, and whether societies are becoming more similar. These two kinds of diversity often move in opposite directions. When one society trades a new artwork to another society, diversity within society goes up (consumers have greater choice), but diversity across the two societies goes down (the two societies becomes more alike). The question is not about more or less diversity per se, but rather what kind of diversity globalization will bring."

27. Contrary to the principles of his fictional avatar, the real-life Stanley Fish tried to assemble a distinct and high-profile English department of literary theorists when he got the chance at Duke in the 1980s.

28. Edwin Smith, "New English Chair Proposes More Diversity in Literature, Changes in Writing Program," *Southern Register: The Newsletter of the Center for the Study of Southern Culture*, Winter 2007, 4.

10

Linguistics from the Left:
The Truth about Black English That the
Academy Doesn't Want You to Know

John McWhorter

Black English is "bad grammar," right? Take the way that it doesn't conjugate the verb "to be." Well, here's a pop quiz. Consider this Black English sentence: *I be eatin' candy every day*. Now: what would be the negative version of the sentence?

I ain't be eatin' candy every day. Right? No!

If you listen to black people who use the dialect, you will never hear them saying *ain't be*. The correct negative version of the sentence is *I don't be eatin' candy every day*.

Of course, no speaker who did not happen to be a linguist could tell you that, anymore than we, unless linguists, could explain why if we were planning a trip to the store, we would tell someone *I'm going to the store tomorrow* but not *I will go to the store tomorrow*. *Will* is, after all, a future marker, and yet you would never, in telling someone your plans, say *I will go to the store*—it would sound like you were a foreigner, and indeed that is a mistake foreigners make. Part of the miracle of human language, standard or nonstandard, is that so much of its complexity is mastered and wielded unconsciously.

So it is with Black English's *be*. It is a piece of grammar, used in a systematic way that requires effort for outsiders to master just as English's future marking does. In her book *Ghettonation*, Cora Daniels, a black author, writes generally in standard style but occasionally states "I be ghetto!" to signal an allegiance with street black culture.[1] In fact, this usage

175

of *be* is incorrect. *Be* in Black English has a particular, systematic function: marking regular, habitual action, such as eating candy every day. This means that one cannot say *I be a postal worker*, because being in this context is not something one does on separate but regular occasions like bathing. Black English grammar is not a matter of lapses in standard English grammar; it is a system of its own. One can, therefore, use it incorrectly: *I be ghetto* is incorrect.

Yet it is entirely reasonable that the reader is unaware that Black English is much of anything except curses and lapses. In the media, what we hear about Black English is that it is one part hip-hop slang and one part "bad grammar." That was certainly the case during, for example, the controversy over the Oakland school board's proposal to use Black English in the classroom in 1996. An informal coalition of academic linguists, education specialists, and speech therapists, mostly black, have been devoted since the early 1970s to the idea Oakland proposed, and they saw the 1996 controversy as a precious opportunity to teach the American public that the way black people often speak is not a conglomeration of bad habits, but an alternate system to standard English, just as regular and just as complex—and sometimes more.

They largely failed, and one of the main reasons was that the study of Black English has proceeded according to conventions different from those that usually apply among linguists seeking to analyze a nonstandard dialect and demonstrate to the wider world that it has legitimacy. Namely, since the late 1960s, the study of Black English in the academy has been so deeply colored by the narrow ideological obsession with policing the world for racism that the basic task of describing the dialect in a scientific fashion, separate from sentiments of identity, crusading, and therapy, has been all but forgotten.

This approach to Black English is a symptom of a left-leaning undercurrent in a particular subfield of linguistics, sociolinguistics. This subfield was founded by scholars such as Dell Hymes and William Labov in the 1960s and was originally intended simply to show how grammar and the usage of language vary according to cultural and sociological factors. For example, in some cultures, extended silences are a normal part of social interaction, while in others, constant chatter is considered a sine qua non of humans occupying the same space. Or, as Labov demonstrated in a classic study in the 1960s, there was more to be said at that time than simply that "New Yorkers leave the r off of the ends of syllables" in words like store and corner. Labov showed more precisely that certain New Yorkers spoke this way: in the 1960s, "r-less" speech was most typical of lower-class people, less common among the working class, and least common among the middle; it was less common the younger people were, showing that this way of speaking was on the wane; and it was more common among men than women, showing that women have a tendency to strive for more "correctness" in their speech.[2]

This was the first time that linguistic work of this kind had ever been done, and it lent crucial insights into how humans use language. However, starting in the 1970s, what viscerally stimulated a great many people working in this new subfield was less the basic, empirical agenda set by scholars like Hymes and Labov than something more specific: a mission to defend the ways of speaking of disadvantaged populations. This was the explicit mission of much early work on Black English, for example, including that by Labov himself, and that mission is, in itself, crucial. It is, however, inherently founded in a left-leaning political orientation, and in the study of Black English, this orientation, stoked by the ideologies left over from the Black Power era, has often distracted scholars from the kind of analysis that would conclusively demonstrate the legitimacy, both current and historical, of the dialect.

The case of the Dutch dialect of the Limburger region in the Netherlands is instructive. This dialect is so different from standard Dutch that it is, essentially, a different language. Limburgish is spoken with tones like Swedish; standard Dutch is not. Making the plural is often different in Limburgish: in standard Dutch, *brother* is *broer,* and *brothers* is *broeren*; in Limburgish, *brother* is *broor,* and *brothers* is *breer.* It is easy for a standard Dutch speaker to hear Limburgish as "mistakes," but when one and a half million people have been making the same "mistakes" for several centuries, speaking in a way that standard Dutch speakers can often barely comprehend at first, there is a case for recognizing a new language entirely.

Thus, there are linguists currently spearheading a project to compile a full-length dictionary of Limburgish words and a detailed description of its grammar. These will show that even if history happens not to have put Limburgish in the shop window, so to speak, it is a systematic variety of human language, just as standard Dutch is. This process is how countless nonstandard dialects have been demonstrated to be more than "mistakes" or "quaint"—with hard work done by people who are certainly moved to legitimize a dialect they likely speak, but are also moderately obsessed with the details and intricacies of how language works. Linguistics is, in fact, a science. We linguists are not etymologists (a subject not even taught), nor are we grammar police: we study and describe how grammar works—and we can even tell you why you wouldn't say *I will go to the store*.

In the wake of the Black Power movement of the late 1960s, assorted scholars embarked on a quest to show Black English as a legitimate variety of English. Ideally, this would have entailed at the outset the careful compilation of a full-length grammatical description of the dialect. However, the tenor of the times, focused on asserting blacks' legitimacy as people, got in the way of science. Specifically, many of those interested in Black English were attracted to the idea that it is not even English at all but an African language in disguise, having African sound features and sentence structure, with English words plugged in. There are black schoolteachers and administrators who remain convinced of this to this day, cherishing the idea that Black English is a cultural link to Mother Africa.

This led to some bizarre claims about the decidedly English-sounding dialect we hear around us. Smitherman had it that Black English does not have final consonants, such that *hood* is pronounced *hoo'* and *bed* pronounced *beh*.[3] However, there are no black Americans telling their children to put on their *hoos* or to go to *beh*. The attractiveness of this notion was that African languages often do not use final consonants; most familiar to Americans are Swahili words and expressions like *hakuna matata* ("no worries"), *jambo* ("hello"), and *Kwanzaa*. Of course, Black English often allows a final consonant to drop when there is another one right behind it: *bes'* for *best*. But there is a long way from that to *hakuna matata*.

Overall, Black English does not parallel African languages in any significant way in terms of sound or structure. There actually are languages that plug English into African structure, but they are nothing like Black English. When African slaves were brought to New World plantations and learned English quickly, they created creole versions of English which are often completely distinct languages, combining African grammar with English words.

On plantations in Surinam, for example, the creole language of this kind is called Sranan, and it indeed has a very African way of putting things.

Take the sentence *Dogs are walking under the house*, which in the Ewe language of Togo and Benin is *Avu le tsa yi xo te*. Thus:

Ewe:	Avu	le	tsa	yi		xo	te
Sranan:	Dagu	e	waka	go	na	oso	ondro
English:	dog	is	walk	go	at	house	under

Obviously, however, black Americans are not given to saying *Dog is walk go house under, yo!* Black English is a dialect of English, not Yoruba or Wolof. All ink spilled to prove otherwise has distracted people from the real work of describing the grammatical patterns of this thoroughly English dialect.

At no time was this elevation of "Black is Beautiful" ideology over empiricism more damaging to perceptions of Black English than during the Ebonics controversy in 1996 and 1997. The Oakland school board, misled by Ernie Smith, a charismatic black medical school teacher with little formal linguistics training who has long had legions of black schoolteachers in his thrall, incorporated the African idea into its manifesto, calling Black English one of several "West and Niger-Congo African Language Systems" and "not a dialect of English." Black linguists backed up Oakland to a man (with the exception of the man writing this) and sat in front of television cameras saying "Black English looks like English but it isn't," a case so plainly absurd that it only reinforced the general idea that Black English is indeed nothing but slang and mistakes.

Because I happened to be the black linguist working nearest to Oakland at the time, the media sought me out for my opinion on whether black students' problems with learning to read were based on problems negotiating the difference between Black English and standard English. I said that Black English was a systematic grammar, but not different enough from standard English to impede learning to read, nor in any way African. Much to my surprise—this was my first experience with the PC police in university culture—I was condemned roundly for this by Black English specialists. One of them refused to write a letter recommending me for tenure, out of disgust with my breaking ranks.

Yet the ranks in question are composed of people lying to the public in the name of a crusade to legitimize Black English—a crusade that, in the very act of lying, they sabotage. In the years afterward, I learned that most of the linguists amidst such ranks are well aware that Black English is not an African language. No one with a doctorate in linguistics does work arguing that Black English is not English: rather, the notion thrives among educators and people with degrees in other areas, who have inferred from superficial likenesses between some African languages and Black English that the similarities are causal rather than accidental (there are superficial accidental likenesses among the grammars of all languages). However, the linguists saw it as an imperative to wink and let the African notion pass in public.

This also happens at conferences attended by both linguists and educators, where those working according to the African idea are not told that the idea is hopeless. Biologists do not politely allow creationists to present papers in their midst without directly and relentlessly criticizing the flaws in the creationists' argumentation. Among Black English specialists, however, the tacit sense is that identity politics—the linking of the dialect to Mother Africa—are more important than engaging with the empirical reality of what Black English is. To actually get down to particulars at one of these conferences and specify in what ways the African idea does not hold up would be considered highly improper—the behavior of some persnickety martinet not with the program.

An example of linguists' willingness to look the other way is offered by John Baugh, now of Washington University, who in a book published years after the Ebonics controversy (one not widely read nor intended to be) quietly but firmly stated: "Any suggestion that American slave descendants speak a language other than English is overstated, linguistically uninformed, and—frankly—wrong."[4] Yet in 1996, he was the "pro" to my "con" on an early episode of the Fox News show *Hannity and Colmes*, grimly insisting that Black English was indeed different enough from the standard to make learning how to read difficult. One senses that Baugh saw this as a tolerable bit of collateral damage amidst a general imperative of ensuring that the so-called "linguistic needs" of black students were met.

Another example appears in an article by Charles DeBose and Nicholas Faraclas tracing Black English's use of the verb "to be" and some other parts of its grammar to languages of southern Nigeria like Yoruba.[5] DeBose and Faraclas would not be inclined to term Black English an African language with English words. However, they make a clear argument that African languages had a decisive role in determining the grammatical structure of

Black English, a role that must be acknowledged if Black English is to be correctly understood. They present themselves as having a "willingness to approach the study of [Black English] without the Anglocentric biases that have clouded much of the previous work," and assert that "to ignore the role of the West African substratum in the motivation of the [Black English] system would be analogous to trying to motivate Modern English from French without acknowledging the Germanic roots of the English language."[6] That is, although English has a massive battery of words from French, the historical source of its grammatical structure is in the Germanic ancestor that also yielded German and Dutch; in the same way, DeBose and Faraclas imply, Black English has English words, but its structure is, to some highly significant extent, rooted in the languages of West Africa.

However, the simple facts are that 1) there is very little resemblance of any importance between the parts of Black English grammar they address and the same ones in Yoruba and its relatives; and 2) slaves from southern Nigeria were not imported to the United States in significant numbers. Yet this article appeared in an important anthology. The editor of the anthology is well aware in his work that Black English is a form of English, yet this article was treated as a passable contribution nevertheless.

One does not need to be a linguist to see that the difference between *She isn't at her desk* and *She ain't at her des'* is not African, and has nothing to do with why a young black child may not be able to make out either written sentence at all. In fact, perhaps only a linguist could begin to fashion a delicate mental equipoise within which the whole idea makes any kind of sense at all. In the wake of the Ebonics controversy, few in America knew much more about Black English than they had before—today just as before, the typical response when the topic comes up is the cute scene in *Airplane* when a white woman offers herself as speaking "jive" in order to translate for two black passengers.

There has been a corollary effort to demonstrate that Black English grammar is a development from a creole language spoken in the United States, Gullah, the "Geechee talk" of the Sea Islands and Charleston in South Carolina. Presumably, the idea is that Gullah was once the language of slaves throughout the South and even up the East Coast, but that after Emancipation, black people had more contact with whites and their Gullah "bleached" into Black English, closer to whites' English but still carrying the Gullah "legacy."

This, again, is attractive in linking Black English to a historical process in which Africans "retained their identity" by creating creoles, making do with European words for pragmatic reasons but using them amidst the African grammars they had been born to. And unlike the idea that Black English is an African language, the idea that Black English is the outgrowth of what was once a creole is promulgated by respectable linguistic specialists.

The problem with this hypothesis, however, is that for forty years, neither linguistic nor historical evidence has borne it out. Just a look at Gullah alone shows how fragile the idea has always been. Here is a Gullah sentence:

Ah bin uh tawk nawmo.   "I was only talking."

The grammar in this thoroughly ordinary sentence is clearly quite un-English. The *uh* is a shortened form of a word *duh*, which in turn began as *does: I does talk* meant *I am talking*. The *bin* places the sentence in the past; there is no *-ed* past marker in Gullah. *Nawmo* is from *no more*, which has developed a related meaning *only*, as in *I want two chickens, no more*—i.e., only two.

The proposition is that the Black English rendition of the same sentence, *I was jus' talkin'*, is somehow derived from *Ah bin uh tawk nawmo*. Of course, one might draw a hypothetical step-by-step pathway wherein *I was jus' talkin'* "morphs" out of *Ah bin uh tawk nawmo*, and things of that kind have, predictably, been proposed.[7] However, there is no evidence of this morphing from Gullah to Black English in records of black people talking over the past two hundred years. Quotations from the days of yore show black people talking more or less the way they do now: an 1829 quote from a black woman, for example, is *Soon he want to know how old you be first*. This sentence would be perfectly plausible from black people in St. Louis or Cleveland today.

The hypothesis that Black English derives from Gullah is, in the scientific sense, unnecessary. There is no reason to suppose that the roots of *I was jus' talkin'* are not in, well, *I was just talking*. Yet massive amounts of ink have been devoted to—and scholarly set-tos occasioned by—the pretense that the hypothesis is on some level a worthy one. Because before Emancipation, slaves were sometimes transplanted from the United States to other places, it has been hoped that the descendants of these slaves today might speak Gullah, or at least Gullah Lite, since they have not had as much exposure to whites as black Americans have since the Civil War. Yet again and again, scholars find that descendants of these transplanted slaves sound a lot like black people here in the U.S. In Liberia, one mines sentences like *I done forgot it*. In Nova Scotia, *I never run from nothing else no more*. In the Dominican Republic, *English ain't so easy to learn like Spanish is*.

The simple truth is that despite the sociological line between whites and blacks in America, Black English is largely an offshoot of the regional British dialects that slaves heard working alongside the indentured servants we learn about in middle school history classes. Black Americans' accent has moved far from the way rural Brits speak, but the grammar is often almost uncannily similar. *Even when I be round there with friends, I be scared* sounds like a black teenager in Atlanta, but it was in fact uttered by an Irishman. Those familiar with the black expression *My baby mama* for *My baby's mama* would find Yorkshire English familiar as well, in which one can also not use the possessive *'s*: *My sister husband*, for example. As for double negatives, they are native not just to Black English, but to all known dialects of the English language (including Old and Middle English) except the modern standard one. Therefore, near Manchester one catches sentences like *I am not never going to do naught no more for thee*.

Thus, Black English is a mixture of several regional British dialects, seasoned very lightly with an African sound pattern or two, and festooned with a rich slang reflecting the experience of slaves' descendants in the United States.[8] This, one would think, is an interesting enough story, a tale of a people making the best of the worst in taking on a new language, by wresting from it a new and vibrant dialect. However, because it is not an African or Caribbean story, but instead an "Anglocentric" one, Black English specialists cannot embrace it—even though it is true.

Rather, much work on the history of Black English has proceeded with an almost studiously perfunctory attention to the English of Great Britain, as if musicologists tracing the roots of bebop jazz devoted 95 percent of their attention to the use of drums in African music while giving only genuflective acknowledgment to the fact that bebop is primarily distinct in its innovative approach to Western harmony. It is clear that to most of these Black English specialists, committed to wielding Black English as a weapon in an eternal battle against discrimination, oppression, and the like, the speech of white proletarians in England is simply not terribly interesting. These specialists are like a paleoanthropologist who pays only lip service to the close similarities between humans and apes and proposes that humans instead developed from birds—because both humans and birds have femurs and intestines, and because he has a gut-level dislike of apes.

There has, in fact, arisen a cadre of white Canadian linguists making the case for the roots of Black English in, well, English.[9] Predictably, they are received by much of the old guard, as well as the new guard they have trained, as unsavory nuisances, despite the fact that their argumentation, historical research, and statistical analysis are more thorough than that of all but a few of the scholars who have worked on Black English. One even detects an unspoken speculation that the Canadians' research paradigm has a racist motivation, or at least that it is somehow unsavory in not stressing the roots of the dialect in the African or the Caribbean, or not noting its connection to "the Struggle."

The hold that political correctness has on the study of Black English has had repercussions beyond the public perception of the dialect and its scholarly documentation. A healthy current lives on among education specialists supposing that black students are in some sense "bilinguals" in need of special assistance in learning to read the foreign tongue they encounter in school. For example, John Baugh, although hardly subscribing to the idea that Black English is an African language, espouses in his work the basic assumption that Black English is different enough from standard English that black students have particular linguistic "needs" currently unaddressed in American educational practice.[10]

Or, intermittently since the early 1970s, researchers have sought to show that black students' reading problems could be constructively addressed by teaching them first with Black English materials, and then transitioning them gradually to standard English (naturally this approach is an attractive topic for graduate students). While chance happened to bring this idea to the attention of the media for a brief spell in 1996 and 1997, it had not only been alive decades before this, but it continues to be espoused and addressed.[11] Unsurprisingly, the novelty of reading one's home dialect can result in a minor uptick in reading performance, at least in the short term, and this improvement is presented as demonstrating that Black English truly is a barrier for such children. Yet amidst all of this earnest hand-wringing, there is not a word about the fact that we learned forty years ago an effective method for teaching poor, nonwhite children how to read.

This method was developed by Siegfried Englemann, whose Project Follow Through conclusively showed, with long-term studies covering children of various ages, classes, and colors, living in various places, that phonics-based teaching methods using systematic drilling were the most effective way of teaching children from poor backgrounds how to read. Since then, poorer school districts adopting methods of this kind, called Direct Instruction, regularly see reading scores improve.

The "Ebonics" notion lives on as if this work had never been done, when in fact, any graduate student interested in teaching kids who are poor or black or both should be presented with Project Follow Through and its methods. Project Follow Through has been shown to work far better than any "Ebonics" pilot project; and no work has ever disproven its superiority. Yet I am aware of no argument after the early 1970s citing Black English as a barrier to reading for black kids that even mentions Project Follow Through.

Rather, the "Ebonics" idea marches on in a bubble, with some writers calling standard English a "gatekeeping" oppressor language that must make room for Black English.[12] The rhetorical power of that terminology is allowed to stand in the place of sustained argumentation. No one in this school of thought considers the fact that black students can learn to read thoroughly well without Black English aiding them in the classroom—and this despite media accounts of charter schools successfully teaching disadvantaged black students without anything like the "Ebonics" methods.

The reason Project Follow Through is ignored is because it cannot be fashioned as part of a larger crusade against racism and injustice. Sadly, its neglect reveals a certain self-medicational aspect of the idea that black students need "Ebonics" instruction. The crusaders are interested in black kids learning only if they do so amidst a victory wrested from the oppressor who has been denying them their rights as black bilinguals. But such a victory is unnecessary and shows no signs of ever happening. The academics drawing Black English into a claim about pedagogical practice may consider themselves to be fighting the good fight, but they are disconnected from what actually helps black students learn to read.

In 2002, there did at last appear a book-length grammatical description of Black English.[13] However, the bone-deep assumption among academics studying the dialect that any engagement with it must spring from an oppositional, protective impulse makes this book less than it could be. Grammatical description takes up only roughly the first half of the book, and the brevity of this account (about 120 pages) is such that the dialect remains only preliminarily described, while laymen could easily see it as a mere checklist of colorful "mistakes," rather than a substantial and complex description of what is irrefutably a true system of grammar.

For example, a description that established Black English in a conclusive way as a legitimate dialect would draw attention to its parallels to the dozens of other vernacular English dialects in, especially, Great Britain, underscoring the fact that we are dealing not with a peculiar excrescence emerging among black people in the United States, but with one of countless variations on the basic English template that have arisen since the Angles, Saxons, and Jutes invaded Britain a millennium and a half ago.

Instead, half of the book is devoted foundationally to the more local goal of addressing "racist" conceptions of the dialect in the United States, via pulling the camera lens back and covering topics such as the coherence of Black English conversational patterns, Black English in literature and the media, and of course, the use of Black English in education.

These, however, are aesthetic and/or controversial issues, which have long been amply covered elsewhere. The accepted approach to writing a grammatical description is to stand back from the language or dialect, take a deep breath, and objectively describe its structure—and largely only its structure—as if one were a foreigner encountering the language of an obscure tribe in the Amazon.

It seems that this approach is difficult for most people working on the dialect today. Instead, there is a sense that Black English, because of the unfortunate history of black people in America, is an exception, and that any enlightened approach to the dialect must be channeled by a guiding intention to defend it from racist dismissal. To analyze the dialect in the purely objective fashion of the linguist is seen as somehow beside the point, even though precisely this would accomplish the goal of establishing Black English as a different rather than lesser English.

As a result of political correctness, the following is true regarding Black English:

1. Structural description constitutes an unsuitably small proportion of a bibliography driven primarily by advocacy;

2. The dialect's actual and obvious historical origins are treated as controversial and suspect rather than accepted by all serious researchers and investigated further;

3. It has been misrepresented to the general public so often by academics that they have reinforced the very dismissal they are in battle against.

This kind of confusion between empirical engagement and political advocacy occurs in linguistics beyond the study of Black English. Take, for example, creole languages like Sranan (discussed above), which were born when adult slaves learned a European language orally with no explicit teaching, and used the language with one another more than with whites. The resulting language was, as all languages used everyday and learned by children are, complex, but its grammar, again like such languages generally, is less complex than that of old languages like English or Arabic.

Let us look for example at the sentence *They don't have the resources that could allow them to resist the famine*, first in French and then in Haitian Creole, which has French words but a grammar based on a mixture of French and African languages, and which is less complex than any of those:[14]

French: Ils n'ont pas de ressources qui puissent leur permettre de résister à la famine.

Haitian: Yo pa gen resous ki pou pèmèt yo reziste anba grangou.

In the French sentence, verbs are conjugated; Haitian verbs are not (as in many languages, such as Chinese). French has subjunctive marking (*puissent*); Haitian does not. French nouns have genders; Haitian do not. French has what is called "partitive marking," which students of French know as the pesky use of *de*—"of"—before nouns where it is so often largely untranslatable into English (*de ressources*). Examples go on. Haitian

Creole certainly has grammatical structure, but that structure is less complex than French's, because it began a few hundred years ago as simplified French, and it takes languages millennia to pile on complexities such as inanimate nouns having genders and the like.

Yet what I have just written is considered hasty, heretical, and even morally suspect by many people who study creoles. Most creoles are spoken by African-descended or sociopolitically disadvantaged people, and as such, the idea that the languages they speak natively are comparatively simple grammatically is taken as suggesting the speakers' mental inferiority. This is true even though the issue is—and has been carefully argued to be— that older languages are accreted with complexity that has nothing do with speakers' mental capacity. For example, the fact the nouns in German come in three genders is not an indication that Germans are mentally sophisticated, but rather that their language drags along an unnecessary complication, now meaningless, that arose via a series of accidents.

Yet it is fashionable to point to features in a creole that seem to refute the hypothesis that creole grammars are less complex than older languages', even though, as I have carefully and repeatedly stated, here and elsewhere, the issue is, quite simply, a matter of degree.[15] In fact, the observation that creoles are less needlessly complex than older languages is couched within an assumption that this simplicity could make creoles useful for examining what the heart of the innate human language competence might be.[16] Meanwhile, arguments that creoles are as complex as older languages often simultaneously maintain that this complexity disproves the existence of any grammatically distinct creole language at all, and often imply that creole studies should be devoted only to examining the languages' social histories— which would stretch the definition of what linguistics, as opposed to history or anthropology, is thought to be.

This would not only be less interesting than treating creoles as the novel linguistic creations that they are, but would be based on an empirical fallacy, shored up by the sociopolitics of our moment and evident even to modestly trained undergraduates coming into the subject from outside of any preset ideological assumptions.

It is, then, not surprising that the work on the origins of Black English that proceeds in the fashion considered traditional in the field of linguistics has been done mostly by people outside of the United States, mainly in

Canada and Germany.[17] An ossified sense among black academics and their fellow travellers that to be authentic is to be oppositional has, sadly, left America as a whole no more enlightened on the truly fascinating dialect it has birthed than it was forty years ago.

Notes

1. Cora Daniels, *Ghettonation: A Journey into the Land of Bling and Home of the Shameless* (New York: Doubleday, 2007).

2. William Labov, *The Social Stratification of English in New York City* (Washington, DC: Center for Applied Linguistics), 1966.

3. Geneva Smitherman, *Talkin and Testifyin* (Detroit: Wayne State University Press, 1977), 17.

4. John Baugh, *Beyond Ebonics: Linguistic Pride and Racial Prejudice* (New York: Oxford University Press, 2000).

5. Charles DeBose and Nicholas Faraclas, "An Africanist Approach to the Linguistic Study of Black English: Getting to the Roots of the Tense-aspect-modality and Copula Systems in Afro-American," in *Africanisms in Afro-American Language Varieties*, ed. Salikoko S. Mufwene (Athens: University of Georgia Press, 1993), 364–87.

6. Ibid., 385.

7. See, for example, Ralph Fasold, "One Hundred Years from Syntax to Phonology," in *Parasession on Diachronic Syntax*, ed. Sanford B. Steever, Carol A. Walker, and Salikoko S. Mufwene (Chicago: Chicago Linguistics Society, 1976), 79–87.

8. See John H. McWhorter, *Word on the Street: Fact and Fable about American English* (New York: Plenum, 1998), 155–99.

9. See, for example, Shana Poplack, ed., *The English History of African American English* (Malden, MA: Blackwell, 2000).

10. See, for example, his article in a respected anthology on Black English, "Linguistics, Education and the Law: Education Reform for African-American Language Minority Students," in *African-American English: Structure, History, and Use*, ed. Salikoko S. Mufwene, John R. Rickford, Guy Bailey, and John Baugh (London: Routledge, 1998).

11. See McWhorter, *Word on the Street*, 219–21, for studies in this vein through 1998; studies after this include H. Fogel and L. C. Ehri, "Teaching Elementary Students Who Speak Black English Vernacular to Write in Standard English: Effects of Dialect Transformation Practice," *Contemporary Educational Psychology* 25 (2000): 212–35; A. Pandey, "TOEFL to the Test: Are Monodialectal AAL-Speakers Similar to ESL Students?" *World Englishes* 19 (2000): 89–106; and the study described in John R. Rickford, "Linguistics, Education, and the Ebonics Firestorm," in *Georgetown University Round Table on Language and Linguistics: Linguistics, Language, and the Professions*, ed. J. E. Alatis, H. E. Hamilton, and A-H Tan (Washington, DC: Georgetown University Press, 2002), 25–45.

12. One example: Arnetha F. Ball, "US and South African Teachers' Developing Perspectives on Language and Literacy: Changing Domestic and International Roles of Linguistic Gatekeepers," in *Black Linguistics: Language, Society, and Politics in Africa and the Americas*, ed. Sinfree Makoni, Geneva Smitherman, Arnetha F. Ball, and Arthur K. Spears (London: Routledge, 2003), 186–214.

13. Lisa J. Green, *African American English: A Linguistic Introduction* (Cambridge: Cambridge University Press, 2002).

14. Ralph Ludwig, Sylviane Telchid, and Florence Bruneau-Ludwig, eds., *Corpus créole* (Hamburg: Helmut Buske, 2001), 164.

15. See John H. McWhorter, *Defining Creole* (New York: Oxford, 2005); for attempts at refutation, see various response articles in *Linguistic Typology* 5, no. 3/4 (2001) and Umberto Ansaldo, Stephen Matthews, and Lisa Lim, eds., *Deconstructing Creole* (Amsterdam: John Benjamins, 2007).

16. Most explicitly, Derek Bickerton, *Roots of Language* (Ann Arbor, MI: Karoma, 1981).

17. From Germany, for example, a sustained and quantitative analysis of historical data shedding light on the historical relationship of Gullah and Black English in South Carolina is offered by Alexander Kautzsch and Edgar W. Schneider, "Differential Creolization: Some Evidence from Earlier African American Vernacular English in South Carolina," in *Degrees of Restructuring in Creole Languages* (Amsterdam: John Benjamins, 2000), 247–74. The authors have a traditional, objective, and apolitical dialectologist's orientation that is all but foreign to American specialists' work on the history of Black English.

11

History Upside Down

Victor Davis Hanson

What is politically correct history? And what is so wrong with it?

Narratives that emphasize, or are even devoted to, the contributions of the poor, the disenfranchised, the nonwhite, non-European, and nonmale are most certainly not politically correct history. Instead, politically correct histories are a more recent genre of academic history that aims to use the past to achieve social change in the present. They seek to show, by using selective evidence, applying asymmetrical standards of criticism, and employing various race, class, and gender theories, that the West—and the United States in particular—is inherently pathological, and has habitually oppressed the "other" (at least, when it was not borrowing or stealing the latter's culture and superior ideas).

Once we understand the great wrong that we've done others in the past, we can begin to make amends by radically rethinking our own contemporary culture, politics, and traditions.

Michael Bellesiles, for example, won the Bancroft Prize for *Arming America*—it was later rescinded because of "scholarly misconduct"—by slanting and inventing evidence about early American gun ownership. He sought to "prove" that guns were not common in colonial times and during the American Revolution, thus weakening the case for our long-held but dangerous notion of the right to bear arms as reflected in the Constitution.

Martin Bernal wanted to diminish the supposed cultural arrogance of the West by arguing in *Black Athena* that the Greeks derived much of their cultural heritage from Black African peoples in Egypt.

In *Orientalism,* Edward Said claimed that much of what we know about Asia and the Middle East is arguably false and misleading. The "Orient" was invented by a long tradition of prejudicial Western scholarship, eager to denigrate a culture in some ways superior to the West—and one whose present miseries are in large part attributable to Western biases.

The Conquest of Paradise, written by Kirkpatrick Sale, argued that the Americas were essentially ruined by the arrival of Europeans, who brought disease and environmentally destructive practices, and who exploited the nonwhite natives in ways that plague us still. In contrast, indigenous peoples, massacred or killed off through European diseases, had practiced a more environmentally sound way of life that would have kept the Americas in their pristine state.

Howard Zinn advanced his revolutionary views about contemporary America in *A People's History of the United States,* which rewrote the history of the United States as primarily a story of a white male capitalist class at war against blacks, Native Americans, other countries, socialists, women, and workers.

For William Appleton Williams, author of *The Tragedy of American Diplomacy,* the twentieth-century foreign policy of the United States was a matter of capitalist greed. The Cold War was unilaterally prompted by American desires to preserve markets, increase profit, and deny others access to their own natural resources—all unduly at the expense of the Soviet Union and its mostly blameless Communist and third-world allies. This thesis is updated by Chalmers Johnson in *The Sorrows of Empire*: once we decided not to retrench after the fall of the Soviet Union, America showed that its imperialism was innate and not an artifact of the Cold War. When we expanded military bases all around the globe to better use force to bend the world to our economic advantage, Williams's "tragedy" became Johnson's "sorrows"—as America sold out its own people for arms profits, oil, and Israel.[1]

Two themes dominate all these diverse histories. The contemporary white male, Western, capitalist establishment does not deserve its present privilege, which either is a product of exploitation in the past or was stolen from others. Second, history should be used to trace and document Western pathogens in hopes of remedying their pernicious legacy in the present. The anti-Western and anti-American authors of these histories, of course, choose to live in the democratic and capitalist West precisely because there they are uniquely free to write and say what they wish, while enjoying the benefits of a prosperous economy that provides scholars the support network necessary for serious research. This irony is entirely lost on these historians.

Western historians, of course, have always been critical of their own institutions and popular culture. Long before the rise of postmodern fashions and theories, Westerners were intellectually curious about—and even praised fulsomely—those outside the European male power structure. This interest in a diverse array of non-Europeans is as old as Herodotus, the father of history. The second book of his *Histories* (c. 430 BC) offers a sympathetic account of a far older—and in some regards materially more impressive—Egyptian culture of the pharaohs. Xenophon wrote admiringly of Persian customs in his *Cyropaedia*. Tacitus's *Germania* is not just a descriptive account of tribal culture, but is written with explicit admiration for natural German vigor and innate courage—despite past German annihilation of Roman legions and mutilation of legionaries' remains.

Tacitus's imperial contemporaries, particularly Juvenal, Petronius, and Suetonius, offer savage portraits both of a bankrupt, amoral Roman elite and a new grasping mercantile class completely lacking traditional agrarian virtue. Note that their buffoons and villains—the "esurient Greekling," the monstrous Sejanus, the crass Trimalchio, the perverted Caligula, and the psychopathic Nero—are not merely presented as the bad apples found in any society, but as templates of something inherently defective in the values of imperial Roman society itself.

Montaigne's romance about the "cannibal," Shakespeare's depiction of a monstrous but occasionally sympathetic Caliban, and Rousseau's notion of a "noble savage," all shorn of Western civilization's cultural baggage of religion, government, science, and constructed manners, ultimately go back to classical Greek and Roman curiosity about the untamed—whether Homer's and Theocritus's Cyclops or Euripides' Bacchae, or Catullus's Attis. These accounts provided philosophical support for two subsequent centuries of fierce criticism of Western exploitation and colonialism in Africa, the Americas, and Asia.

So criticism of the West is inherent in Western historiography. We know of the abuses of Hernan Cortés during the Spanish invasion of Mexico largely because of the narratives of Bernal Díaz del Castillo, Bartolomé de

Las Casas, or Fray Bernardino de Sahagún—Spanish veterans and clerics who felt the Spanish conqueror had been ruthless to his men, or to the indigenous Mexica, or to both. To Edward Gibbon, Christianity offered ancient society no blueprint for ethical improvement, but instead had destroyed Roman civic militarism without offering any consistent, superior morality in its place. Bishop John William Colenso and his daughters published scathing attacks on the British and Boer treatment of the Zulus and provided a contemporary critique of the entire British colonial policy in South Africa. *Heart of Darkness* was not the beginning, but the logical culmination, of Western reflection upon the damage Europeans did abroad.[2]

Self-critical European historians thrived in a wider landscape of literary angst about perceived Western moral lapses. Slaves appear smarter than their Greek masters in both Old and New Comedy. Aristotle assumed the existence of an entire body of contemporary critics of slavery (their writings are now lost) when he argued for the apparently controversial notion of a "natural" slave. Writing in the fourth century BC of the liberation of the Messenian helots by the Theban Epaminodas, the rhetorician Alkidamas asserted that "nature had made no man a slave." Aristophanes and Euripides assumed that an Antigone or Lysistrata is not only brighter but more courageous than the men in her midst.[3]

Contemporary politically correct history is, however, something altogether different from this tradition of disinterested criticism of Western customs and protocols, which was intellectually curious rather than bent on finding, in deductive fashion, proof about preexisting theories of Western pathology and moral decline. In inquisitorial fashion, the politically correct historian selectively evokes the past to advance a contemporary political agenda of social change. The point is to indict Western culture as culpable for much of the nation's, and indeed the world's, present sins—from global warming to failed states in the former third world. Historians focus on class, race, and gender issues—often at the expense of individuals, and classical topics like war and politics—to sort out (i.e., "deconstruct" or "unpack") implicit past oppression of people of color, women, and gays. When facts intervene, they are ignored or explained away.[4]

When contemporary historians, as part of this drift away from political, diplomatic, and military history, indict those of the past as illiberal, they do so largely by drawing on the prevailing absolutes and standards of present-day

Western society, which is—ironically—assumed to possess both superior wisdom and morality. We are to reappraise the moral character, and indeed the contributions, of Thomas Jefferson not because of some new reinterpretation of the Declaration of Independence or his administration's foreign policy, but because, like some Virginia estate owners of the age, he held slaves and supposedly fathered children by one. We are to look askance at Abraham Lincoln, not because on reexamination his war strategy may have been flawed or too costly, but because some of his early speeches reveal a realist determination to save the union, rather than first to abolish slavery. The lack of perfection in our past heroes on matters of race suggests to us, the moral gods of the twenty-first century, that they may well not have been good at all.

Of course, while past Westerners are now found guilty of racism, imperialism, or colonialism, the same standards of scrutiny rarely apply to the so-called other. To accuse the West of introducing deadly diseases such as smallpox into the Americas is commonplace; rarely discussed is the fact that indigenous peoples exposed Europeans to cocaine, coffee, sugar, tobacco, and even syphilis. The early nineteenth-century Zulu king Shaka, who may have killed off tens of thousands of Africans through war, mass executions, and forced migrations, could hardly be considered as pernicious as the British colonialist Cecil Rhodes.[5]

Similarly, slavery is not seen as a universal evil common to all cultures and finally outlawed due to Western pressures. Such a generic acknowledgment of that human frailty and its belated remedy would have little political currency today. Today, to whom does it matter that the Arab world may have shipped out as many black African slaves to the Middle East and Asia as Europeans once did to the New World, or that African slavery in the Arab world persisted well into the late twentieth century? Such acknowledgment of the long nexus of the Arab Middle East and black African slavery would mean little to the contemporary House of Saud, to most of the citizens of the autocratic Middle East—or even to Westerners themselves.[6]

Sometimes these assumptions of politically correct historians are overtly expressed by campus facilitators as they make their way into the mainstream of university life. At the University of Delaware, for example, as O'Donohue and Redding note in an earlier chapter, cultural reeducation was recently mandated for thousands of undergraduates. Diversity trainers were given precise written instruction about how to characterize white culture—

dubbed "a melting pot of greed, guys, guns, and god."[7] Indeed, the Delaware diversity program's written manual offered official definitions of various European pathologies:

> A racist is one who is both privileged and socialized on the basis of race by a white supremacist (racist) system. The term applies to all white people (i.e., people of European descent) living in the United States, regardless of class, gender, religion, culture, or sexuality. By this definition, people of color cannot be racists.[8]

Such asymmetrical reasoning is often immune from countervailing facts, since postmodern theory comes to the rescue by reminding us that our sources of knowledge and, when convenient, our sense of morality are subjective, predicated on the privileged position of those who hold power. Through such distorted lenses, we could hardly hold the Aztecs culpable for sacrificing thousands each year, or for the mass murder of between twenty thousand and eighty thousand war captives in 1487 at the Great Pyramid of Tenochtitlan. After all, much of the evidence survives secondhand in Spanish chroniclers, and thus was serially interpreted by a long tradition of Western historians either ignorant of, or uninterested in, the mentality and religious mind-set of natives. More to the point, Aztecs, unlike the oppressive colonizing conquistadors, were not sailing into the harbor at Barcelona to find gold and force Spaniards to worship Huitzilopochtli.[9] Power, remember, also adjudicates morality: the West is uniquely culpable because its white male power structure had the ability (rarely are we told why that was so) to reify its prejudices, while its victims remained powerless and thus their own shortcomings largely irrelevant.

Numerous problems arise when academics seek to inflate the importance of their politically correct research by using it to warp the larger society outside the campus. About a decade ago, the Davis (CA) City Council voted to change the name of Sutter Plaza—dozens of streets and parks in the state are named after the California pioneer—on the plea of a nearby University of California professor who alleged that Sutter was "an immoral man who kept Native Americans as slaves." But was Sutter merely immoral or something a bit more complex, a man who braved all sorts of natural and human challenges to open a trading post that facilitated exploration and settlement? And where does such revisionism end—with the Trotskyization of thousands of things named "Sutter"? Or do we go on to other now dethroned heroes, such as the illiberal Catholic priest Father Junipiero Serra (the namesake of many major freeways, roads, churches, and schools), or cutthroat railroad magnate Leland Stanford? Are we to assume that Native Americans themselves did not in turn practice slavery, or torture and mutilate their victims, or treat women as less than equals?[10]

What drives this effort to see the past solely as melodrama rather than tragedy, in which cultures, peoples, and nations sometime collide? Why act as if ideas, individuals, and whole peoples should be rounded up, indicted, tried, and sentenced in a court of presentist historical morality? Who benefits from politically correct history?

Most obviously, the answer is anti-Western, anticapitalist leftists who profess to hate the system of a free market and consensual government that has made Western society so uniquely successful. One objective of politically correct history is to make contemporary Westerners accept that much of their present material privilege is not based on any positive thing they did or on the adoption of successful protocols such as free markets, private property, constitutional government, rationalism, or freedom of the individual—but rather derives from long profiteering on the backs of the poor, slaves, women, and foreigners. That way, dividends of various sorts (from affirmative action and race-based preferences in hiring, to de facto racial quotas and entitlements) follow when perpetrators are identified, and their successors are asked to show contrition, or provide redress and reparations for their inherited privilege—as the University of Delaware diversity manifesto reveals.

If Western success cannot entirely be explained through the conquest and exploitation of the non-European, perhaps it can be attributed to sheer luck. Jared Diamond, who argues that the geography and natural landscape of Europe, not its cultural practices, accounted for Western dynamism, holds that Europeans were simply fortunate to be born where they were, especially when their own brains were genetically inferior to indigenous peoples who unfortunately started out at a disadvantage with less favorable natural environments:

> New Guineans . . . impressed me as being on the average more
> intelligent, more alert, more expressive, and more interested in

things and people than the average European or American. At some tasks that one might reasonably suppose to reflect aspects of brain functions, such as the ability to form a mental map of unfamiliar surroundings, they are considerably more adept than Westerners.[11]

Whether the West is culpable or only lucky, the result is the same: it does not deserve its present bounty, and should be shamed or coerced to give it up. Once the anti-Western narrative is canonized, all sorts of curriculum experts, community activists, special consultants, and politicians are needed to translate the new academic wisdom from the university to the pragmatic applications in the real world.

The devolution of thought is well known, but examine a few examples of how political correctness in the university now becomes embedded within our popular culture and schools: a statue commemorating the 9/11 New York firefighters, and based on a famous photograph from Ground Zero, was to be altered to include an Hispanic and African American not originally in the picture; professionals from doctors to police personnel must pass cultural competency tests to ensure us that they understand the past and present oppressions of their own dominant culture; and the efforts of race and gender facilitators to force mandatory diversity training continues even though there is little evidence it creates greater sensitivity rather than backlash.[12]

In short, beyond the university professoriate, an entire layer of social engineers finds lucrative employment in translating academic "research" to practical indoctrination: their continued employment, in turn, depends on their more theoretical brethren in the university uncovering ever more evidence of oppression of minorities, women, the poor, and gays to fuel new tutorials, handbooks, and counselors in the public schools and workplace.

Another related catalyst of politically correct history is simple politics, and this process works out in two ways. First, with the fall of Communism, and the emergence of a renewed conservative presence in both the executive and legislative branches, liberals in the university sought to offer a pessimistic counternarrative to a supposedly false version of America peddled by an exploitative government, corporation, church, and traditional family. The university styled itself as fighting a rearguard action, until the more formal forces of progressivism could regroup and refashion a post–Cold War promise of state-induced egalitarianism.

If students from kindergarten to graduate school could be versed in the "other side" of the American or Western story, then they would be equipped to see contemporary politics as a continuum: in this eternal war between the powerful haves and the vulnerable have-nots, a slave-owner, speculator, or polluter of old simply has assumed a new contemporary face as a racially insensitive college president, Enron executive, or environmental exploiter. In the increasing intrusion of politically correct history in policymaking at both the federal and state levels, liberal politicians sought academic expertise to further their own progressive agendas.

Second, politically correct history provides immunity to either defective scholarship or no scholarship at all. Being on the right side of past debates—and thus current politics—is a guarantee of good intentions. As a veteran of some twenty years on university retention, tenure, and promotion committees, I can attest that intangibles such as "being a role model," "being an advocate for community service," or "providing a platform for alternative voices" are frequently invoked when a weak candidate without a record of serious scholarship can adduce even slight evidence of a politically correct paper trail.

Another impulse that drives politically correct history is more psychological and less obvious. There is among Western elites—never more so than in the age of instant globalized communications—great guilt over their privileged positions vis-à-vis others both abroad and at home. But in the post–Cold War era, that angst is increasingly difficult to translate into concrete political change that might somehow legislate or coerce greater egalitarianism.

One mechanism for reconciling the elite position of the tenured professor— who is guaranteed lifelong employment, good pay, and a nine-month teaching cycle—with concern for the less fortunate is through empathy for the downtrodden of the past and anger at their oppressors. Not only does politically correct history, then, gain an author currency among his peers, but it also offers symbolic psychic penance at relatively little material cost. By exposing past prejudices of sexist and racist males against women or minorities, the politically correct historian can square the circle of a long tradition of oppression that resulted in his own rather rarified existence. If one is an endowed professor, say, at Stanford University—originally created by the largess of a nineteenth-century robber baron, and more recently maintained by generous contributions from Wall Street and Silicon Valley multimillionaire capitalists—a sense of revolutionary self is more easily obtained by writing about past oppressions than by driving five miles to East Palo Alto to tutor ghetto children or to live in a nearby Redwood City barrio.

What is wrong with this mechanism—other than commonplace hypocrisy and the usual academic irrelevance?

At the most basic level, politically correct history pushes to the side other far more important topics and approaches. In the zero-sum game of university-press-subsidized publications, or the 120 units of the undergraduate experience, not all history is equal. To understand how the American nation came into being, knowledge of Gen. Nathaniel Green or Henry Knox might offer more instruction than the canonization of Crispus Attucks. Harriet Tubman and Sojourner Truth—now familiar to all high school students—were remarkable women of color, but they did not change the course of the Civil War in the manner of William Tecumseh Sherman, who between 1864 and 1865 sliced through Georgia and the Carolinas and humiliated the Southern plantation class, but who is now in comparison mostly unknown to our high school graduates.

I once surveyed courses listed in the University of California at Santa Barbara catalogue, and found sixty-two classes concerning Chicano history and culture, but not a single one devoted to the American Civil War, in which one could learn much of anything about the conflict's major campaigns, or how the United States was saved from bisection. Among the obvious losers created by such an imbalance are Hispanic students themselves, inasmuch as knowledge—at least through a course or two—of how the Union was torn apart and saved would offer a far better insight into their country than courses such as "Methodology of the Oppressed," "Decolonizing Cyber-Cinema," or "History of the Chicano Movement."[13]

Recently, a popular survey of politicized university courses singled out a class on "Queer Musicology" offered at University of California–Los Angeles. But why focus on UCLA when nearby Occidental College offers classes such as "The Phallus" (stressing "the relation between the phallus and the penis, the meaning of the phallus, phallologocentrism, the lesbian phallus, the Jewish phallus, the Latino phallus, and the relation of the phallus and fetishism"), and "Blackness" (with explorations of "new blackness," "critical blackness," "post-blackness," "unforgivable blackness" and "queer blackness")? The latter requires a mandatory prerequisite class in "Whiteness" (which examines "the construction of whiteness in the historic, legal and economic contexts which have allowed it to function as an enabling condition for privilege and race-based prejudice").[14]

When New York University offered a recent conference on topics like "Sex, Gender and the Public Toilet: Outing the Water Closet," the tuition-based revenues were not only squandered but diverted away from subjects that might better ensure that New York students were well versed in American and world history. And this is the tragedy of politically correct history in the end—the squeezing out of what matters by what does not.[15]

In the Newton, Massachusetts, school district, teachers complained that "there is a curriculum overload—simply too much to teach with too little time."[16] And why not, when hundreds of new names and places are introduced largely on the basis of race, class, and gender, and on the supposition that those criteria alone account for past silence about a particular person, event, or place?

In the Newton schools, first-graders were required to study the biographies of four of six persons: Benjamin Banneker, Yo-Yo Ma, Rachel Carson, Selma Burke, Mae Jemison, and Thomas Edison. No Lincoln or Roosevelt here. There could hardly be any systematic explanation of the selection process (other than on the merits in the case of Thomas Edison), no account of why or how these figures played preeminent roles in American history—other than their race, gender, or politics. Based on comparable accomplishment in these fields, one could have just as easily selected a Benjamin Franklin, Leonard Bernstein, James Watson, Andrew Wyeth, and Neil Armstrong as the five most important Americans in our history. But these men would not have been selected, either because they are white males or a logical argument could be raised that their accomplishments don't quite rank with those of a Jefferson, Lincoln, or Roosevelt; in the case of Selma Burke or Mae Jemison, their stature beneath these three greats would be irrelevant.[17]

Because politically correct history involves questions of methodology in addition to themes and topics—emphasis on theory over mastery of dates, places, individuals—we have seen an aggregate loss among our high school and college graduates in basic knowledge of key events and people of our past. Students without a mastery of the inductive method, or lacking historical data to draw upon for exempla, are asked to accept sweeping notions of race, class, and gender oppressions based on theory, in which facts are either ignored, derided as rote memorization, or dismissed as hopelessly biased. I would wager that those who attended "Sex, Gender and the Public Toilet: Outing the Water Closet" gained very little knowledge of the history and role of public sanitation engineering and its effects on the quality of life in cities of the past.

In the late 1980s, during the uproar over E. D. Hirsch Jr.'s *Cultural Literacy: What Every American Needs to Know*, I used to circulate to my students studying classical literature in translation a list of Hirsch's terms that applied to the ancient world. I noted two reactions. First, the students at California State University–Fresno knew almost none of them, whether *deus ex machina* or Demeter. Second, the students were grateful for the list because it gave them confidence in obtaining a knowledge-based architecture—so much so that they themselves began to compile their own similar lists of "need to know" expressions and proper nouns from the assigned reading. A third reaction was from the professors to whom I showed the list: they knew little more of the terms than did the students and thought the exercise trite.[18]

So we have reversed entirely the classical order of education: the accumulation of information, the acquisition of the inductive method, and the final presentation of ideas based on sound reasoning and supported by illustrative examples. Instead, students learn the correct conclusions first, then a basic sense of how to refute critics through deductive thinking, and rarely, if ever, bothersome facts at all: Mae Jemison is de facto one of six Americans worth studying; but she has not received proper acknowledgement because she is a woman and an African American in a sexist and racist society; and a history of the space program, study of other astronauts, or analysis of their contributions to the American experience compared with others' would be tedious or irrelevant to Ms. Jemison's status. True, the knowledge of facts without the ability to theorize may be only half an education; but theory without facts is no education at all.

Moreover, because of increasing public perception that the university is failing to impart a comprehensive education in which students graduate acquainted with the details of the past—at a time when university tuition rises faster than the rate of inflation—our schools are losing the public's confidence. There is a growing sense that the worldwide American reputation for higher educational excellence exists largely despite, rather than because of, our humanities and social science departments. Physics, information science, chemistry, engineering, or medicine may be influenced by political correctness in the methods by which they are explained or presented, but so far these disciplines remain largely apolitical and their content mostly empirical and traditional.

One result is that the study of history—from home schooling to casual reading—is increasingly accomplished divorced from the university itself. The notorious theoretical obtuseness of politically correct history is not entirely responsible for the poverty of modern academic prose, given that overspecialization has also contributed to technological jargon, pseudoscientific vocabulary, and incoherent grammar and syntax. But the result is the same: the general reader does not wish to wade through "phallocentric," "fetishization," and "queering." As a consequence, university presses struggle to justify their rising subsidies, and are desperate to find titles and prose styles that might make their books accessible to a popular audience.

Journalists and freelance authors fill the void. A David McCullough or Rick Atkinson writes about topics of interest to the public and is able to communicate his ideas successfully, in no small measure because neither is currently employed full time by a contemporary graduate history department, where advancement, publication, and reputation hinge on politically correct approaches and expression. In classics, nonacademics now write the most widely read historical work on the ancient world, whether biographies of Cicero or histories of the Persian War. And it is C-SPAN, not satellite television from university campuses, that is most likely to convey to the public the most recent research from historical scholars.[19]

Finally, we forget the aesthetics of history, a discipline that is as much an art as a science. When history becomes preaching, when it turns entirely utilitarian and policy driven, and when it becomes dreary and cold in its expression, it begins to whither. Faces of the past are no longer presented as unique individuals, but reduced to underappreciated women, or stock capitalists, or cardboard-cutout homosexuals, or collectively victimized blacks. We then lose all sense of individual difference and exceptional accomplishment that transcend daily oppressions and capture our empathy or earn our disgust.

Not all of the brave souls who died crossing the frontier, suffering hunger and disease, were exploiters of the environment or murderers of Native Americans. The Greeks who died at the pass of Thermopylai cannot be reduced to mere slave owners. Who could sort out the rival claims for victimization among striking nineteen-century coal miners—were they primarily victims of greedy capitalist mine owners, or themselves racist in their exclusion of African Americans in their unions, or sexists who ran their own meager households in tyrannically paternalistic fashion, or simply hard-working laborers who tried to raise their families in poverty while fueling the American Industrial Revolution? Or again were they parties to systematic desecration of the environment in short-sighted fashion, supplying fossil fuels to a polluting industrial complex? Or finally, to paraphrase the Roman novelist Petronius, were they just humans, not gods, who in a pretechnological society felt lucky to survive another day of drudgery?

There is a rarely remarked-upon irony in politically correct history, as the deskbound class passes judgment on those who struggled in an unforgiving physical world. Most now dead withstood physical challenges and pain that we probably could not imagine, much less endure—and in that sense were far braver than are we academics who chose to stand in condemnation of them. What they did or what they wrote deserves to be interpreted on its own merits, without our passing judgment on lives that may not measure up to the more refined standards of our own day.

In this regard, studies show that most professors identify themselves as liberal and progressive, as detailed in previous chapters of this volume. Why that is so is not entirely clear. But perhaps one explanation is structural: the contemporary university—with a thirty-two-week period of actual class-time instruction, performance audits largely conducted through faculty governance, and lifelong employment through tenure—has shielded thousands of academics from the realities of what most other Americans face each day. In some cases, professors have simply gone from being undergraduates to graduate students to professors without ever leaving for long the university campus. And while academics pride themselves on their worldly experiences of overseas travel and visiting lectureships, they nevertheless often have very little idea how their own country works—and most importantly why it usually works extremely hard and effectively. Laborers outside the campus typically might have only two to three weeks of annual vacation, and might be expected on the job from 8 a.m. to 5 p.m. under the careful scrutiny of a boss, who daily judges the quality of their labor and has the ability to terminate their employment rather quickly. When we add in additional considerations such as the relatively easy physical existence of the professoriate—without the grime of the mechanic or farmer, the danger of the policeman or fireman, or the constant repetition and monotony of the data-entry transcriber—we can appreciate why and how utopian contemplation on campus arises without consequences, theories are not married to reality, therapy trumps the tragic sense, and accusations and condemnation bring no worry over reprisals.

Finally, there is the matter of a common civic education. The United States, even at its zenith of political, economic, and military power, is not immune from the laws of history, which remind us that any state that is to endure—whether Athens in the fourth century BC or Rome in the fifth century AD—must not only collectively embrace an appreciation of a common culture and past, but also foster some confidence and pride in its own exceptionalism.

In contrast, should Americans be convinced that the story of their country is largely one of racist, sexist, and class oppression—rather than an ongoing effort to enact the promise of our Constitution to all citizens of the United States—then there is no reason to believe that any of us would, or indeed should, make the material, intellectual, or spiritual effort to defend and advance the idea of America. And if we should reach the point where our citizens agree that the United States is no better than the alternative, then there would be no intrinsic reason for it to continue—and, if history is any guide, it would not.

Notes

1. M. A. Bellesiles, *Arming America: The Origins of a National Gun Culture* (New York: Alfred A. Knopf, 2000); M. Bernal, *Black Athena: The Afroasiatic Roots of Classical Civilization*, 3 vols. (New Brunswick, NJ: Rutgers, 1988–2005); C. Johnson, *The Sorrows of Empire: Militarism, Secrecy, and the End of the Republic* (New York: Henry Holt, 2004); E. Said, *Orientalism* (New York: Vintage, 1979); K. Sale, *The Conquest of Paradise: Christopher Columbus and the Columbian Legacy* (New York: Taurus, 2006); William Appleton Williams, *The Tragedy of American Diplomacy* (New York: Norton, 1988); H. Zinn, *A People's History of the United States* (New York: Harpers, 2005).

2. On the various criticisms of Cortés, see H. Thomas, *The Conquest of Mexico* (New York: Random House, 1993), e.g., 581–86; and various entries in P. De Fuentes, *The Conquistadors: First-Person Accounts of the Conquest of Mexico* (Norman: University of Oklahoma, 1963). On the Colensos' criticisms of British imperialism, see, for example, S. Marks, "Harriet Colenso and the Zulus, 1874–1913," *Journal of African History* 4, no. 3 (1963): 403–11; J. Guy, *The Destruction of the Zulu Kingdom: Civil War in Zululand 1879–84* (London: Longman, 1979), 81–90, 92–93, 197–98, 235–37. For the general notion of a self-critical Western literature and history, and especially its romantic attraction to the "other," see B. Thorton, *Plagues of the Mind: The New Epidemic of False Knowledge* (Wilmington, DE: Intercollegiate Studies Institute, 1999), 27–52.

3. Alkidamas's fragment is found at the Scholiast on Aristotle, *Rhetoric* 1373B18. For a brief review of the openness of classical societies to self-criticism and introspection, see V. Hanson and J. Heath, *Who Killed Homer? The Demise of the Classical Education and the Recovery of Greek Wisdom*, 2nd ed. (San Francisco: Encounter, 2001), 97–128.

4. "In history, it [postmodernism] is a denial of the fixity of the past, of the reality of the past apart from what the historian chooses to make of it, and thus of any objective truth about the past." G. Himmelfarb, *On Looking into the Abyss* (New York: Vintage, 1995), 133. The first comprehensive critique of contemporary politically correct history and its various manifestations, from postmodern theory to multiculturalist apology, was outlined comprehensively by Keith Windshuttle, *The Killing of History: How Literary Critics and Social Theorists Are Murdering our Past* (New York: Free Press, 1996); on multiculturalism, see especially 253–81.

5. For Shaka's murder of thousands, see E. A. Ritter, *Shaka Zulu: The Biography of the Founder of the Zulu Nation* (London: Longman, 1955), 310–15; D. Morris, *The Washing of the Spears: A History of the Rise of the Zulu Nation under Shaka and Its Fall in the Zulu War of 1879* (New York: Simon and Schuster, 1965), 98–108.

6. On the nature of African slavery in the Middle East, which both predated and outlasted European enslavement of African peoples, see M. Gordon, *Slavery in the Arab World* (New York: New Amsterdam, 1987), e.g., 155–68; B. Lewis, *The Middle East: A Brief History of the Last 2,000 Years* (New York: Scribner, 1995), 174–46. And

for modern slavery in Islamic Sudan, see Mende Nazer and Damien Lewis, *Slave* (New York: Public Affairs, 2005).

7. Quoted in Stuart Taylor Jr., "Opening Argument. Academia's Pervasive PC Rot," *National Journal Group Inc.*, November 12, 2007, http://nationaljournal.com/taylor.htm.

8. Quoted in ibid.

9. For a review of the estimates of the numbers killed in Aztec human sacrifices, see M. Harner, "The Ecological Basis for Aztec Sacrifice," *American Ethnologist* 4, no. 1 (February 1977), 119–20.

10. "Politically Correct History," *Press Democrat* (Santa Rosa, CA), December 30, 1998.

11. Jared Diamond, *Guns, Germs, and Steel: The Fate of Human Societies* (New York: Norton, 1997), 20.

12. "Firefighters Seek Accurate Depiction of Flag-Raising Heroes," January 12, 2002, NewsMax.com, http://www.papillonsartpalace.com/firefigh.htm; James Ahearn, "Mandating Race Instruction," *Record* (Hackensack, NJ), July 3, 2005; Lisa Takeuchi Cullen, "Employee Diversity Training Doesn't Work," *Time*, April 26, 2007, http://www.time.com/time/magazine/article/0,9171,1615183,00.html.

13. See V. Hanson, *Mexifornia: A State of Becoming* (San Francisco: Encounter, 2003), 105.

14. Charlotte Allen, "I got an A in Phallus 101," *Los Angeles Times*, January 7, 2007, 6765169.story?page=1&coll=la-opiniocenter>http://www.latimes.com/news/opinion/la-op-allen7jan07,0,6765169.story?page=1&coll=la-opinion-center.

15. R. Kimball, "The Groves of Academe, or You Can't Make It Up, Episode 8,968," *Roger's Rules*, November 3, 2007, http://pajamasmedia.com/rogerkimball/2007/11/03/the_groves_of_academe_or_you_c/.

16. M. Viser, "Survey Targets History Program," *Boston Globe*, October 2, 2005, http://www.boston.com/news/local/articles/2005/10/02/survey_targets_history_program/?page=1

17. Ibid.

18. The text in question is E. D. Hirsch, *Cultural Literacy: What Every American Needs to Know* (New York: Houghton Mifflin, 1987).

19. See D. Brooks, "Brian Lamb's America: In Praise of C-SPAN, Our National Historian," *Weekly Standard*, November 8, 1999, 21–25. For recent popular accounts of the ancient world, see for example two works by Tom Holland, *Persian Fire: The First World Empire and the Battle for the West* (New York: Anchor, 2007) and *Rubicon: The Last Years of the Roman Republic* (New York: Anchor, 2005); see also A. Everett, *Cicero: The Life and Times of Rome's Greatest Politician* (New York: Random House, 2002).

12

Why Political Science Is Left But Not Quite PC: Causes of Disunion and Diversity

James W. Ceaser and Robert Maranto

Some facts are so obvious that not even a behavioral political scientist would demand proof. One of these is that the vast majority of card-carrying political scientists in America today are on the left of the political spectrum. The result is that the general orientation of the discipline's professional association, the American Political Science Association (APSA), and of the major research university departments in political science is decidedly liberal. This ideological disposition is so pervasive and deep-seated that it usually goes unnoticed. For most political scientists, as for most social scientists, the intellectual sun rises on the left and sets on the right.

The liberal caste to the political science profession is no way contradicted by a series of well-publicized outbursts that have taken place within APSA over the years in which many charged the association with being too "conservative." A cursory examination of these incidents reveals that this epithet served only as a figure of speech. These conflicts have all been internecine feuds among liberals, with those on the far left attempting to supplant those on the moderate left. They have never involved *genuine* conservatives—those who might have thought well of, or even voted for, a Republican like Ronald Reagan or George W. Bush. There have never been enough of them in the profession to matter.

An initial draft of this chapter was presented at the annual American Political Science Association meeting in Chicago, September 1, 2007.

Universities are not, or at any rate should not be, representative institutions that are asked to meet the criterion of what political theorist Hannah Pitkin once called "descriptive representation,"[1] or a mirroring of the society at large. Still, it is impossible not to be struck by the extreme discrepancy between the percentage of conservatives in academia and that found within the American public at large. Our universities today clearly suffer from a "conservative representational deficit" (CRD). CRD would probably not be a matter of concern in most technical or humanistic disciplines if professors in fact kept to their subject matter (which, alas, they often do not). But things are different in the social sciences, where a basic social philosophy (liberalism or conservatism) falls so close to the subject of inquiry that it often cannot help but affect what is thought and taught. This is above all the case in political science, where the absence of a reasonable "political" balance in the profession would seem to pose the greatest threat to the overall objectivity of the profession.

In a discipline that prides itself today on the sophisticated study of causality, it is regrettable that no major work seeking to explain CRD has appeared since Seymour Martin Lipset and Everett Ladd's *Divided Academy* over thirty years ago, in an era in which regression analysis was still uncommon.[2] Scientific inquiry into explaining variance, it appears, still usually finds its genesis in researchers' intuitive reaction to what they perceive to be an anomaly or a problem. But in a profession that now unreflectively thinks in a liberal way, the presence of so few conservatives probably does not strike many as anomalous or problematic. On reflection, most would probably count it a blessing. As for the concerns raised by some conservatives about the absence of diversity within the field, the liberal mainstream has generally responded by arguing that diversity involves matters far more important than differences of viewpoint; it is a question instead of representing different racial, ethnic, and sexual groups. Finally, on the rare occasions when members of the profession have been forced to confront the question of CRD, they invariably attribute it in the first instance to "self-selection," arguing, for example, that because political science focuses on government and the state, and because conservatives don't think much of the state, it is only natural that conservatives would disdain the profession and prefer to earn their livelihood in the market. (Of course, as previous empirical chapters demonstrate, there is more than *just* self-selection going on.) Or liberals will congratulate themselves on the fact that the political science profession does much "better" in representing conservatives than does sociology, anthropology, or history, occasionally even honoring prominent conservatives with high offices in the APSA. Many political scientists can plausibly boast—and they do—that some of their own best acquaintances are conservatives.

For conservatives, this grab bag of excuses for explaining CRD is apt to appear woefully inadequate. True enough, conservatives do receive more equitable treatment in political science than in many other disciplines in the social sciences. But the real question should then be why they fare so poorly in these other disciplines, not why they suffer less in political science. In any case, the most important consideration in the end is not the causes of CRD (a matter which is treated elsewhere in this volume), but its consequences for members of the profession and for the academic enterprise as a whole. Does the limited number of conservatives result in injustices for conservative political scientists, and does it diminish the intellectual vitality of the discipline?

Perceptions

Underrepresentation resulting from pure self-selection is one thing; outright discrimination—of which there are only a few blatant cases today—is something quite different. But in between these two alternatives is a larger and vaguer category, one of systematic bias produced by attitudes and practices that emit distinct and perceptible signals. One point is clear. Political scientists who are conservative often fear that their ideological orientation can harm them in hiring and advancement. Are they merely being paranoid, or is this a case where the paranoids also have real reason to be worried? As Rothman and Lichter suggest in a previous chapter, data indicate that such concerns are not mere paranoia.

Moreover, if the plural of anecdote is data, at least a certain amount of evidence exists showing a systematic anticonservative bias that might make the profession less inviting to conservatives. With names withheld to protect the innocent, here are a few incidents:

- A talented young graduate student, conservative in his political views, was reluctant to apply for fellowships at the American

Enterprise Institute and the Heritage Foundation for fear that either one would make it more difficult for him to get an academic job. One of the most respected figures in the discipline, a liberal, advised him that AEI might pose no problem, but that the Heritage Foundation could indeed prove a problem at many places. Further inquiries at both of these institutions reveal that those who run these fellowship programs are acutely aware of this problem. By contrast, no such stigma attaches to fellowships at the liberal-leaning Brookings Institution, or even at the farther left Economic Policy Institute.

- A number of conservative assistant professors were told to be highly circumspect in expressing their political views during their probationary period. While the same might be said to someone holding certain radical views on the left, mainstream liberal views almost never present any problems.

- Some conservatives are proudly displayed as the "house conservative" and used to prove the broad-mindedness of the department. They may even enjoy a certain iconic status and be good-naturedly referred to as "our conservative." By contrast, no one ever treats a liberal in this manner in a major university. Conservatives who have left academia, often for a position in a Washington think tank, are known to greet conservative friends still in the academy with some version of the question, "Are they treating you well there?"—with the implication that a conservative faculty member resembles a spouse in a potentially abusive marriage. Even if the relationship starts well, it could go south at any time.

- Spouses (mostly wives) of conservative professors report highly unpleasant experiences with other departmental spouses. As the wives have less need to be careful, what they say is more revealing of the general atmosphere of the academy. Many wives of conservatives have reported being berated for having husbands who voted for Ronald Reagan or George W. Bush. They have been made to feel as out of place as liberals in certain country clubs.

More explicit tales, of course, could be cited. On leaving his political science department at Northern Arizona University for a free-market think tank, conservative professor Michael Sanera lamented that "our department has Marxists, communitarians, people who think that Castro has the only democracy in the world, and then it's got moderate liberals and Kennedy-Mondale kind of liberals, but the only two people that were right of center were driven out."[3] This is perhaps an extreme version of what many conservatives often experience in a less cataclysmic way. If conservatives were inclined to use such language—which they normally resist—they might even complain of being "marginalized" within political science. To the neutral observer, it can be said that they sometimes display behavior patterns similar to those of other marginalized groups, which include attempting to signal identity to potential confederates in perceived hostile territory by such means as dropping the name of a certain author, or mentioning in passing a group like the National Association of Scholars, to see if it evokes a sympathetic response.[4]

Do these anecdotes amount to a genuine anticonservative bias? Let a candid world judge.

Realities: History and Data

Abused or not, conservatives have generally been on the outside of the profession. Their second-class status goes all the way back to the foundation of the APSA, which was created by progressives. The association's founding fathers, led by Frank Goodnow, broke away from the American Economic Association, which they judged to be too laissez-faire, and the American Historical Association, which they considered to be too politically uninvolved and conservative.[5] APSA was founded not with a distant academic objective in mind, but with the practical aim of putting the knowledge of science to work in the furtherance of rational social policy. The association's pro-government viewpoint is nicely captured in John S. Dryzek's account of the genesis of APSA, which commences with the phrase "In the beginning was the state."[6] Indeed, for the founding generation of APSA, the state did loom as a kind of deity, invoked at every turn. Frank Goodnow told the association in his inaugural presidential address in 1904 that political science had a role to play in promoting the "realization of State will."[7] Of course, there was to be nothing overtly partisan in this effort. The fulfillment of progressive aims was to take place in accord with the strict canons of social science, which the founding generation of political scientists was convinced supported state-oriented measures. As John Gunnell describes this delicate political program, "the dilemma that faced the founders of [APSA] was how to eschew partisanship but gain authority in matters of public policy."[8]

The liberal orientation of the profession also helps to account for some of the official stances taken by the association itself over the years. In the most notable case, the association endorsed a report, written by E. E. Schattschneider, that favored "responsible party government" and an executive-centered approach unfriendly to traditional separation of powers.[9] The report embodied the standard liberal view of the period, which continued in effect until the 1970s, when liberals, fearing they had lost control over presidential majorities, became less enamored of executive power and began to sing hymns of praise to the old doctrine of checks and balances. (For those unaware of the history, the attraction of the responsible party position for liberalism is that it was thought to help remove obstacles that stood in the way of rapid action, thus favoring planning and a more active federal government.)

Following the full confirmation of the behavioral revolution in political science in the 1960s, which sought to introduce strict canons of neutrality into scholarship, APSA became more "professional" in its orientation and avoided taking explicit stands. But a push for reengagement in the world has since reemerged, and the association has taken to forming task forces to study critical issues. The first of these task forces appeared in 2004 and was devoted to a topic of special concern to liberals, the rise of economic inequality in America.[10] The authors concluded that they had discovered "disturbing deficits and trends that undermine the promise of American democracy in an era of persistent and rising social inequalities." In the tradition of Frank Goodnow, they embraced numerous "pro-state" positions to solve the dire problems they had identified. Perhaps because of its liberal argument, the report appeared with the strange caveat, reminiscent of a radio station before a talk show, that it expressed the "opinions solely of the task force members . . . [and that] no opinions, statements of fact, or conclusions in the report should be attributed to the American Political Science Association."[11] It nevertheless bore the imprimatur of APSA and was widely promoted by it.

The report was interesting for having either ignored or never considered the objections that one kind of conservative was certain to raise. In a commentary, Robert Weissberg of the University of Illinois issued a rejoinder that was as spirited and lively in its style as the report was pompous and dull. Entitled "Politicized Pseudo-Science," Weissberg's article contended that the whole report was an exercise in leftist "agitprop." He wrote: "Conceptual sloppiness—a bizarre vision of democracy, a politics-as-the-source-of-all-wealth cosmology, equating accomplishment with unearned 'privilege,' and so on—[is] sufficiently fatal to relegate the project to history's dustbin. . . . Such foolishness would probably have disappeared if a few 'conservatives' joined the Task Force, but inclusiveness might, regrettably, have doomed the report at conception."[12]

The orientation of the professional association only reflects the disposition of the membership and, more broadly, of the profession. Data gathered on members of the profession clearly establish its liberal leanings. Going back to 1959, a survey showed that political scientists in America preferred Democratic over Republican presidential candidates by a 70 to 19 percent (3.7 to 1) margin; they were even better disposed toward the Democratic party, favoring it over the Republican party by a 74 to 16 percent (4.6 to 1) margin.[13] An October 1980 survey by Walter B. Roettger and Hugh Winebrenner found that Democrats outnumbered Republicans by 4.3 to 1 in the field, with 51 percent of political scientists expecting to vote for Carter, as compared to 16 percent for Reagan and 13 percent for Anderson.[14] Similarly, Christopher J. Bosso's 1987 survey of presidential and congressional scholars, not known as the most liberal scholars in the discipline, found Mondale preferred over Reagan by a 77 to 21 percent margin.[15] A previous chapter by Klein and Stern (chapter 2) finds Democrats outnumbering Republicans among political scientists by a ratio of 5.6 to 1, which is well under the 28 to 1 ratio in sociology, and the 8.5 to 1 ratio in history. (Economics, the most conservative, is still 2.9 to 1 Democratic.) Conventional party-identification figures may actually understate the degree to which conservative ideas are underrepresented in the academy. In examining views on specific economic and social issues, Klein and Stern showed that both Democratic and Republican academics are generally farther to the left than their counterparts within the mass public.

In the same vein, the 2007 annual APSA meeting preliminary program included, by a very conservative count, forty-eight panels whose titles and constituent paper titles strongly suggested topics preferred by the Left, such as racial inequality, gender inequality, gay rights, the horrors of the American empire, leftist political activism (always in a positive light), the rights of children (though not rights to school choice, nor for the unborn), anti-immigrant prejudice in the U.S., and even the long-lamented Florida recount. Twenty-five panels seemed to show more conservative or libertarian approaches and dealt with such matters as economic freedom, positive contributions of religion and the military, the late but still influential Leo Strauss, and the movies of John Ford. This seems a reasonable balance, save for the fact that eighteen of the twenty-five were sponsored by external groups: the Claremont Institute (fifteen), AEI (two), and the Cato Institute (one). Without such foreign intervention, a 48–7 score seems likely. (We invite others to replicate this admittedly casual research.)

The problem of CRD is manifested in another way. There is some evidence to suggest that the more prominent political science programs, the ones that teach the most gifted undergraduates and produce the graduate degrees, are particularly deficient in conservative representation. Some enterprising researchers were able to discover that Harvard's Department of Government had but one registered Republican (wish to guess who?) as against twenty members registered with the Democratic Party or smaller parties to its left). Similarly, a 1987 study showed the Stanford Political Science Department having a 22–2 distribution.[16] The well-regarded UC-San Diego program pitched a perfect liberal shut-out, 27–0![17]

It is possible only to speculate on the costs of an ideologically skewed discipline. A monochrome field limits the sort of public policy questions asked, retarding the pursuit of knowledge. As Maranto et al. note in the first chapter, sometimes the effects are not even subtle. For example, as Steven M. Teles shows, the public had determined by the 1970s that AFDC was not working, and yet policy analysts continued to deny it.[18] Similarly, as George Kelling and William Sousa write in *Do Police Matter?*,[19] political science professors (among others) refused to study the success of the New York City Police Department's reforms and failed to encourage other cities to adopt like reforms. In so doing, the academic establishment failed to acknowledge what Heritage Foundation political scientist Robert Moffit calls "the greatest public administration success story of the last 25 years."[20]

But a more important toll is no doubt exacted in the form of a political uniformity that is found among the faculties of so many academic departments. As such critics as Martin Anderson point out, this situation makes for a less interesting environment for both faculty and students, and favors a dull careerism over energetic debate about the many great political issues that confront the nation.[21] It is an obvious fact that some of the finest minds in political science on the conservative side, including Charles Murray, William Kristol, and Peter Berkowitz, have exited, voluntarily or involuntarily, from regular academic positions to serve within the think-tank world in Washington, DC, or in government positions. The academy's loss may be the nation's gain, as the "conversation" in the nation's capital has been greatly enlivened as a result.

Sources of Diversity

There are two ways of looking at the problem of CRD in political science. One, common up to now, is to consider the glass as four-fifths empty; the other, to which we now turn, is to regard the glass as one-fifth full. And in fairness to the profession of political science, it is one-fifth full, at least.

Representatives of book publishers who are sentenced by their superiors to attend the professional meetings of academic disciplines confirm an opinion held by many academic refugees from other professions who visit the annual APSA convention. This opinion is that the political science meeting is by far the most lively and interesting of all the professional association conventions. The reason is not only the variety of approaches and methods employed in the profession, but also the diversity of perspectives, stemming in part from the solid contingent of conservatives (both in a political and cultural sense) found within the profession. The panel programs put on by some of the conservative groups, most notably by the Claremont Institute, often produce some of the best-attended sessions of the whole convention. This is only one example of the richness that differences in political and social viewpoints bring to the profession.

Political science, in this respect, *is* different from most of the other disciplines in the social sciences. If one considers conservative representation in academia from a comparative and longitudinal perspective, not only is the problem of CRD less acute in political science than in other disciplines, it has also been getting worse more slowly than in other fields. In chapter 2, Klein and Stern show that the social sciences and humanities as whole moved from a 4-to-1 liberal-to-conservative ratio in the 1960s and early 1970s to an 8-to-1 ratio today. Political science, meanwhile, has moved just marginally to the left, and conservatives are only slightly less in evidence in the profession than they were a half-century ago.

Why this relative stability, rather than the more pronounced left turn that occurred in fields such as anthropology, sociology, English, psychology, and education, which some of the previous chapters detail? Why isn't political science as uniformly left as critics like David Horowitz maintain?[22] Why have certain fads of political correctness seemingly had less traction within political science than in some of these other professions? There are a number of possible reasons, none of which alone is sufficient to explain the result. Perhaps the most important factor over the years has been the influence exerted by certain individuals in the profession, among them Eric Voegelin, Leo Strauss, Edward Banfield, Samuel Huntington, James Q. Wilson, Harvey Mansfield, Aaron Wildavsky, Martha Derthick, William Riker, and Paul Peterson, who, while not themselves all conservatives, helped to make many conservative positions respectable. Even though the number of conservatives has been limited, the illustriousness of the names on this list testifies to their enormous influence within the discipline.

The more general reasons include the following.

First, one section of political science has a connection to philosophy and to the classics, which has kept alive certain older "conservative" ideas dating back to Aristotle. As Allan Bloom observed, "Political Science is the only discipline in the university (with the possible exception of the philosophy department) that has a philosophic branch. . . . Political philosophy . . . provides at least a reminiscence of those old questions about good and evil and the resources for examining the hidden presuppositions of modern Political Science and political life."[23] From the political philosophers have come both some of the most radical leftists in the profession as well as some of the most important conservatives, among them Ellis Sandoz, Harvey Mansfield, Harry

Jaffa, and, of course, Leo Strauss. To this connection to the major political philosophers must be added the special connection of many American political scientists to the political thought of America's founders. The main works of the founding, above all *The Federalist*, certainly lead the mind in the direction of sober and realistic thought that is more conservative than not in its temperament. Say all that one might wish about the thought of Alexander Hamilton, James Madison, and John Jay, but "politically correct" is not a term that would ever come to mind.

Second, there is the subject matter of political science itself, a large part of which deals with the real world and which must confront the tough issues of war and peace, terrorism, and revolution. While other disciplines too treat reality, they do not treat quite these harsh aspects of it. The study of such matters will often sober the mind and produce a highly realistic approach. International relations scholars have been all over the map, so to speak, in their ideological orientations, but there is no doubt of the lingering power of certain conservative strands in this area, including those of Herman Kahn, Henry Kissinger, and Albert Wohlstetter. There were even outside institutional supporters promoting this tough or realist perspective, with funds over the years coming from the Department of Defense and foundations having conservative perspectives.[24]

Third, American political science remains dominated by various versions of the pluralist paradigm. As Richard M. Merelman makes plain in *Pluralism at Yale*, a fascinating study of the leading department during the 1955–70 period, a commitment to pluralism as a political theory encouraged leading professors to tolerate "disrupters," mainly of the left, but at least occasionally of the right.[25] Pluralist thought seemingly made the field too laissez-faire to purge dissenters. Although the Yale Political Science Department had essentially no conservative professors after the inflammatory Wilmoore Kendall, a mentor to William F. Buckley Jr., was paid to surrender tenure and depart in 1961,[26] the department did not enforce an ideological orthodoxy, and produced such prominent center-right political scientists as Aaron Wildavsky, William K. Muir, and Fred Greenstein.

Fourth, political science is, in fact, less a single discipline with one approach than a holding company for a number of disciplines with a variety of approaches. It is characterized, in comparison to the other social sciences, by its incoherence. Allan Bloom in 1987 described political science as resembling "a rather haphazard bazaar with shops kept by a mixed population."[27] A similar account was soon afterward developed by Gabriel Almond in his famous "Separate Tables" essay.[28] Indeed, as Theodore J. Lowi pointed out, from 1981 to 1984 three of the four APSA presidents (Lindblom, Lipset, and Converse) had PhDs in fields other than political science.[29] Under political science's big tent, there has been space for different ideological views, and APSA itself seems open to incursion by outsiders.

Two prominent incursions, coming from the fields of law and of economics, have kept political science open to conservative and libertarian ideas. Constitutional law was an important area of study long before the founding of APSA, and it has connected political science not only to the American Constitution, but also to what Edward Corwin called the "higher law tradition" of natural law found in the medieval and ancient sources. While this part of the discipline has declined somewhat in influence in the past two decades, it remains alive and important, producing such preeminent scholars as Michael Zuckert, Robert George, and Keith Whittington. As for the influence of economics, the approach known widely in the field as "rational choice" had its origins in ideas of political economy that emerged from the libertarian "Virginia school" of James Buchanan and Gordon Tullock, and the significantly less promarket "Rochester school" founded by William Riker. To different degrees, each has expressed skepticism of traditional left-of-center approaches to public policy.[30] To this could be added a third import from economics, principal-agent theory, which has stimulated considerable research on public bureaucracy.[31] Arguably, the intellectual framework for the reinventing government movement came from the economics invasion, particularly principal-agent theory.[32] Further, the school choice movement owes much of its intellectual leadership to political economists, particularly to John Chubb and Terry Moe of the Hoover Institution and the Brookings Institution.[33] Indeed, one could argue that this particular branch of political science has changed the world more than it has been changed by the world.

Finally, the field of political science is influenced by elections and the general play of elite ideas to a greater degree than other social sciences. In an era when Republicans have won a substantial number of national elections, political scientists studying elections, Congress, and executive branch policymaking will naturally focus much of their attention on right-leaning ideas. Moreover, to a much greater degree than sociologists, political scientists are actually likely to have served in government. The second author's experience suggests that service in the U.S. bureaucracy, and in places like the Brookings Institution, has a moderating impact on left-of-center academics. This could plausibly make those in the field more open to tolerating conservatives in their midst, in a way that academic sociologists, for example, might not. Further, conservative dominance in government and certain foundations provides opportunities for research that could in some instances burnish the scholarly credentials of right-leaning political scientists.[34]

Conclusion: Reforming Political Science

Although American political science is overwhelmingly left or center-left, conservative and libertarian thinkers have kept a toehold in the field, one that is unlikely to soon disappear. The discipline is thus not so unrepresentative as a few conservative critics have charged. Still, a toehold is different from a real place at the table. So long as conservatives are denied this, the disadvantages of ideological homogeneity remain.

So what do to? Conservatism counsels that the world is not easy to change, but that change is always needed. To paraphrase one of the preeminent conservatives, Edmund Burke, a profession without the means of some change is without the means of its conservation. In this spirit, and while APSA is so fond of task forces, the association should consider establishing a study group to examine whether the current deficit in conservative ideological representation reflects merely the sum of personal choices or is influenced by more systemic factors found in the recruitment and training of PhD candidates, and the hiring and promotion of faculty. Part of this research might involve surveys and focus groups of conservative political scientists and graduate students to measure the degree to which they have perceived ideological discrimination. This research should be conducted in a way that does not publicly compromise individual institutions. Ideally, the profession of political science should clean its own house before it invites the criticisms of others.

The health and vibrancy of political science today, especially in comparison to some of the other social sciences, stems in large part from its greater openness to different political and social viewpoints. In the end, it is the whole profession that will gain by an enhanced presence of conservatives in its ranks. Fairness in this case is also self-interest rightly understood.

Notes

1. Hanna Fenichel Pitkin, *The Concept of Representation* (Berkeley and Los Angeles: University of California Press, 1967).

2. Everett Carll Ladd Jr. and Seymour Martin Lipset, *The Divided Academy: Professors and Politics* (New York: McGraw Hill, 1975).

3. Robert Maranto, "For True Diversity, Include Conservatives," *Baltimore Sun*, July 31, 2003, 17a.

4. Notably, the APSA has recognized caucuses for women, Latinos, and Asian Pacific Americans; for lesbian, gay, and bisexual political scientists; and for those interested in a "New Political Science"—but none for conservatives, nor for the religious. See APSA, "Caucuses in Political Science," http://www.apsanet.org/section_444.cfm.

5. John G. Gunnell, "The Founding of the American Political Science Association: Discipline, Profession, Political Theory, and Politics," *American Political Science Review* 100, no. 4 (November 2006): 481.

6. John S. Dryzek, "Revolutions without Enemies: Key Transformations in Political Science," *American Political Science Review* 100, no. 4 (November 2006): 487.

7. Quoted in ibid., 488.

8. Gunnell, "Founding of the American Political Science Association," 483.

9. "Toward a More Responsible Two Party System. A Report on the Committee on Political Parties," *American Political Science Review* 44 (September 1950). For a critique of similar approaches within a subfield, public administration, see Vincent Ostrom, *The Intellectual Crisis in American Public Administration* (Tuscaloosa: University of Alabama Press, 1973). See generally Raymond Seidelman with Edward J. Harpham, *Disenchanted Realists: Political Science and the American Crisis, 1884–1984* (Albany: State University of New York Press, 1985); and John Marini and Ken Masugi eds., *The Progressive Revolution in Politics and Political Science* (Lanham, MD: Rowman and Littlefield, 2005).

10. APSA, "American Democracy in an Age of Rising Inequality," 2004, http://www.apsanet.org/imgtest/taskforcereport.pdf.

11. Ibid.

12. Robert Weissberg, "Politicalized Pseudo-Science," *PS: Political Science and Politics* 39, no. 1 (January 2006): 35.

13. Henry A. Turner, Charles G. McClintock, and Charles B. Spaulding, "The Political Party Affiliation of American Political Scientists," *Western Political Quarterly* 16, no. 3 (September 1963): 650–65.

14. Walter B. Roettger and Hugh Winebrenner, "The Voting Behavior of American Political Scientists: The 1980 Presidential Election," *Western Political Quarterly* 36, no. 1 (March 1983): 134–48.

15. Christopher J. Bosso, "Congressional and Presidential Scholars: Some Basic Traits," *PS: Political Science and Politics* 22, no. 4 (December 1989): 839–48.

16. Martin Anderson, *Impostors in the Temple* (Stanford, CA: Hoover Institution Press, 1996), 140–41.

17. John M. Ellis, "How Serious Is the Damage?" *Academic Questions* 20, no. 1 (Winter 2006): 14–15, 21.

18. Steven M. Teles, *Whose Welfare? AFDC and Elite Politics* (Lawrence: University Press of Kansas, 1996).

19. George Kelling and William H. Sousa, *Do Police Matter? An Analysis of the Impact of New York City's Police Reforms Civic Report* 22 (New York: Manhattan Institute for Policy Research, 2001).

20. Personal communication, July 15, 2007.

21. Anderson, "Imposters," 146.

22. David Horowitz, *The Professors* (Washington, DC: Regnery Publishing, 2006).

23. Allan Bloom, *The Closing of the American Mind* (New York: Simon and Schuster, 1987), 366.

24. Anne Norton, "Political Science as a Vocation," in *Problems and Methods in the Study of Politics*, ed. Ian Shapiro, Rogers Smith, and Tarek Masoud (Cambridge: Cambridge University Press, 2004), 67–82.

25. Richard M. Merelman, *Pluralism at Yale* (Madison: University of Wisconsin Press, 2003).

26. Kendall founded the politics program at the (then) new Catholic University of Dallas. See the Willmoore Kendall site, http://members.tripod.com/~batesca/kendall.htm.

27. Bloom, *Closing of the American Mind*, 375.

28. Gabriel Almond, "Separate Tables: Schools and Sects in Political Science," PS 21, no. 4 (Fall 1988): 828–42.

29. Theodore J. Lowi, foreword to *Disenchanted Realists: Political Science and the American Crisis, 1884–1984*, by Raymond Seidelman with Edward J. Harpham (Albany: State University of New York Press, 1985), xii.

30. Almond, "Separate Tables," 832–33.

31. See, for example, Terry M. Moe, "The New Economics of Organization," *American Journal of Political Science* 28 (November 1984): 739–77.

32. Ibid.

33. See John E. Chubb and Terry M. Moe, *Politics, Markets, and the Organization of Schools* (Washington, DC: Brookings Institution, 1990).

34. Robert Maranto, *Beyond a Government of Strangers: How Political Appointees and Career Bureaucrats Can Work Together* (Lanham, MD: Lexington Books, 2005).

PART IV

Needed Reforms

13

The Route to Academic Pluralism

Stephen H. Balch

America's opinion leadership is probably more ideologically divided today than at any time since the Great Depression.[1] Left and Right find vociferous voice in virtually every public medium, and while there is rarely balance, there is also nothing like monopoly, whether in publishing, broadcasting, or the "new media." Moreover, despite an overall liberal/left dominance, the general trend has been toward increasing heterogeneity. The main exception has been the academy, where the edge of Left over Right in politically and culturally sensitive fields ranges from about 3 to 2 in economics to well over 10 to 1 in English and philosophy. And the evidence suggests that these academic asymmetries are, in all likelihood, worsening, as noted by Klein and Stern in chapter 2 and by Rothman and Lichter in chapter 4 of this volume.

The nearly closed intellectual shop that has developed on our campuses should be a source of major concern for all Americans who appreciate the educational value of competition between ideas, but most especially for conservatives of every stripe whose thought bears the brunt of the exclusion. Since the academy educates future generations of citizens and leaders, houses an army of "expert" commentators, and, perhaps most significantly, establishes what counts in elite circles as "respectable opinion," conservatives should recognize that reopening it is highly desirable not only for education's sake, but for the future of the principles and ways of life they cherish.

There is only one feasible path to greater intellectual pluralism in academe, and that leads through the faculty. "Personnel is policy" as much in academe as elsewhere, and only when the composition of faculties begins to alter—when faculty members who dissent from prevailing orthodoxies can be hired and make careers in appreciable numbers—will fresh breezes start to blow.

Lesser measures will have but marginal effect. Even the most provocative speaker is but a flash in the academic pan, a comet streaking across a firmament whose fixed stars are the tenured professoriate. Likewise for alterations in the curriculum. What's taught is far more a matter of who's teaching it than anything the catalogue describes.

Materially changing the composition of faculties is a daunting task. Fortunately, a massive overhaul may not be required to achieve results. The admission of a significant cohort of dissenters to secure career prospects should have effects far beyond what their numbers might suggest. The flabbiness, triviality, and incoherence of so many academic orthodoxies, the very nature of postmodernism's métier, opens the real possibility of their destabilization once serious internal debate gets under way. Still, to reach even this point will entail challenging some central assumptions upon which the constitutional system of academe is founded, assumptions taken for granted because of long and undisputed usage and the formidable professional and ideological interests that they've come to anchor. Dislodging them will require not only dogged application of organizational pressure, but an ability to reimagine the sum and substance of academic life.

Governance in the Humanities and Social Sciences: The Need for Countervailing Power

The near academic monopoly enjoyed by the liberal Left has many roots. But it could never have established itself unless nearly all those with any title to cultural respectability assumed that the professoriate (unlike other professions) could be trusted to intellectually police itself. Whereas bureaucratic experts must be held responsible to elected officials, and business executives to the marketplace (as well as government regulators), scholars are thought answerable to virtually no one except their own colleagues for the intellectual quality of their work. This has naturally led to cozy arrangements, the academic equivalent of an industrial trust restricting the competition of ideas for the sake of insider advantage.

Yes, colleges and universities possess governing boards and, in theory, legislatures retain fiduciary responsibilities over public institutions. Yet their powers are almost never exercised about questions of academic quality and content. Trustees, although seasoned and tough-minded in their chosen spheres, turn to putty when contemplating charges of restricting academic freedom, which certain interventions are bound to evoke (as Anne Neal discusses in a later chapter). Ditto for politicos, who, however hardened to the dangers of the legislative jungle, liquefy on approaching those of the blackboard. (Grantors, to be sure, have influence *over the direction research takes*, meaning that, in the natural and applied sciences especially, the questions researched—though not the findings—are substantially determined by defense and commercial interests. But this has minor impact on the *cultural content* of academic life.)

These enviable immunities to outside criticism have been largely acquired through the juxtaposition of superficially similar but distinct concepts. Essentially, professors have persuaded the laity, as well as themselves, that all the intellectual marketplaces of academe are created equal and are thus to be governed by identical rules. Specifically, the marketplaces of the humanities and social sciences have been successfully equated with those of the natural sciences, where, as is well known, truth inevitably outs.

Although this equation of domains had some plausibility in the heady springtime of the modern research university, more than a century of subsequent experience, and the growing political correctness of the last forty years, have demonstrated its inadequacy. On its reconsideration the success of reform depends.

The first step to wisdom lies in appreciating how anomalous among the intellectual arts natural science actually remains. The true sciences have developed systems of experiment and close observation that allow for dispositive tests in the trial of alternative explanations, permitting consensuses about facts and theories to emerge among practitioners.[2] Even more impressively, the true sciences can translate many of their results into powerful utilities widely employed and appreciated by the outside world. Scientists have unusually clear-cut ways of knowing when they've got it right, and are highly rewarded both individually and as a guild for so getting it.

Needless to say, this doesn't come merely as a gift to those who choose to be physicists, chemists, geologists, and biologists. It derives instead from

the character of the problems they attack. Although sometimes madden-
ingly difficult, they are nonetheless amenable, with great ingenuity and
technique, to the isolation, simplification, and clarification of key elements
in a manner cumulatively leading to general insights of precision and
power. It is for this reason that the language of mathematics becomes their
practice so well. Reduced to clear, crisp, interchangeable bits, the conceptual elements of natural science give numbers true fit.

But the observation of human beings doesn't work this way. While quantification has its uses in humane scholarship, they are usually confined to the
definition of massive terrain features such as aggregate economic resources,
or the great divides of public opinion. Quantification reveals as much of a
society's detailed interior decor as does a room covered in furniture cloth.

When, in imitation of the natural sciences, numbers are force-fed into
humane discourse, they often fail to reveal even as little as this, wreaking
instead an artificiality that trivializes or obscures. However enabled by survey
research, cliometrics, or economic analysis, the bottom line in humane discourse remains judgment, informed by breadth of learning, creative intelligence, and that primordial empathy with one's fellow creatures sometimes
called common sense. In these key respects, the sciences proper part company
with the realms of humane learning, even those that assume science's title.

They part company in another respect as well. Although natural sciences' discoveries have produced the most revolutionary of social effects,
they have, for the time being at least, also assumed a somewhat taken-for-
granted character within the larger culture. Perhaps this represents a
momentary lull in science's history of induced upheaval, but, for the most
part, the newest revelations in physics, astronomy, chemistry, and geology,
however unsettling or extraordinary, are not directly fed into the maw of
politics. Environmental science is, of course, an exception. And sometimes
biology, too, since issues pertaining to health, the environment and, increasingly, human identity are of interest to activists. But no interest groups—
apart from those enthusiastic about intelligent design—are as yet critical of
biology's actual findings, just their possible misuse.

The "findings" of humane learning enjoy no such privilege. They're
comestibles for political consumption, often under suspicion of being
cooked to taste. Politics is, after all, argument—at its higher levels argument
about history, the nature of justice, the character of man, the workings of

the economy, or simply the fairness and efficiency of everyday social arrangements. The authority scholars marshal can tilt these arguments. Thus, while the natural sciences generate utilities whose universal appreciation humane learning can only envy, humane learning in some sense compensates by producing polemical utilities whose value is assessed along partisan lines. The fields of force in the natural sciences pull strongly toward truth; nothing more will serve, and everything less will eventually be found out. In humane learning they pull at cross purposes, sometimes toward truth, but frequently toward serviceability for, and reward from, causes.

Moreover, these causes, as the data on professorial allegiances indicate, are not evenly distributed across the spectrum. As already noted, it's the Left that recruits the big battalions. This is not because the Right lacks interest in employing scholarship, but because humane scholarship, so much the artful conflation of words, merges far better with the projects of the Left.

The Left, to vastly but usefully simplify, is about visions of change, while the Right is about protecting things as they are. Humane learning also tends toward visions—visions of the good, beautiful, and true. Especially when it comes to the production of "theory"—feminism, the utopian variants of ecology, and the numerous epigones of Marxism—the symbiosis between visionary thinkers on the one hand and activists on the other can be smooth and mutually rewarding. (Had we a significant utopian Right, it might also be well served.) By enmeshing themselves in the causes of race, gender, and class, the most vocal and driving segments of the academic Left have been enabled to gain a support and sense of purpose their less politicized peers generally lack. This zeal has, time and time again, translated into institutional power.

The constitutional principles of academe, entrusting intellectual decision making almost exclusively to academics, make good sense in the natural sciences. Unfortunately, their proponents generally assume that the natural sciences' self-correcting qualities hold equally well in all other scholarly domains. In the natural sciences, consensus about theory represents the piecemeal aggregation of individual consents, one hypothesis crowding out others as observers evaluate the respective congruence of each with growing bodies of evidence. Scientific powers-that-be may sometimes hinder this progression, but, given the multiplicity of research centers, and the existence of relatively conclusive tests, they have never been able to halt it. Scientific curricula and personnel decisions are also anchored in this process of rationally assembled consensus. From the perspective of lay overseers, such a record has made *laissez faire, laissez passer* seem by far the best practice.

The dynamic in humane learning has proved otherwise. Potent bodies of theoretical knowledge recognized as such by "laity," as well as practitioners, have not developed. There are kernels of theory to be sure, as well as large bodies of well-attested facts and an enormous amount of interesting and sometimes penetrating insight and judgment, but no one looks for a flow of universally conceded and powerful utilities from fields like literature, sociology, anthropology, history, philosophy, political science, or, for the most part, economics. Instead, one too often finds creeds—socially constructed beliefs (in the true spirit of postmodernism)—that reflect causes served rather than truth attained. And where one has creeds, authoritarianism often follows, because only thereby does a creed's arbitrariness get masked and its reward system preserved. The academy's naive extension of the natural science model of internal governance into humane learning has made it easier for this authoritarianism—commonly called political correctness—to develop.

The critical factor in the erection of ideological authoritarianism has been academe's almost total reliance on a co-optation process, dominated by faculty majorities, to control hiring and tenure. The exclusion of external lay oversight was more or less accomplished by the mid-twentieth century through the triumph of the contemporary notions of academic freedom and shared governance incorporated in the *1940 Statement on Academic Freedom and Tenure* and subsequent resolutions by the American Association of University Professors and American Association of Colleges.[3] (The firings of the McCarthy era constituted oversight's last discrediting gasp.) Since in humane learning hiring and tenuring decisions are heavily imbued with creedal and cause desiderata, ideologically dominant coalitions, once sufficiently established, have been able to use them to drive dissident perspectives toward extinction,[4] a phenomenon the authors of *The Federalist Papers*, together with other seasoned political hands, would have hardly found surprising.[5]

Withdrawal of supervision and majoritarian decision making are far from the whole story. If they were, different universities and colleges within the extended universe of American higher education should have moved in a variety of ideological directions. That they largely did not suggests that the driving factor has been the appeal of left-liberal visionary creeds for status-seeking intellectuals otherwise light on useful knowledge. But the nullity of governing boards, and the hiring power of departmental majorities, has lent the process a runaway character that might otherwise have been avoided, resulting in the ideological monoculture now to be seen virtually wall-to-wall on campus after campus.

Strategies for Unseating PC

Like it or not, the intellectual governance of academe, if not quite hermetically sealed against lay influence, is entrenched against it within multiple defensive rings. The first ring is comprised by the reigning concept of academic freedom, eliding the distinction between the natural sciences and humane learning, and thereby also between the liberties of searchers after truth and the privileges of guild self-interest. Governing boards and legislatures are fully snared by these confusions. One can envision, of course, some national crisis in which the academy's general incivism becomes politically intolerable. But failing this, it is hard to imagine any massive arousing of slumbering fiduciaries in the foreseeable future. At particular institutions, however—perhaps those buffeted by scandal or an especially galling ideological outrage—adventuresome trustees may seize an occasion for pressing against the perimeters.

To yield any profit, this assault will have to involve close collaboration with senior administration—and university presidents rarely arrive in their positions without substantial vetting by the ideologically committed. Although the great majority therefore espouse academe's corporate values with enthusiasm, as men and women of practical affairs most are also capable of recognizing the institutional downsides of skewed intellectual climates. Given their control over budgets and staffs, and their quasi-academic status, they have access to many more leverage points than do trustees in isolation.

Unfortunately, significant intellectual reform, even under these best of conditions, will still require protracted pressure, and while presidents and trustees come and go, professors are, more or less, forever—bringing us to the status quo's second ring of intellectual defense, tenure. Tenure has a significance for the lives of individual faculty quite different from that which it possesses for the balance of university power. For the individual scholar, tenure serves as advertised, protecting dissident opinion and, as such, is frequently a lifesaver for conservatives. (Although without new intake, there are fewer and fewer such creatures to be saved.) But viewed in its relation to academic governance, tenure has the effect of creating a semipermanent faculty, which, much like any other civil service, can delay, unravel, or roll back the efforts of transient reformers. Even with the best of wills, a university president contemplating a challenge to ideological vested interests must reckon on what can be realistically accomplished in the time he has available, together with the considerable damage the predictable hubbub will inevitably inflict on his subsequent advancement.

If trustees and chancellors are uncertain reeds, can donor power provide the needed oomph? Again, alas, hope is more often hope against hope than any realistic expectation, as we here reach the status quo's third ring of fortification, endowment.

By "endowment" I mean not just the surpassing fortunes on which many elite institutions rest, though these make the contributions of most donors weigh much less against considerations of internal politics than might otherwise seem likely (as was most famously witnessed in 1995, when, following faculty protest, Yale returned a $20 million gift from Lee Bass intended to support new programs in Western civilization). Beyond money, it is the lavish endowments of psychological preferment and social benefaction that allow universities and colleges many cuts below the Ivy League to so contain donor unrest. The appeals of alma mater as the cherished scene of youth's morning (and evenings) are difficult to ignore. Big hitters are assiduously courted. Meetings with the president, seats on the fifty-yard line, seats on the board—each carries sizeable cachet and has a way of turning potential critics into self-blinded insiders preferring to believe the best and told little else. Moreover, America is a land in love with education as the engine of mobility at the heart of the national dream. This aspirational font showers prestige on virtually every reputable university and college in the land.

There are, of course, doubters, but they scarcely know what to do with their doubts. Those who give get appreciation, even honor. Walking away leaves little but a bad taste. The better course—finding ways to give against the grain—requires a cleverness hard to come by without instruction, a service that development offices are unlikely to provide.

This is not a message of despair, but realistic expectation. Too strong to be taken at a rush, the citadels of political correctness are nonetheless vulnerable to patient siege. For all their apparent buttressing, their cloud-capped towers are mainly mental gossamer, false positions liable to collapse once under protracted squeeze. The key is to concentrate reform's modest current forces on the points of maximum vulnerability. Where then to begin?

The first step lies in providing reliable guideposts for those wondering what can be done to foster change. Trustees need to understand that their responsibilities don't end with fund-raising and cheerleading. Donors must learn that there is more they can do than just walk away in disgust. Dissident academics require direction and inspiration to take advantage of the opportunities before them.

Let's begin with trustees. They should be reminded that many of the reasons why ultimate control over America's universities and colleges was originally lodged outside the faculty remain good ones. Specifically, they should understand that concentrations of power tend to corrupt wherever they occur, even where such power lies in the hands of the intellectually elevated. The weaknesses of the current laissez-faire regime, the gulfs that separate scholarly practice in different domains, and the governance implications of these gulfs must be clarified for them.

There won't be any sudden epiphany. The best to be hoped for is a gradually deepening immersion by particular boards in the intellectual problems of their institutions, which will in turn breed an increasing confidence in addressing them and enhanced resources for continuing to do so. Most boards are virtually unstaffed, leaving them dependent on the institutional apparatus they are supposed to supervise. A moment in American academic history will thus have been reached when a board decides it needs to "staff up" to better exercise its intellectual responsibilities, as discussed by Anne Neal in the next chapter. The creation of academic advisory councils made up of distinguished scholars and scientists would be a splendid way to begin. Such blue-ribbon bodies commissioned to investigate the state of intellectual practice across disciplines could start educating trustees, to say nothing of the larger university community, about the true corollaries of academic freedom. This, in turn, might lead to the further elaboration of standard-setting mechanisms, perhaps in the form of university offices—similar in status to those that now sustain "diversity"—charged with uplifting the overall tenor of the academic culture, assisting weaker fields in rising toward the levels of the stronger, and embedding an understanding of best intellectual practice in the graduate training of every doctoral student.

Could one actually imagine such a process unfolding? It would necessarily require intimate collaboration between trustees and an unusual university CEO—suggesting that the best initial move for an enterprising board is to hire such a pathfinder. A scandal or public outrage, like the "Affaire Ward Churchill" at the University of Colorado, that dissipates, even temporarily, a university's endowment of psychological capital, would certainly also contribute to feasibility. But however put in motion, a single successful example of constructive trustee engagement could lead to others and then, just possibly, to a genuinely broad-based campaign for the academic uplift of ideologically crimped fields.

In mediating this uplift, governance reform on the principle of "different strokes for different folks" is essential. Exceptional deference to insider governance has powerful justification in the natural and applied sciences. The fields of humane learning may not only warrant a good deal more lay oversight, but also the introduction of some institutionalized forms of adversarialism. The spreading movement to create new and intellectually diverse academic programming offers one very promising way of accomplishing this.

The courtroom, perhaps, provides a better guide for the governance of humane learning than does the laboratory. In academe, as in court, the discovery of truth is the transcending objective. In court, however, partisanship isn't disguised, but admitted, institutionalized, and turned to truth's advantage. Lawyers, as officers of the court, can't struggle "no holds barred." But though they are obliged to play by the legal rules, they are also expected to make their client's best possible case. It is this clash of rival efforts, mediated by a neutral judge and jury, that operates to deliver enlightenment.

Unlike attorneys, professors do not understand themselves as the pliers of causes. Yet they easily slip into such roles. Perhaps then, in order to keep them honest—to the greater intellectual good of all—it would be useful to import into their midst something like the courtroom's deliberately structured theater of contest. A recognition of contending "schools of thought" as an accepted, indeed, cultivated organizational element within universities—kept, to be sure, within the rules of reason and civility by higher university authority—poses an attractive way of accomplishing this purpose.

New programs, representing conservative, traditional liberal, and libertarian perspectives are now springing up and are prospering at institutions like Princeton, Duke, and Brown. These, together with smaller sprouts at other universities, sponsor speakers, conferences, courses, and even modest programs of study outside the academic mainstream. Some of these programs are also experiencing significant fund-raising successes, mainly because they have finally provided disgruntled donors with that long-sought-after means of "constructively" giving to alma mater. And since university presidents and development offices often seem pleased with this win-win arrangement, "psychological endowment" is finally being turned into a facilitator rather than a barrier to reform. In addition, the creation of new programming provides frustrated faculty dissidents with a way to precipitate institutional change that does not leave them at loggerheads with their higher-ups, as James Piereson indicates in a previous chapter.

New programs of modest dimension can have intellectual impacts significantly exceeding their size. But to become genuine paths to intellectual pluralism, they need to climb toward a much higher organizational plateau. Crucially, they need to be able to hire, train, and provide secure career venues for dissenting scholars, and serve as launching pads for entry into the scholarly profession. Given the tensions that can rise between rival viewpoints, effective intellectual pluralism probably requires more than just official blessing; it demands firm institutional ground on which to stand. At a minimum, there is a need for new programmatic entities constituting departments-in-fact, if not departments-in-name, because only at the departmental level, or higher, does semiautonomy of function confer the requisite degree of career control embodied in the possession of faculty lines.

Programs limited to the sponsorship of extracurricular events are relatively easy to establish, especially if money is available. So long as courses are not offered or, of greater moment, curricula and degrees are not involved, administrative approval is usually enough to confer official status. Beyond that, faculty bodies must give sanction, and given the likely influence of zealots, herein will lie the rub. In unusual circumstances, trustee and presidential decisiveness may allow the creation of a major program through pure *coup de main*. Otherwise, a steady clambering upward will be required, moving from lectures, through courses, to minors, to majors, before reaching for the final prize. It is not an easy assignment, though with art and diplomacy, as well as demonstrations of student, donor, and political interest, from step to rising step, it is probably feasible at least at some places. And once it is accomplished, it will become easier elsewhere by virtue of the demonstration effect.

This is not a call for "affirmative action" for ideas or ideologues, nor for the authorization of self-contained intellectual ghettos that ignore everything beyond their walls. Too many already exist. In order to justify their purpose, new programs and departments must be committed to freewheeling intellectual engagement and a readiness to examine the assumptions favored by their own membership, to which occasional gadflies might be useful additions. There is a fine line to be drawn here: common sensibility rather than a common doctrine being the thing to be sought. For example, in the current university environment, a department devoted to the integrated study of Western civilization would probably bring together scholars whose interests were sufficiently overlapping to provide a strong sense of professional fellowship (and risk reduction), without simultaneously creating any stale unity of thought. The same might be true of a department focused on studies of what could be called "free institutions"—the history and interconnection of constitutionalism, market economics, and the variety of social, cultural, and philosophical arrangements associated with them. There is hardly a single way of pursuing such studies, but the subject matter alone is sufficiently heterodox to make a strong feeling of community among practitioners almost inevitable. Both of these subject areas would also resonate with disaffected donors, since each clearly communicates a challenge to politically correct habits of thought.

In an environment of deliberately fostered intellectual contest, the academic responsibilities of senior university administration would necessarily expand. Ensuring reasoned discourse in an atmosphere of civility will take an attentiveness, concentration, and even imagination not now frequently displayed. There might, for instance, be a variety of interesting ways in our era of electronic communication to put the interrogation of opposing perspectives on full public display. Administration will need to cultivate them. More venerable formats might also be taken off the shelf. A revival of the medieval university practice of periodic open disputations between rival perspectives has a potential worth considering.

Perhaps all this is just whistling in the dark. Although hardly a revolution in the intellectual climate of academe, the creation of departments or other programming of similar heft may require more gumption than any governing board or university president is ever likely to summon. So, looking further down the road, there may yet be another hope. The information revolution holds the potential to make higher education—all education—a much more capital-intensive and much less labor-intensive business than it presently is. Conceivably, it will be mass marketing of virtual classrooms and faculties that finally breaks the grip of the ideological guilds. But before the Internet becomes the academic route of choice, the better part of a generation is likely to pass, to the enduring loss of both liberal education and our civic culture. Let us then seize the moment.

Notes

1. See James Q. Wilson, "How Divided Are We?" *Commentary*, February 2006, 15–21 for a forceful presentation of this view.

2. Anthony T. Kronman has recently made a similar set of distinctions between the sciences and the humanities, although he regards the social sciences as more like the sciences than the humanities in these respects than do I. See *Education's End: Why Our Colleges and Universities Have Given Up on the Meaning of Life* (New Haven, CT: Yale University Press, 2007), chapter 3.

3. For these documents, see AAUP, *Policy Documents and Reports*, http://www.aaup.org/AAUP/pubsres/policydocs/contents/1940statement.htm. The most explicit avowal by the AAUP of the "scientific justification" for the exercise of academic freedom can be found in that organization's founding document, *The 1915 Declaration of Principles*. Interestingly, this can no longer be found in *Policy Documents and Reports*, but is included in Louis Joughin, ed., *Academic Freedom and Tenure* (Washington, DC: AAUP, 1969), 155–76.

4. I expand on this point in "The Antidote to Academic Orthodoxy," *Chronicle Review*, April 23, 2004, B7–B9.

5. Not surprisingly, negative selection not only weeds out dissidents, but also creates disincentives against their attempting to enter the most politicized fields.

14

The Role of Alumni and Trustees

Anne D. Neal

Should alumni and trustees remain silent when academic freedom is threatened, educational standards decline, or political agendas drive academic decisions? Yes, according to long-standing tradition.[1]

The logic behind the tradition is deceptively simple. Academic decisions should be made on academic grounds; hence, they should be made by academics. And there are sound reasons for this logic. The McCarthy era demonstrated how the scholarly pursuit of truth can be threatened by coercive, extra-academic interference.

But it's also the case today that academic decisions are frequently made on anything *but* academic grounds. And alumni and trustees must take notice, and take action.

Too often, the contemporary academy focuses on faculty interests at the expense of student needs, academic freedom without academic responsibility, political agendas in the name of teaching students to think critically. Institutional policy and campus culture are alarmingly hostile to a wide range of viewpoints.[2] Course offerings often center on a narrow, politicized part of the disciplinary spectrum.[3] A survey conducted for the American Council of Trustees and Alumni found that 48 percent of students at America's top colleges complained of campus presentations that "seem totally one-sided," while 42 percent faulted reading assignments for presenting only one side of a controversial issue.[4]

Over the last fifty years, higher education has gone from a post–World War II boom to an era of limited public resources, from decades of low tuition to tuition increases far in excess of inflation, from a system that exposed students to broad areas of knowledge to one where students pick and choose from a veritable smorgasbord of narrow and trendy offerings. Meanwhile, political correctness—what former Yale law professor Anthony Kronman defines as "a stifling culture of moral and political uniformity based on progressive ideals"—has become commonplace.[5]

Academics themselves have long noted these unhealthy trends. In a 1994 poll conducted by the Organization of American Historians, historians cited "overspecialization" and "political correctness" as undermining their profession.[6] Today, the problem is even more entrenched. In 2006, Princeton's Stanley N. Katz lamented the professoriate's progressive fragmentation, its inability to "develop and maintain . . . norms of conduct or of intellectual substance," and its loss of faith "in the relevance of teaching undergraduates for the health of our democracy."[7] Katz was not just describing his personal experience; he was also responding to a plethora of recent polls showing a decline in public faith in higher education, along with a growing "public squeamishness about the ideological orientation of faculty members."[8]

As other chapters in this book show, the politically correct university is not the invention of outsiders; rather, it is a very real problem, one created and propagated by those inside—administrators and academics who hold their students and colleagues to ideological standards rather than academic ones. As early as 1991, Yale president Benno Schmidt warned that "the most serious problems of freedom of expression in our society today exist on our campuses. The assumption seems to be that the purpose of education is to induce correct opinion rather than to search for wisdom and liberate the mind."[9]

Most institutions—and their internal constituencies—need checks and balances, and higher education is no exception. That is why informed alumni and trustees must articulate their concerns about academic trends that threaten American higher education's future. Unlike university insiders, who are part of a complex and often deeply politicized environment, alumni and trustees can exercise independent judgment and speak freely—without reprisal. Able to bring fresh insight and energy to old, entrenched problems, they can actively support fundamental academic values and steward their contributions to ensure students learn what they need to know.

Why Should Alumni and Trustees Help?

According to a 2007 survey by the National Center for Public Policy and Higher Education, 87 percent of the public believes that a college degree is key to getting ahead.[10] But at the same time, public confidence in our institutions of higher education has waned. A 2006 poll conducted by the American Association of University Professors found that 58.4 percent of the American public have only some or hardly any confidence in American colleges and universities; 59.1 percent believe higher education imposes low educational standards; 45.7 percent say political bias is either a very serious problem or the biggest problem facing higher education. Over 80 percent say the high cost of tuition is a "very serious" problem.[11]

While improving higher education should matter to all Americans, alumni and trustees have a vested interest in their alma maters. In 2008, alumni were the largest private source of higher education financial support, giving 27.5 percent of the total.[12] Many alumni serve on governing boards and advisory committees or otherwise stay active in their schools' affairs long after graduation. And this is all to the good: though they are often defined as "outsiders," alumni and trustees are—by virtue of their education and subsequent life experience—qualified to participate in college and university affairs. As University of Wisconsin emeritus professor Charles Anderson rightly notes, "graduates of the university are members of the guild . . . competent to participate, as citizens, in its affairs."[13]

Alumni are often more strongly committed to good teaching, a coherent curriculum, affordable tuition, and academic freedom than are faculty or administrators. While professors offer expertise acquired over years of specialized research and scholarship, educated alumni bring with them a broader perspective and the ability to focus on the bigger picture. As successful individuals with a wide range of experience, moreover, alumni are well positioned to understand what graduates need to know if they are to have meaningful, informed, and thoughtful lives.

Engaged alumni can press administrators and trustees to be accountable in ways no one else can. They can keep a vigilant eye on the breadth and quality of academic programs—and thus help guarantee that the value of the education offered by their alma maters remains consistently high. They can take notice and speak out when institutions lower academic standards or enforce political correctness. Indeed, unless alumni speak out, too often the primary source of pressure on administrators will continue to come from the faculty—and administrators will continue to accommodate them accordingly. Without alternative voices, administrators often lack the support necessary to address concerns such as academic excellence and accountability. As former Harvard dean Harry Lewis has observed: "The stakeholders can force change. . . . The alumni, trustees and professors who recognize what has happened can apply enough pressure to steer the ship to a new heading."[14]

The American Council of Trustees and Alumni (ACTA) was launched a decade ago to mobilize thoughtful alumni and trustees on behalf of rigorous general education, good teaching, high standards, and academic freedom. The last ten years have marked a renaissance in alumni and trustee engagement and influence. And those who serve as fiduciaries—aided by alumni pressure and support—are now acknowledging that they need to refocus the academy, and its faculty, on higher education's pedagogical and intellectual mission.

The following examples suggest how alumni and trustees are changing academic culture for the better.[15]

Committee for the CUNY Future. A group of concerned alumni coordinated by ACTA formed the Committee for the CUNY Future in 1998 to press for the return of high academic standards to an institution that was becoming mired in remedial programs. The committee's high-profile membership and articulate defense of educational excellence provided the impetus trustees needed to vote for curricular reform, which has raised CUNY's educational quality and institutional profile. Some years later, when Brooklyn College's acclaimed core curriculum was attacked by deans and the president, the alumni group fought to preserve the model curriculum—and won. In 2006, the committee successfully urged Governor George Pataki to reappoint the reform-minded CUNY trustee Jeffrey Wiesenfeld.

Scholars for the University of Chicago. In 1999, with ACTA's assistance, a coalition of University of Chicago faculty, students, alumni, and trustees came together to oppose the president's efforts to weaken Chicago's famed core curriculum. Scholars for the University of Chicago—which numbered among its members Nobel laureate Saul Bellow, sociologist David Riesman, and philosopher Mortimer J. Adler—persuaded Chicago to retain the curriculum, and the president who announced the proposed changes resigned.

Dartmouth Alumni for Open Governance. For over a decade, Dartmouth alumni have worked to preserve their governance of their college. First through Dartmouth Alumni for Open Governance, founded during the late 1990s, and now through other groups pursuing the same goals, Dartmouth alums have been at the forefront of a struggle that regularly draws headlines. Dartmouth's governance structure is unique; its board of trustees is small, and alumni have historically elected half its members. In recent years, alumni have asserted their influence by electing four straight dark horse petition candidates to the board, on platforms dedicated to improving educational quality, cutting costs, and encouraging the free exchange of ideas. To weaken the influence of the petition trustees, a majority of the board decided to double the number of board-appointed trustees. Meanwhile, the dispute has drawn public attention to a governance system where conflicts of interest reign, and opened a new frontier in higher education reform. Reform-minded Harvard alumni are following in the Dartmouth reformers' footsteps, mounting petition-backed bids for that institution's Board of Overseers.

A Better Colgate. In 2004, as Colgate trustees moved to eliminate fraternity life and dilute the core curriculum, concerned Colgate alumni launched Students and Alumni for Colgate—now A Better Colgate—with ACTA's help. The effort includes a Web site and newsletter where Colgate alumni showcase curricular decline and administrative attacks on the free exchange of ideas and free association. The group has also developed an extensive mailing list to provide alumni with an alternative perspective on their alma mater. In its latest initiative, the group has opened an escrow account where alumni who would normally give to the university can deposit funds. A protest against Colgate's failure to offer alumni an adequate role in governance, the account will stay in place until independent alumni voices receive greater representation on Colgate's board.[16]

Hamilton College Alumni for Governance Reform (HCAGR). Hamilton College alumni have long been concerned about dubious standards and political correctness run amok at their alma mater. In recent years, a president has resigned after admitting to plagiarism, and deans and faculty have invited such academic frauds as Ward Churchill and convicted felon Susan Rosenberg (of the Weathermen) to speak and teach. In 2005, concerned alumni founded Hamilton College Alumni for Governance Reform, launching a prominent Web site and—working with ACTA—playing a major role in promoting petition candidacies for the board of trustees. Most recently, HCAGR has helped establish the Alexander Hamilton Institute, a scholarly center focusing on the study of Western civilization and the college's namesake. When faculty scuppered a new campus center because of its traditional subject matter, alumni took their dollars elsewhere and established the institute off-site.

Alumni as Donors

The essays in this volume amass much troubling evidence that educational excellence and intellectual openness are under attack. Disciplines are eroding into "interdisciplinary studies," and the study of "culture"—a tremendously broad umbrella category—is overtaking the humanities and social sciences. Meanwhile, core areas of knowledge such as American history and the literary canon are no longer reliably required or responsibly taught. A fifty-college study conducted by ACTA in 2004 revealed that more than 60 percent of elite institutions no longer require math, and that 30 percent do not require a common writing course. None require students to study economics. In another study by ACTA, 80 percent of elite college seniors received a D or an F on a basic, high school–level history test. In still another, ACTA learned that many English departments do not require majors to study Shakespeare.[17]

But thoughtful alumni can help turn things around by funding core disciplinary study themselves. They can earmark their gifts for specific programs and projects, and they can ensure that students have the opportunity to study ideas, authors, and works that have fallen out of favor in the politically correct climate of contemporary academe. "The much maligned 'strings' attached to restricted funds," explains former Yale provost Frank Turner, "are in truth the lifelines that link colleges and universities to the marketplace of ideas within a democratic society."[18] As donors attend more closely to how schools use their gifts—and cry foul when those gifts are misappropriated—those lifelines become ever more substantial.[19]

Too many colleges and universities have a lemming-like tendency to adopt unquestioningly the latest scholarly, ideological, or pedagogical fads. It's then up to donors to set the standard for excellence. An outstanding program financed by alumni can put constructive, competitive pressure on other programs. Excellent alumni-funded programs are already doing just this, inspiring students with a taste of real intellectual seriousness, and motivating them to choose more demanding courses of study. Examples include Duke University's Gerst Program in Political, Economic, and Humanistic Studies;[20] Brown University's Political Theory Project;[21] Princeton's James Madison Program in American Ideals and Institutions;[22] and the Alexander Hamilton Institute for the Study of Western Civilization,[23] most of which are discussed in earlier chapters by Piereson and Balch.

Donors who are active stewards provide an invaluable service to their colleges and a priceless benefit to their country. By insisting that their money be spent wisely, donors can make a huge difference in the campaign to reclaim higher education.

Alumni as Trustees

Of course, when all is said and done, one group of alumni is particularly critical to reform: trustees. As fiduciaries of their colleges and universities, trustees are legally and financially responsible for the well-being of their institutions. According to statutes in the public system and charters in the private one, they hold plenary authority for the institutions' financial and academic operations. "We need to be periodically reminded," former University of Wisconsin regent Phyllis Krutsch has explained, "that the mission and performance standards for our campuses and the ultimate fiduciary responsibility and accountability for results rests, not with academicians or experts of any kind, and not with government employees or even elected officials, but with lay boards."[24]

By custom, however, the reality has been far different. As early as 1992, Hoover Institution scholar Martin Anderson charged college and university trustees with the "chief responsibility for the current sorry state of affairs."[25] More recently, federal judge José Cabranes—a former Yale trustee—laid much of the blame for current problems in higher education at the feet of disengaged and uninformed trustees.[26]

Higher education constituencies have long treated alumni and trustees as outsiders, telling them to put up or shut up. And, for the most part, trustees have gone along. Trustees are not trained or encouraged to question the status quo and are—effectively—prevented from doing their job responsibly. As a consequence, faculties have virtually unlimited power over academic concerns. It has become commonplace for boards and presidents to exercise little or no oversight over academic hiring and curricular matters on the grounds that such things fall outside their appropriate purview. Meanwhile, there is mounting evidence of declines in academic accountability, scholarly rigor, and pedagogical quality—as these matters go unaddressed by the academics themselves.

The federal accreditation process has exacerbated the problem. While accreditors are charged with guaranteeing academic quality, there is ample evidence that these teams of faculty and academic administrators have used their power instead to apply intrusive, prescriptive—and often ideological—standards that infringe on institutional autonomy and self-governance.[27]

Until recently, resources available for trustees have reinforced the notion that governance is an essentially passive exercise. Until ACTA was formed, only one other national organization—the Association of Governing Boards (AGB)—focused in any way on boards of trustees. Despite its name, the organization largely reaches trustees through presidents who "sign up" their boards for membership. "The overwhelming message of AGB is for trustees to cheerlead for the campus administration," explains a former trustee. The organization "too often adopts the proposition that any disagreement with the administration is micromanaging or intolerable failure to support the president."[28] In its 1997 annual report, AGB went so far as to criticize "activist trustees," suggesting that "activism means insisting on sources of information independent from that provided by the chief executive" and amounts to "an attack on the university's integrity—not responsible trusteeship."[29]

Given the current norms, it's not at all surprising that 40 percent of trustees surveyed by the *Chronicle of Higher Education* in 2007 said they were "slightly" or "not at all" prepared for the job. Eighty-six percent of public college trustees and 73 percent of trustees at private, nondenominational schools agreed that their institutions "should be held more accountable for what their students learn."[30]

Fortunately, forces are building that make the go along–get along culture ripe for substantive reforms. During the past decade, limited state budget resources, spiraling costs, and mounting concerns about graduates' lack of basic skills have prompted a demand for accountability. Taxpayers are being asked to foot increasingly higher bills, with no guarantee that their dollars are being spent well. Meanwhile, the scandals surrounding such figures as Ward Churchill and Lawrence Summers have raised public awareness of how politicized higher education has become. In response, the public is ever more vocal about quality and costs and ever more receptive to change.[31] Trustees are rightly feeling pressure to bring rigorous accountability to their work.

One source of pressure has come from the blue-ribbon commission convened in 2005 by Margaret Spellings, secretary of education under President George Bush. Intended to initiate a national dialogue on higher education, the commission's report, *A Test of Leadership: Charting the Future of U.S. Higher Education*, faulted education leaders for complacency and called for "urgent reform." While America rests on its laurels, the commission noted, other nations are "educating more of their citizens to more advanced levels than we are."[32]

Pressure has also come from Capitol Hill. While the Sarbanes-Oxley Act does not apply to nonprofits, the Senate Finance Committee has spent the past several years analyzing whether nonprofits merit similar rules. Bad press about corrupt student loan practices, presidential malfeasance, administrative cover-ups, and excess compensation have drawn increasing attention to the challenges and responsibilities of higher education trusteeship. Each new scandal underscores how urgently college and university boards need to get their house in order. As more and more commentators are observing, if they don't do so soon, it will be done for them.[33]

Stakeholders—taxpayers, students, parents, donors, and alumni—want to know that institutions will not misuse or squander their investments. They want to know that dollars are going to instruction, not high living, and that funding—public and private—is being used to provide the best education possible at the lowest possible cost. When American University students—who pay over $30,000 a year in tuition and fees—learned their president was eating gourmet meals and hiring French chefs on their dime, they and their parents rightly questioned what was really going on. Likewise, reports on conflicts of interest at respected institutions such as Dartmouth College and the University of California make the public wonder whether bad practices are the rule rather than the exception.[34]

When trustees reflexively defer to faculties on academic matters, they risk betraying the very lifeblood of the academic enterprise.[35] By law, college and university trustees are legally responsible for the academic and financial well-being of their institutions. This does not mean boards should review course syllabi or interfere with reading lists. But it does mean that trustees must know about academic programs hosted by their institution, and it means, too, that they should judge those programs impartially and pragmatically. They should have a clear sense of what graduates attending their institutions are expected to know, and they should decide whether those expectations are appropriate. That, in turn, means that they should determine whether their institutions ensure that their students acquire the knowledge and skills they will need to be informed and engaged citizens.

The same goes for the classroom climate. In 2005, ACTA issued *Intellectual Diversity: Time for Action* in response to mounting evidence that professors were allowing their politics to interfere with their teaching.[36] While scrupulously respecting academic freedom, the report urged boards to ensure the robust exchange of ideas in the classroom—that is, to protect the academic freedom of students as well as faculty. Rejecting the common assumption that a proactive board is a wrong-headed one, the report underscored trustees' right and duty to ensure that faculty members live up to their professional responsibilities, and insisted that while "institutional autonomy" is a central value of academic freedom,[37] it does not mean the academy is exempt from outside input or trustee involvement. Institutional autonomy exists not as an end in itself, but as a means of protecting the freedom of students and faculty to pursue the truth—wherever it may lead.

There are already promising signs of reform. The AGB's 2007 *Statement on Board Accountability* is almost a confession against interest, noting "a deep appreciation of the gravity of concerns regarding governance, threats to board authority, and institutional autonomy" and aiming to "place college and university governing boards at the forefront of the nonprofit sector's response to concerns about governance and accountability." Particularly noteworthy is the statement's position on academic freedom: "The board is the prime guarantor of academic freedom and of institutional autonomy in educational matters," the AGB notes in language that neatly dovetails with ACTA's position.[38] Where the threat to academic freedom comes from the inside, trustees must protect the freedom of faculty members whose points of view may be unpopular—as well as the freedom of students to learn.

These shifts within the academic establishment reflect shifts beyond it. Governors across the country—and across party lines—are taking steps to ensure that higher education trustees do a better job. Former Virginia governor James Gilmore personally interviewed all public university trustees and instructed them to stress the importance of engaged and thoughtful stewardship. Former Massachusetts governor Mitt Romney reenergized the Public Education Nominating Council to identify the most able and dedicated citizens to serve. And Ohio governor Ted Strickland gave Ohio regents authority to overhaul and unify the state university system. In such instances, we see how strong extra-academic leadership begets strong academic leadership.[39]

And legislators are also getting involved. Faced with growing evidence of problems in higher education, the nation's largest nonpartisan, individual membership association of state legislators has passed model legislation encouraging trustee training from outside experts and calling upon institutional leaders to provide the public greater measures of accountability.

Trustees as Reformers

As demand for accountability grows, examples are also mounting of higher education boards doing their jobs responsibly and well—and, thereby, initiating needed reform.

The boards of Colorado's public institutions have undertaken an impressive statewide effort to develop a strong core curriculum, end grade inflation, improve teacher quality, and limit tuition increases. In response to the Ward Churchill scandal, the University of Colorado also undertook a review of its procedures for hiring and promotion.[40] The State University of New York Board of Trustees has moved to mandate general education, to measure learning outcomes, to insist on high-quality teacher education, and to identify strong presidents. The South Dakota Board of Regents is requiring professors to inform students on syllabi that they will be evaluated solely on the basis of their academic performance—not their opinions or extracurricular conduct. And the University of Missouri Board of Curators is not only requiring such statements on syllabi, but also authorizing special ombudsmen to review student complaints concerning doctrinaire administrative and professorial behavior.[41]

Boards are also recognizing that they are obligated to identify and select innovative leaders who are unafraid to question the status quo. Executive search firms are notorious for recycling candidates from a small, predictable pool. Some consultants also base their fees on the size of the president's salary, an arrangement that undermines efforts to rein in salaries paid by public funds. Already, two massive state systems—CUNY and Cal State—have ceased employing "headhunters" to fill all vacancies and have instead relied on internal resources to do so. Their pathbreaking example illustrates how boards can regain control over searches of immense institutional importance.[42]

There is also growing recognition that private colleges and universities must address the irregularities that mar their governance structures. In 2005, the Senate Finance Committee convinced Independent Sector, a coalition of leading nonprofits and foundations, to recommend best practices for nonprofits. Advocating strong policies on governance, auditing, conflict of interest, travel reimbursement, and whistleblower protection, the report stated that "failures by boards of directors in fulfilling their fiduciary responsibilities may arise when a board leaves governing responsibility to a small number of people, some of whom may have conflicts of interest that mar their judgment."[43] Scandals at congressionally chartered American University prompted major governance changes designed to diminish conflicts of interest.[44] Dartmouth's recent, highly publicized governance struggles offer a further case for review. Far from modeling best practices, Dartmouth's move to create a self-perpetuating, unaccountable board runs counter to federal and regulatory calls for transparency and independence—not to mention the desires of the thousands of alumni who have voted repeatedly for independent oversight.[45]

Conclusion

Rather than blaming the messenger and denying the problem, the academy must take responsibility for its actions, its integrity, and its future. Whether academic insiders will admit it or not, higher education's runaway costs, inadequate curricula, political correctness, and unethical behavior have everything to do with the closed and clubby mind-set of most higher education leaders. That mind-set must change.

Universities receive special privileges such as subsidies and tax exemptions on the condition that they serve the public good. The trust we place in them entails both extraordinary rights and heavy responsibilities. Ideally, faculty and administrators will take the initiative to make sure they fulfill that duty, but, failing that, trustees and alumni can and should step in.

Far from being an "attack" on the academic enterprise, recent cases of alumni and trustee activism have, in fact, been in defense of it. Concerned alumni have come to save universities from themselves. Colleges ignore them at their peril.

Notes

1. This chapter incorporates in part, adapts, and expands an article by Jerry L. Martin, the founding president of the American Council of Trustees and Alumni, entitled "Alumni Have More to Offer Colleges Than Just Cash," *Chronicle of Higher Education*, October 13, 1995, B1–2. Thanks also go to Dr. Erin O'Connor, ACTA research fellow, for her assistance.

2. This hostility is most openly registered in cancellations of talks by controversial speakers, one-sided speaker panels, campus speech codes, disciplinary double standards, and the punishment and persecution of conservative and religious student groups. See Anne D. Neal, "Is Intellectual Diversity an Endangered Species on America's College Campuses?" testimony before the U.S. Senate Health, Education, Labor and Pensions Committee, October 29, 2003, as well as the case archive maintained by the Foundation for Individual Rights in Education, http://www.thefire.org, for a number of examples. Remarkably, this hostility sometimes even extends to trustees who dare to speak their minds. Individual trustees at the University of California, Princeton, and Dartmouth were reprimanded by their boards when they criticized higher education generally and raised questions about specific policies. See "Moores Suddenly Quits UC Regents Board," *San Diego Tribune*, November 13, 2007, http://www.signonsandiego.com/uniontrib/20071113/news_1n13uc.html; "Trustees criticize Forbes, reaffirm commitment to academic freedom," *Princeton Spectator*, December 1, 1999, http://www.princeton.edu/paw/archive_old/PAW99-00/06-1201/1201notx.html#story3.; and the letter of censure Dartmouth's board issued against Todd Zywicki in December 2007, http://www.dartmouth.edu/~trustees/docs/Trustee%20Statement%20on%20Zywicki.pdf.

3. Brooklyn College history professor Robert "KC" Johnson has documented the consequences of postmodernism in his field. Compared to the history departments of old, the postmodernist history department is one where many advocates of the new social history have been successfully pushing fields like diplomatic history, military history, and constitutional history to the margins of the profession. See Anne D. Neal's presentation at the Notre Dame Center for Ethics and Culture on December 2, 2006, https://www.goacta.org/publications/downloads/NealNotreDame12-06.pdf. See also KC Johnson, "Intellectual Diversity and the Historical Profession," *Historically Speaking*, forthcoming.

4. See American Council of Trustees and Alumni, *Politics in the Classroom: A Survey of Students at the Top 50 Colleges and Universities* (Washington, DC: ACTA, 2004), https://www.goacta.org/publications/downloads/PoliticsintheClassroom_pdf.

5. Anthony Kronman, "Why Are We Here?" *Boston Globe*, September 16, 2007, http://www.boston.com/news/globe/ideas/articles/2007/09/16/why_are_we_here/?page=full.

6. David Thelen, "The Practice of American History," *Journal of American History* 81 (December 1994): 933–60.

7. Stanley N. Katz, "What Has Happened to the Professoriate?" *Chronicle of Higher Education*, October 6, 2006, http://chronicle.com/article/What-Has-Happened-to-the-Pr/22680/.

8. Ibid.

9. Benno C. Schmidt Jr., "The University and Freedom" (speech presented at 92nd Street Y, New York, 1991), 1, 3. Quoted in Craig R. Smith, "Academic Freedom vs. Civil Rights: A Special Report of the Center for First Amendment Studies, California State University, Long Beach," March 2004, http://www.csulb.edu/~crsmith.acadfree.html.

10. John Immerwahr and Jean Johnson, *Squeeze Play: How Parents and the Public Look at Higher Education Today*, National Center for Public Policy and Higher Education, May 2007, http://www.highereducation.org/reports/squeeze_play/index.shtml.

11. Neil Gross and Solon Simmons, "Americans' Views of Political Bias in the Academy and Academic Freedom," American Association of University Professors, June 2006, http://www.aaup.org/NR/rdonlyres/DCF3EBD7-509E-47AB-9AB3-FBCFFF5CA9C3/0/2006Gross.pdf.

12. Higher education institutions collectively raised nearly $28 billion in 2005–6, according to the Council for Aid to Education's annual "Voluntary Support of Education" report; the largest portion of contributions came from alumni, amounting to 30 percent of the total. See data compiled by the Council for Aid to Education at http://www.cae.org/content/pro_data_trends.htm.

13. Charles W. Anderson, *Prescribing the Life of the Mind: An Essay on the Purpose of the University, the Aims of Liberal Education, the Competence of Citizens, and the Cultivation of Practical Reason* (Madison: University of Wisconsin Press, 1993), 150.

14. Harry R. Lewis, *Excellence without a Soul: How a Great University Forgot Education* (New York: Public Affairs Press, 2006), 18.

15. See ACTA's press archive for background on CUNY, Chicago, Dartmouth, Hamilton, Colgate, and Smith alumni efforts: http://www.goacta.org/press/press-releases.cfm.

16. The association's Web address is http://www.votecolgatetrustees.org.

17. See Barry Latzer, *The Hollow Core: Failure of the General Education Curriculum* (Washington, DC: ACTA, 2004), https://www.goacta.org/publications/downloads/TheHollowCore.pdf; American Council of Trustees and Alumni, *Losing America's Memory: Historical Illiteracy in the 21st Century* (Washington, DC: ACTA, 2000), https://www.goacta.org/publications/downloads/LosingAmerica'sMemory.pdf; and American Council of Trustees and Alumni, *The Vanishing Shakespeare* (Washington, DC: ACTA, 2007), https://www.goacta.org/publications/downloads/VanishingShakespeare.pdf.

18. Quoted in Jerry L. Martin and Anne D. Neal, *The Intelligent Donor's Guide to College Giving* (Washington, DC: ACTA, 1998), 63, https://www.goacta.org/publications/downloads/IntelligentDonorsGuide.pdf.

19. A case in point: the Robertson family, whio were engaged in a protracted legal dispute with Princeton over its use of a major donation.

20. "The Gerst program aims at fostering an understanding of the central importance of freedom for democratic government, moral responsibility, and economic and cultural life. It focuses on the theoretical foundations of freedom and responsibility, the development of liberty in the Western and particularly the American historical context, the role of freedom in political and economic institutions, and the character of morally responsible behavior." See http://www.poli. duke.edu/gerst.

21. "The Political Theory Project currently is organized around three main themes: The American Experiment; Market Society and Social Order; and Globalization and Development. The Project sponsors a variety of activities: new courses for undergraduates, a University-wide lecture series, weekly Open Seminar Luncheons for undergraduates, academic conferences, research fellowships for graduate students, support for faculty research, and a postdoctoral fellowship program." See http://www.brown.edu/Departments/Political_Theory_Project.

22. The Madison Program is "dedicated to the pursuit of scholarly excellence in the fields of constitutional studies and political thought." See http://web.princeton.edu/sites/jmadison.

23. See http://www.theahi.org.

24. Phyllis M. Krutsch, "Seven Principles for Effective Boards," testimony before the Governor of Virginia's Blue Ribbon Commission on Higher Education, September 8, 1999, http://www.epi.elps.vt.edu/BRC/K.html.

25. See Martin Anderson, *Impostors in the Temple: The Decline of the American University* (New York: Simon and Schuster, 1992), 195–96.

26. "University Trusteeship in the Enron Era," in *For Trustees Only*, ed. American Council of Trustees and Alumni (Washington, DC: ACTA, 2004). See also José Cabranes, "How to Make Trustees Worthy of Their Constituents' Trust," *Chronicle of Higher Education*, October 18, 2002, http://chronicle.com/article/How-to-Make-Trustees-Worthy/6459/.

27. See American Council of Trustees and Alumni, *Why Accreditation Doesn't Work and What Policymakers Can Do About It: A Policy Paper of the American Council of Trustees and Alumni* (Washington, DC: ACTA, 2007), https://www.goacta.org/publications/downloads/Accreditation2007Final.pdf; George C. Leef and Roxana D. Burris, Can College Accreditation Live up to Its Promise? (Washington, DC: American Council of Trustees and Alumni, 2002), https://www.goacta.org/publications/downloads/CanAccreditationFulfillPromise.pdf.

28. Drew Miller, "What Trustees Must Do, After A.U.," *Inside Higher Ed*, May 16, 2006, http://www.insidehighered.com/views/2006/05/16/miller.

29. Richard T. Ingram, "Are You an Activist Trustee?" *Annual Report* (Washington, DC: Association of Governing Boards, 1997).

30. See Jeffrey Selingo, "Trustees More Willing Than Ready," *Chronicle of Higher Education*, May 11, 2007, http://chronicle.com/article/Trustees-More-Willing-Than/15883/.

31. See Immerwahr and Johnson, *Squeeze Play*, Gross and Simmons, *Americans' Views of Political Bias in the Academy and Academic Freedom*, and Zogby Interactive's poll of public perceptions of faculty, http://www.zogby.com/news/readnews.cfm?ID=1334.

32. See *A Test of Leadership: Charting the Future of U.S. Higher Education* (Washington, DC: U.S. Department of Eduation, 2006), ix–x, http://www.ed.gov/about/bdscomm/list/hiedfuture/reports/final-report.pdf. The commission's conclusion was devastating, suggesting that parents and taxpayers have no proof that the vast investment they make in higher education is worth it. The commission called upon universities to increase productivity, cut costs, and to improve student learning—goals that trustees are in a unique position to promote. Suggestions for what trustees can do are outlined in American Council of Trustees and Alumni, *The Spellings Commission and You: What Higher Education Trustees Can Do in Light of the Department of Education's Recent Report* (Washington, DC: ACTA, 2007), https://www.goacta.org/publications/downloads/SpellingsFinal-Trustees.pdf..

33. See the letter from the Chairman and Vice Chairman of American University's board to Senator Grassley, then Chairman of the Senate Committee on Finance, http://www1.american.edu/governance/docs/To_Senator_Grassley_5-31-06.pdf.

34. See ACTA's memo to the Dartmouth Association of Alumni, "Dartmouth's Governance and Best Practices," http://www.goacta.org/press/PressReleases/2007PressReleases/dartmouthmemo7-30-07.pdf. See also *Inside Higher Ed*'s coverage of corruption at the University of California: "Ouster at U. of California," November 7, 2005, http://www.insidehighered.com/news/2005/11/07/uc; and "UC System Chief to Step Down," August 14, 2007, http://www.insidehighered.com/news/2007/08/14/dynes.

35. See Martin, "Alumni Have More to Offer Colleges Than Just Cash": "In fact, overspecialization may make it more difficult for a narrowly focused scholar than for a well-educated alumnus to understand the kind of liberal education that an undergraduate needs to succeed after graduation. . . . Some professors care more about high salaries and low teaching loads than about teaching what students need to learn. Worse yet, some professors are more strongly committed to their own political and ideological agendas than to reasoned debate and the free exchange of ideas. Indeed, some of them now openly contend that all scholarship and teaching are, and ought to be, political. This viewpoint, though, has no visible support among alumni. Compared with such professors, many alumni show a more accurate understanding of academic freedom."

36. American Council of Trustees and Alumni, *Intellectual Diversity: Time for Action* (Washington, DC: ACTA, 2005), https://www.goacta.org/publications/downloads/IntellectualDiversityFinal.pdf.

37. In the abstract, a prescription for institutional autonomy makes good, practical sense. The university should be a place where the robust exchange of ideas takes place, and where professional standards are maintained by rigorous peer review. Professors are rightfully given academic freedom in exchange for a sacred trust—that

they will use the freedom they are given over the classroom and over academic policy for valid educational ends, not to pursue their own pet causes or personal politics. In the recent past, however, the AAUP, American Federation of Teachers, and Ad Hoc Committee to Defend the University have balked at this compact. Both former and current AAUP heads have argued that faculty should be left alone when it comes to academic freedom. "It should be evident," Roger Bowen claimed when general secretary of the AAUP, "that the sufficient condition for securing the academic freedom of our profession is the profession itself." See Roger W. Bowen, "Institutional Autonomy, Academic Freedom and Academic Responsibility," *Montana Professor* 17 (Fall 2006): 25, http://mtprof.msun.edu/Fall2006/bowen.html. AAUP president Cary Nelson has interpreted the AAUP statement *Freedom in the Classroom* as empowering professors to say to anyone who questions them, "You shouldn't mess with me." See "AAUP Goes to Bat for Freedom in the Classroom," *Chronicle of Higher Education*, September 21, 2007, http://chronicle.com/article/AAUP-Goes-to-Bat-for-Freed/2385/. The American Federation of Teachers maintains that "defending academic freedom requires the defeat of government intrusion, or *any external intrusion* [emphasis supplied], into curriculum, teaching, hiring and student assessment." *Academic Freedom in the 21st Century College and University*, 2007, 15, http://www.aft.org/higher_ed/pubs-reports/AcademicFreedomStatement.pdf. See also the Ad Hoc Committee to Defend the University's Web page at http://defend.university.googlepages.com/home.

38. See Association of Governing Boards of Universities and Colleges, "AGB Statement on Board Accountability" (Washington, D.C.: Association of Governing Boards, 2007), 2, 7, http://www.agb.org/user-assets/documents/AccountabilityStatementFinalForWeb.pdf.

39. As the highest-level elected officials in their states, governors are the key to the cultural transformation. In most states, they appoint trustees and state education officials. They can set an agenda for change. They shape priorities for funding, can make use of the bully pulpit to identify key higher education issues, and can give the trustees a mandate to address those issues. Voters, too, have a pivotal role to play. They must demand that their governors appoint informed, engaged higher education officials who have the time and dedication necessary to tackle the absorbing and difficult work of trusteeship. See American Council of Trustees and Alumni, *Accountability in Higher Education: Governors Provide Leadership* (Washington, DC: ACTA, 2004), https://www.goacta.org/publications/downloads/Accountability.pdf.

40. Notably, in his letter to the board of regents recommending that Churchill be fired, President Hank Brown cited the important role of alumni and trustees in higher education reform. Brown wrote: "In 1995, I co-authored an article with Senator Joe Lieberman in which Senator Lieberman and I urged alumni and trustees to speak up on behalf of academic values and to encourage our colleges and universities to teach that, '[i]n the American marketplace of ideas, we should fight ideas with which we disagree by offering a better idea, not by denying others the right to voice their concerns.'" Letter to Patricia Hayes, May 25, 2007, 8, citing

"Academic Freedom: Alumni Can Help Fight the PC War," Sens. Hank Brown and Joe Lieberman, *Roll Call*, July 17, 1995, http://extras.mnginteractive.com/live/media/site36/2007/0529/20070529_012953_5-25-07%20Brown%20-%20Regents%20(dismissal).pdf.

41. Kavita Kumar, "UM Websites Will Track Grievances against Professors," *St. Louis Post-Dispatch*, October 5, 2007; "SUNY General Education Requirements", http://www.suny.edu/student/academic_general_education.cfm; "South Dakota Board of Regents Policy Manual: Academic Freedom and Responsibility," http://www.sdbor.edu/policy/1-Governance/documents/1-11.pdf.

42. Clara Lovett, president emerita of Northern Arizona University, issued a pioneering criticism of search firms in the *Chronicle of Higher Education* and has worked with universities around the country, including CUNY, Cal State, and the University of Colorado, to produce better searches. See Clara M. Lovett, "The Dumbing Down of College Presidents," *Chronicle of Higher Education*, April 5, 2002, http://chronicle.com/article/The-Dumbing-Down-of-College/35826/.

43. See Panel on the Nonprofit Sector, *Strengthening Transparency, Governance, Accountability of Charitable Organizations*," 2005, 75, http://www.nonprofitpanel.org/final/Panel_Final_Report.pdf.

44. See http://www1.american.edu/trustees/statements/05192006-1.pdf. See also Anne D. Neal, "Ensuring Quality Trusteeship in Higher Education," statement to Senate Finance Committee Roundtable, March 3, 2006, https://www.goacta.org/publications/downloads/NealSenateFinance3-3-06.pdf.

45. A common conflict of interest involves presidents who serve as voting board members. The issue was taken up by the Urban Institute in a 2007 study: "Having the CEO/executive director serve as a voting board member was negatively related to board activity level in financial oversight, setting policy, community relations, and trying to influence public policy, and positively related to none." Francie Ostrower, *Nonprofit Governance in the United States* (Washington, DC: Urban Institute, 2007), 16, http://www.urban.org/UploadedPDF/411479_Nonprofit_Governance.pdf. Also instructive is the example of the Nature Conservancy. After negative publicity exposed irregularities in the organization's governance practices, an independent panel that included former Harvard president Derek Bok recommended that the president/CEO not serve on the governance or any other committee. The conservancy took the panel's advice and now announces on its Web site that the full board handles major strategic issues. See "Accountability and Transparency of The Nature Conservancy," Nature Conservancy, http://www.nature.org/aboutus/leadership/art15505.html.

15

Openness, Transparency, and Accountability: Fostering Public Trust in Higher Education

Hank Brown, John B. Cooney, and Michael B. Poliakoff

Results of a recent national survey affirm that the American public remains steadfast in the belief that higher education is an important pathway for creating economic opportunity; confidence in the value and cost-effectiveness of higher education, however, shows signs of weakening.[1] Almost three-fourths of survey respondents expressed concern about paying for college, and 44 percent believe that waste and mismanagement are driving costs for higher education beyond their reach.

Colorado has felt the impact of the crisis of confidence in higher education, especially among its research universities, through dramatic decreases in funding.[2] Colorado has faced a systematic decline in the percentage of the state general fund that is allocated to higher education, from 22.4 percent in FY 2003 to 10.3 percent in FY 2008. In contrast, the percentage of the general fund that is allocated to K–12 education has increased over the same interval. Although the forces driving the decrease in funding for higher education in Colorado are multiple and complex (e.g., rise in health care costs, constitutionally mandated increases for K–12 education), the message is clear: we have not made a convincing case to those responsible for our funding that our system of higher education is a good investment.

Many of us looking at the university from the inside are puzzled by this public perception of higher education because we know firsthand the extraordinary accomplishments of students and faculty, the groundbreaking research that enhances the quality of life on a global scale, and the selfless service of faculty members to their communities. The disconnect between the perceptions of the public and of higher education communities exists because the public has basic questions about the practices of colleges and universities that have not been answered in a way that is open, transparent, and accountable. The simple proposal that we advance in this chapter is that colleges and universities should strive to make their practices open and transparent, and should hold themselves accountable to the taxpayers and parents who support them. We will discuss four interrelated areas where we believe modest changes could significantly restore public confidence in higher education: administrative costs, political bias, awarding of tenure, and student achievement.

Fiscal Management in Higher Education

The finding that a significant proportion of the American public believes that waste and mismanagement in higher education are driving tuition costs beyond their means indicates that higher education needs to be much more transparent about its sources of revenue and expenditures. The federal government collects a great deal of financial information from the majority of higher education providers, including revenue by source (e.g., tuition, fees, grants and contracts, private gifts) and expenses by function (e.g., instruction, research, academic support, institutional support). Although the data are publicly accessible on the Integrated Postsecondary Education Data System (IPEDS) website,[3] it may not be immediately apparent how to use the data to address the question of waste and mismanagement of resources.

Administrative Overhead. The functional expense category of *institutional support* is a key indicator of the expenses most directly related to how much an institution spends on administrative overhead, that is, on expenses not directly related to instruction. Examples of expenses in this category include expenses associated with executive-level management, legal and fiscal operations, general administrative services, public relations, and the cost of information technology related to these services. Understanding total expenditures for institutional support is only the first step in addressing concerns about waste and mismanagement of resources. Because institutions vary widely in their total expenses and the number of students served, it is useful to standardize expenses for the different functional expense categories in terms of percentage of total expenses and expense per full-time equivalent student (FTE). The IPEDS routinely reports expenses per student FTE by functional expense category, and it is simple enough to compute the expense for any given functional category as a percentage of total expenses.

Although these measures can serve as the basis for productive discussions about how an institution allocates resources, it is the comparison of the measures among peer institutions that is most informative. Knowing that an institution spends $3,500 per student FTE, or 7 percent of its total budget, on central administrative functions is not meaningful by itself. Knowing that the peer average is $2,800 per student FTE, or 5 percent of total expenditures, however, invites an open discussion about the reasons for this discrepancy. It may be a conscious and justifiable decision; the average is not necessarily the norm for which an institution should strive. Rather, what we want to know is that the institution is open about the cost of certain functions, the cost is transparent, and the institution is held accountable for explaining variances in cost relative to similar institutions.

Instructional Cost and Productivity. Additional benchmarks that could be useful for building public confidence in the fiscal management practices of universities include those associated with instructional cost and productivity of faculty members. Institutions of higher education routinely report to IPEDS expenditures in the functional expense category of *instruction*. As the name implies, these are expenditures directly related to teaching. Expressed as a cost per student FTE and as a percentage of total expenditures, these metrics convey useful information about how an institution allocates its resources relative to administrative overhead and its peer groups. Unlike *U.S. News & World Report*, which aggregates expenditures per student for *institutional support* and *instruction* with expenditures for academic administrative support, student services, and operation and maintenance of plant (i.e., wealth), we believe it is important to consider these measures separately because they represent different management objectives: allocating resources to enhance student achievement versus minimizing overhead costs. Furthermore, we recommend in the interest of openness, transparency, and accountability that instructional expenditures be broken out into specific categories of faculty and academic programs.

The National Study of Instructional Costs and Productivity (i.e., the Delaware study) is an ongoing effort with voluntary participation that provides a reliable framework for comparing expenditures related to instruction across institutions at the program level.[4] That framework includes measures such as the following, which would address public concern about fiscal management:

- Direct instructional expenditures per credit hour.

- Direct expenditures for instruction as a percentage of total expenditures.

- Direct instructional expenditures per student FTE.

- Faculty FTE, including a breakout of tenured, tenure-eligible, and other faculty.

- Expenditures for research per tenured and tenure-eligible faculty FTE.

- Expenditures for public service per tenured and tenure-eligible faculty FTE.

- The number of organized class sections (upper *vs.* lower division) taught per faculty category.

- The number of student credit hours (upper *vs.* lower division) taught per faculty category.

The focus on expenditures for faculty, especially tenured and tenure-eligible faculty, is purposeful. According to the Delaware study, tenured and tenure-eligible faculty a) are the most visible and subject to criticism from the government, media, and parents; b) represent the fixed costs of the institution; and c) represent the greatest investment by a college or university (often 80 percent or more of the resources available). Although the fine-grained analysis of the Delaware study does not disaggregate the teaching responsibilities of tenure-eligible faculty members from those who are tenured, we believe that such disaggregation could be useful in addressing concerns about the quality of undergraduate education. What former Yale University dean Donald Kagan says about Harvard faculty—for them, "undergraduate education is at best of secondary interest"[5]—might be said of other faculties as well; the Boyer Commission and others have voiced similar concerns about the level of involvement of senior faculty in undergraduate education on a national scale.[6] During his time as dean, Donald Kagan particularly emphasized the role that senior faculty should play in introductory-level courses. Senior faculty members bring a mature and comprehensive vision of their fields to the classroom, a vision rarely brought by the graduate students and assistant professors who are routinely assigned to the introductory courses. Parents and taxpayers, moreover, expect that undergraduates will have the benefit of the institutions' finest scholars, who are certainly played up in the publicity materials that the university disseminates. These are the same faculty, however, who are expected to generate revenue through research grants and the transfer of knowledge to the private sector, and who are the lifeblood of intellectual progress; they account for much of the scientific and medical advances of recent decades. The grants they receive, to a greater or lesser degree, enable them to "purchase" a lighter teaching load in order to have time for their research. Any valid system of benchmarking credit hours by faculty category would need to incorporate data about released time for funded research: its usefulness would depend on being exceedingly fine-grained. The reporting system for the Delaware study takes this issue into consideration.

Although the surveys of postsecondary faculty conducted in 2002 by the U.S. Department of Education National Center for Education Statistics are useful for answering questions about faculty involvement in undergraduate teaching at a national level, they do not specifically address the openness, transparency, and accountability needed at the institutional level.[7] The federal government could play a useful role in developing policies that expand participation in the type of data collection exemplified by the Delaware study. Presenting data on patterns of faculty involvement in undergraduate and graduate education and associated cost, in a way that is accessible and understandable to supporters and critics alike, invites open and productive discussions about how colleges and universities manage their resources to fulfill their mission.

A lynchpin in the analysis is the formation of peer groups that serve as the basis of comparison. There is an extensive body of research concerning the formation of peer groups for the purpose of comparison,[8] and we cannot overemphasize that the basis for the peer groups must be scientifically valid and credible in the eyes of the public and lawmakers. Here again, the federal government could play a key role in establishing a process for the formation of peer groups that is open and transparent and not subject to the criticism that the institutions were biasing the results in their favor. The U.S. Department of Education could, for example, appoint a panel comprising of members of external nonpartisan agencies with expertise on the formation of peer groups to work with members from the business and higher education communities to develop a methodology for institutions to select their peers.

Our proposal is not revolutionary. It requires simple comparisons with groups of peer institutions, determined by independent and reliable methods, and objective information about administrative and instructional costs, as well as patterns of faculty involvement. Yet we believe that it is a vast improvement over the widely publicized peer comparisons based on perceived prestige, wealth, and exclusivity in *U.S. News & World Report*.[9]

Imbalance of Political Views in Higher Education

Public perception that faculty members at U.S. colleges and universities are predominantly liberal or center-left in their political orientation and predominantly affiliated with the Democratic Party is well founded; the public itself, of course, is far less homogeneous politically. Lawmakers, business leaders, and the citizens who pay taxes and tuition are concerned that the imbalance of political orientation is self-perpetuating through policies and procedures that tilt the recruitment, retention, promotion, and tenure processes in favor of liberal faculty members, and that liberal faculty members create a chilly classroom climate for students who may hold more conservative viewpoints than their own. Until those concerns are effectively addressed, colleges and universities will pay a high price.

A first step toward addressing concerns about the absence of intellectual pluralism is for colleges and universities to be open and transparent about their commitment to promoting intellectual diversity as part of broader campus efforts to promote cultural diversity and academic freedom. The leadership of the institution, from the governing board to department chairs, must publicly affirm their commitment to each of these ideals. Second, institutions will need to demonstrate that they are accountable for making progress toward improving intellectual diversity. This will require institutions to formulate their goals in ways that are measurable. Although some may find our proposal uncomfortable, recent surveys indicate that the majority of faculty (69 percent) at U.S. colleges and university campuses agrees with the idea that "the goal of campus diversity should include fostering diversity of political views among faculty members."[10] The path for achieving the goals of intellectual pluralism, however, is less clear.

Faculty Recruitment. Problems with recruiting an intellectually diverse faculty begin with the educational pipeline, as Woessner and Kelly-Woessner show in a previous chapter. The unwitting discrimination against prospective graduate school students expressing viewpoints that differ from the mainstream of the department or discipline may be one of the most difficult challenges. The problem is illustrated by a survey-based experiment that asked faculty members of clinical psychology programs to evaluate mock applicants to their PhD programs.[11] Three sets of application materials used in the study were identical in all ways but one. In one set, the student disclosed that he had become an evangelical fundamentalist Christian early in his college career. In a second set, he disclosed that he intended to integrate his Christian beliefs into his practice of psychology. In the third set, the control materials, there was no reference to his religious beliefs. For both sets of application materials where the student disclosed his religious beliefs, faculty expressed lower positive feelings and greater doubts about the student's ability to become a good clinical psychologist, a greater need to interview the candidate in comparison with other candidates, and a lower probability of admitting him to the program. Although we are not aware of similar studies in other fields, there is considerable evidence that this pattern of reasoning is commonplace. Confirmation bias is a well-known phenomenon in the research on reasoning; it involves selection and interpretation of information consistent with one's beliefs and ignoring or discounting information inconsistent with them.[12]

A particularly striking demonstration of confirmation bias was con-ducted among a group of Republican and Democratic partisans a few months prior to the 2004 election.[13] Study participants read a series of statements about George W. Bush, John Kerry, and a more politically neu-tral individual such as Tom Hanks. The first statement, usually a quotation from the individual himself, was followed by a contradictory statement showing the person's words or actions to be inconsistent. Next, participants were asked to consider the inconsistency of the two statements and then to rate the extent to which the two statements were contradictory on a four-point scale (strongly disagree to strongly agree). Analysis of the ratings shows that Democrats and Republicans drew very different conclusions from the same information. Republicans rated Kerry's statements as more contradictory than did Democrats, whereas Democrats rated Bush's state-ments as more contradictory than did Republicans. Democrats and Repub-licans, however, did not differ in their evaluation of contradictory statements made by neutral individuals.

The researchers also used functional neuroimaging (fMRI) to study pat-terns of neural activity during the reasoning task. Results from the analysis of participants' brain activity during the tasks show that there was no increase in activity in the areas of the brain that are normally active during conscious reasoning. Rather, there was an increase of activity in the regions of the brain that are typically associated with regulating negative emotions and conflict resolution. When the participants reached their biased conclusions, the activ-ity in these regions decreased, followed by an increase in activity in brain regions normally associated with reward. Results from this investigation are consistent with the idea that the participants' biased judgments are the result of emotion-based processes that occur outside of awareness.

Confirmation bias may also operate in the selection process for new fac-ulty members and in the process for awarding tenure.[14] As noted in previous chapters of this volume, the bias in faculty selection may be less unwitting than we suggest above. Nevertheless, overcoming highly automated patterns of thought is a challenge. Notwithstanding the considerable body of research on confirmation bias and related phenomena, very little of that work is focused on the conditions that mitigate confirmation bias. Hence, it is diffi-cult to formulate policy recommendations to counteract biased reasoning processes that operate outside of awareness and are strongly reinforced at a biological level. Raymond Nickerson suggests that "a critical step in dealing with any type of bias is recognizing its existence," and argues for the importance of awareness:

> Perhaps simply being aware of the confirmation bias—of its pervasiveness and of the many guises in which it appears—might help one both to be a little cautious about making up one's mind quickly on important issues and to be somewhat more open to opinions that differ from one's own than one might otherwise be.[15]

Unfortunately, merely cultivating awareness about biases in reasoning is not sufficient to minimize these biases.[16] Universities need to take additional steps.

First, when university committees are charged with selecting students for admission to graduate programs, recruiting new faculty members, and evaluating faculty members for tenure, members should be reminded of the commitment of the institution to intellectual diversity and should be sensitized to biased reasoning processes. Moreover, they should know the requirements for accountability that have been shown to lead to more accurate impressions and predictions about the performance of others.[17] Second, universities should recognize that including individuals with expertise who hold a minority opinion in a group discussion has been shown to lessen confirmation bias.[18] Department chairs and deans should thus take initiative to compose search and screen committees that are ideologically diverse; the comparable strategy has been helpful in increasing ethnic, gender, and cultural diversity. Given the absence of intellectual pluralism in some disciplinary areas, this approach will be a challenge and will add to the workload of those who are in the minority. Third, universities might try to lessen biases with repeated presentations of information inconsistent with strongly held beliefs. An investigation of scientists' reasoning processes during their weekly laboratory meeting found that repeated presentation of data that are inconsistent with strongly held theoretical views eventually leads them to modify their theories to account for the inconsistent data, a finding that was replicated under controlled conditions.[19] A fourth technique universities can use for minimizing biases in social judgment is the consider-the-opposite strategy. Research suggests that explicit directions to consider information that is opposite to one's perceptions and beliefs are more effective in altering social judgment than explicit direction to be as fair and unbiased as possible.[20] The essence of the consider-the-opposite strategy is "Here is how it [bias] happens and what you can do about it," versus "Here's what can happen. Don't let it happen to you."[21] It is also important to note that periodic prompts and challenges may be necessary to sustain unbiased reasoning.[22] Other suggestions for protecting against biased reasoning are described in texts on critical thinking.[23]

Political Bias in the Classroom. Students' perceptions about the political climate on campus, reflected in a 2004 survey conducted by the Center for Survey Research and Analysis (CSRA) at the University of Connecticut, are cause for concern.[24] For example, 46 percent of students report that professors use the classroom to present their personal political views; 29 percent report courses on their campus in which students feel they have to agree with the professor's political or social views to get a good grade; and 22 percent perceive there are courses in which the professor creates an environment that is hostile to certain political or social views. If a professor displayed bias against a student based on race, nationality, or gender, there would be an outcry and a full-scale investigation. Yet according to 83 percent of students, the forms they fill out to evaluate faculty do not ask whether a professor shows social, political, or religious bias. Other large-scale programs that assess classroom climate, such as the National Survey of Student Engagement (NSSE),[25] are not designed to address political bias as a dimension of the classroom environment; however, an institution may include questions about intellectual diversity and academic freedom on the NSSE.

Our proposal for openness, transparency, and accountability begins with the institution affirming a commitment to principles of intellectual pluralism and academic freedom as one pillar of the principles, policies, and procedures developed to advance diversity of race, national origin, age, ability or disability, and gender. Second, it must be clear how progress in this area is measured. We recommend use of a standardized set of survey questions and sampling methodology because this would enable institutions to establish baselines for improvement and to benchmark the climate in their classrooms against those of their peers. Like the NSSE, this survey focuses on how well the institution as a whole fares in promoting intellectual diversity and academic freedom. Thus, the institution, rather than the student or faculty member, is the unit of analysis. Questions concerning the instructor's balanced and fair presentation of social issues (when such issues are germane to the topic of the course), treatment of students who express social or political views out of the mainstream, and the extent to which the instructor avoids comments on politics unrelated to the course material are reasonable starting points for the development of a classroom survey designed to assess classroom climate for intellectual diversity and academic freedom.[26]

Third, campus officials must be held accountable for promoting intellectual diversity in the same way that they promote ethnic, racial, and gender diversity. They should be expected to implement appropriate surveys at the classroom level, take steps to improve campus climate, correct legacies of past discrimination, especially in hiring practices, and take aggressive and proactive measures to protect intellectual diversity and academic freedom. Ultimately, the federal government will do much to improve the intellectual life of colleges and universities by requiring and publishing data on intellectual diversity just as it does on racial, ethnic and gender diversity.

Tenure-Related Processes

Tenure is vital to the success of higher education; however, it is not widely understood by the public and is in danger of becoming anachronistic.[27] Recent survey results, for example, indicate that approximately half (55 percent) of the U.S. population is aware of tenure for professors in higher education.[28] The issue of tenure, however, is squarely in the crosshairs of state legislators and leaders in the business community, who see it as a practice that values research over teaching and protects incompetence.[29] Concern that tenure sometimes protects incompetent faculty is shared by the public (81 percent) and professorate (95 percent) alike. Yet the majority of citizens (77 percent), when made aware of the tenure system, believes in spite of such concern that tenure is a good way to reward accomplished professors.

Given that policies and procedures related to awarding tenure are among the least visible and least understood, colleges and universities will benefit from making their tenure-related processes open and transparent and holding the leadership accountable for high standards and unbiased review of tenure cases. An important first step toward an effective tenure system is examining and strengthening what exists. It is imperative that we in higher education take the initiative to examine ourselves. There are many lawmakers at the state and federal level willing to intervene if we do not. Colleges and universities have been less than forthcoming with the public and legislators about tenure, leading to the suspicion that higher education is interested only in protecting its own rather than in guaranteeing the highly effective and productive teachers and researchers students and taxpayers deserve.

The experience at the University of Colorado is instructive. The dramatic decline in public support for and confidence in our university, as well as the rattling of sabers in the legislature to fix the tenure system for us, galvanized the faculty leadership and the governing board into action. We began with the belief that it is necessary to be transparent in our processes and straightforward in our explanations of why tenure is necessary and how it works. Such transparency is crucial to tenure's future, just as tenure is crucial to the academy's and America's long-term well-being and international competitiveness.[30]

The university's board of regents, in consultation with faculty governance leaders, appointed an advisory committee on tenure-related processes to conduct a comprehensive review of the tenure process, beginning with the appointment of a faculty member to a tenure-track position, through the probationary period, to the award of tenure, and ending with post-tenure review. Processes and procedures related to dismissal for cause were also included in the review. Moreover, the regents were clear that an independent review was critical to the integrity of the process. Howell M. Estes III, a retired air force general highly regarded in the state, familiar with complex projects, and not connected to the university or the academic community, was asked to lead the independent review. Two working groups were created: the internal group consisted of fourteen veteran faculty members from across the university system; a nationally known consulting firm formed the external group. The groups received the same charge but worked independently. The external group performed a confidential audit of ninety-five randomly selected tenure files, and both groups conducted nearly 160 interviews with those involved in awarding tenure or conducting posttenure review. The university's processes were also benchmarked against those at nineteen peer universities and ten schools of medicine.

Whereas the two working groups reached many of the same conclusions, they also tended to fill in gaps for each other. The report they produced found a tenure process that is generally well-designed and managed and one that held faculty members to exceptionally high standards. Certain weaknesses, however, emerged, including instances of failure to follow processes and procedures rigorously, either in granting tenure or in posttenure review.[31] The failure in the latter was particularly problematic. In some instances, accountability for faculty performance was lacking, documentation of individual faculty strengths and weaknesses was insufficient, and a meaningful system of incentives and sanctions was absent. The university's dismissal for cause process was also found wanting, particularly in its inability to conduct and conclude processes in a timely manner. Both working groups independently raised concerns about the lack of policies to address removal of tenured faculty from the classroom, especially in those situations when students are being adversely affected. The university has moved aggressively to address the deficiencies noted in the study.

The comprehensive review conducted by the University of Colorado is an important first step toward ensuring tenure remains relevant and effective in tomorrow's universities. Yet discussions must also move beyond tenure processes. It is important to examine the tenure system itself, future career pathways for our increasingly diverse and mobile faculty, and standards of performance in a global academic marketplace. There may be alternative models to explore, and discussions of alternatives must involve a variety of stakeholders who focus on one key question: "How do we create and maintain a rigorous and competitive tenure system that best meets the needs of our students and our publics, and best positions America for long-term success?"[32] Conducting an independent evaluation of tenure processes will require a significant investment of resources, resources that would otherwise be used to support teaching, research, and creative activity. State government can encourage universities to undertake periodic reviews of their tenure system through appropriations earmarked for that activity. Recommendations for such an evaluation might include, but not be limited to, the following:

- Describe the policies and procedures for recruiting, reappointing, promoting, awarding tenure, and conducting post-tenure review in a way that is easily accessible and understandable to internal and external audiences.

- Describe the criteria used in decision making at the lowest level that captures variation among academic units.

- Benchmark the policies, procedures, and criteria against peer institutions.

- Describe any training efforts that are required for faculty members and administrators who are involved in hiring, reappointment, promotion, tenure, and post-tenure review decisions. The earlier discussion of strategies to mitigate confirmation bias applies to tenure review and post-tenure review committees as well.

- Describe the review cycle for policies.

- Describe the process for informing tenure-eligible faculty members about their progress toward tenure.

- Describe how the policies and procedures address diversity, including intellectual pluralism, in recruitment and retention of tenure-eligible faculty.

- Describe the dismissal-for-cause process, including timelines.

- Evaluate the implementation and outcomes of these policies, procedures, and criteria at every level of review through periodic random audits of files, including the tally of votes at each level of review.

- Maintain data on attrition of tenure-track faculty by department or program.

Student Achievement

Greater openness, transparency, and accountability concerning student achievement would greatly strengthen public trust and confidence in higher education. As matters stand now, course grades and cumulative grade point averages (GPA) do not necessarily reflect the true quality of students' academic work.

Grade Inflation. Suspicions that course grades or cumulative grade point averages do not reflect consistent and objective standards of student performance are evident in the claims of widespread grade inflation in the popular press and trade journals alike.[33] Supporting these claims is a substantial body of research showing the upward pressure on grade distributions from the late 1960s to the present.[34] A straightforward definition of grade inflation is "an increase in grade point average without a concomitant increase in achievement."[35] This definition makes it clear that any claims about grade inflation must rule out the possibility that increases in grade point average are not the result of concomitant increases in achievement, such as might occur from changes in selectivity in admission policies. To address this issue, a 1981 study investigated the relationship of GPA to student achievement (as measured by students' SAT scores) between 1964 and 1978.[36] Results from this analysis found evidence of a steady increase in GPA from 1964 to 1974, with GPA remaining relatively stable during the next four years. In contrast, SAT scores generally declined over the same period of time after a spike in 1966. The authors conclude that the observed increase in GPA cannot be explained by a concomitant rise in student achievement and is therefore properly attributed to inflation. The authors are careful to note, however, that the unit of analysis in this study is not individual students. Rather, the results are based on a synthesis of studies of individual colleges that voluntarily participated in a predictive validity study of the SAT and freshman GPA (unweighted mean scores). Therefore, the authors urge caution in interpreting these results due to the differential participation of schools and the possibility that participants were not representative of the population at large.

Research using self-report questionnaires also finds evidence of increasing GPAs between the 1980s (1984–87) and 1990s (1995–97) across institutions and major fields of study.[37] Students also reported a decline in the number of hours devoted to schoolwork and in course learning effort. The increase in GPA coupled with the decline in student effort, and the positive correlation between effort and GPA, constitute another cluster of indicators for grade inflation. A breakout of the different types of institutions found that research universities and selective liberal arts colleges showed the largest increases in GPA, whereas general liberal arts colleges and comprehensive colleges and universities showed declines in GPA. Additionally, there was evidence of grade deflation in the humanities and social sciences. As with the majority of studies in this area, the authors urge caution in drawing firm conclusions about grade inflation due to methodological limitations. One serious limitation of this research is the use of self-reported GPA. A research synthesis involving forty-three studies, for example, found that the average correlation between actual and self-reported GPA was only .34.[38] A second limitation is that the study design is cross-sectional rather than longitudinal. That is, different groups of institutions, rather than the same institutions, were sampled at the two points in time.

A longitudinal analysis of the educational records (i.e., high school and postsecondary transcripts) from national samples of three cohorts of students, referred to as the high school classes of 1972 (N = 12,600), 1982 (N = 8,400), and 1992 (N = 8,900), provides one of the best estimates of changes in grade distributions for the period.[39] The GPA earned by all students for all postsecondary coursework completed is presented in figure 15-1, broken down by institutional selectivity. Three patterns are immediately clear. First, for each decade's cohort, GPA increases as a function of institutional selectivity: the more selective the institution, the higher the GPA. Second, there is pattern of grade deflation between the class of 1972 and the class of 1982. Third, there is a pattern of grade inflation between 1982 and 1992; however, the average GPA in 1972 and 1992 is approximately equal (3.03 *vs.* 3.07).

In sum, grade inflation may not be a universal phenomenon, but where it does exist, it is in itself destructive of academic standards—and hence a catalyst for public distrust of higher education. Where it exists, it evokes the intellectual weakness of the postmodern university, with its fey unwillingness to distinguish merit and its rejection of criteria for objective judgment as "logocentricity" (or the like). Grade inflation destroys challenge, which is one of the key motivations for continuous improvement and higher levels of achievement, and in this way it corrupts both students and faculty and harms the society that higher education is intended to serve.[40]

Given the interinstitutional and intrainstitutional variation in grading practices over time, it becomes even more important for each institution to

FIGURE 15-1

GRADE POINT AVERAGES BY COHORT AND SELECTIVITY OF INSTITUTION

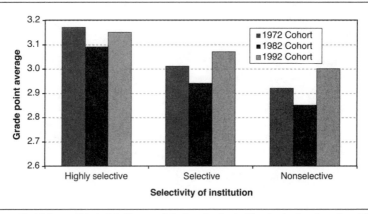

SOURCE: C. Adelman, *Principal Indicators of Student Academic Histories in Post-Secondary Education, 1972–2000*, Washington DC: U.S. Department of Education, Institute of Education Sciences, 2004.

be open, transparent, and accountable about grading practices at the institutional level and among the various academic units and levels of coursework. Institutions can publish grading policies in ways that reaffirm the commitment of the faculty to evaluate students' performance against the intellectual standards of the academic and professional disciplines. Moreover, we recommend reporting grade distributions and GPA at the same program level at which instructional costs and productivity are reported in the Delaware study described in the discussion of fiscal management. In this way, pockets of grade inflation in particular programs or schools cannot be hidden under an institutional average.

Assessment of Learning. As Alexander Astin writes, "An institution's assessment practices are a reflection of its values."[41]

A core curriculum is a ubiquitous feature of American higher education among degree-granting institutions. Institutions often describe their core curriculum as the cornerstone or foundation of the students' education, a means of preparing them to become productive citizens. In some schools, the requirements are constrained to a common set, or nearly common set, of courses, whereas other institutions specify core area requirements that may be fulfilled through a broad array of course offerings. At one end of the spectrum is the comprehensively prescribed course of study at St. John's College required of all students, and at the other end of the spectrum is the modern comprehensive research university, where a seemingly endless array of courses can satisfy the "core" requirements. In the case of the comprehensively prescribed course of study, there are likely to be more narrowly defined expectations about student achievement. In contrast, the core requirements of the comprehensive university may be fulfilled in many different ways. Nevertheless, there are expectations that students will acquire knowledge and skills in those domains. The core curriculum is the most significant requirement next to a student's major and represents a substantial investment of an institution's resources. Often, the core curriculum can amount to one-third of the credit hours required to fulfill requirements for the baccalaureate degree. Consider these statements about the goals of the general education curriculum, taken from the University of Colorado's 2007 course catalogue:

> These requirements are designed to assure that each student has attained a minimum level of competency in each of the areas listed: foreign language, quantitative reasoning and mathematical skills, written communication, and critical thinking.[42]
>
> Specifically, students will be able to read, write, listen and speak in a manner that demonstrates critical, analytical and creative thought.[43]

Although these statements about the purpose of the general education curriculum do not constitute a random sample, the reader will find that most schools use similar language, especially concerning the expectation that the curriculum will develop students' critical thinking and/or analytical reasoning skills. For example:

> These core requirements provide for breadth across the humanities and arts, social studies, biological sciences, and physical sciences; competence in communication, critical thinking and analytical skills appropriate for a university-educated person; and investigation of the issues raised by living in a culturally diverse society.[44]

Unfortunately, higher education has failed to produce a coherent body of evidence showing that it has achieved the noble goals articulated for the core curriculum. One survey of state accountability systems found twenty-eight states reporting a total of 218 indicators of learning.[45] A majority of the indicators (179) includes indirect measures of learning such as retention/graduation rates or self-reports of learning, whereas many fewer learning indicators (39) are direct measures of learning, such as achievement tests (Collegiate Assessment of Academic Progress), graduate school admissions tests (GRE, LSAT, MCAT), and licensure examinations (e.g., for teaching). By other accounts, only nine states present evidence that would enable comparison among states across a broad range of direct indicators of student learning.[46] Given what we know about grade inflation, faculty assurances that students' grades sufficiently measure their learning gains in the core skills are not likely to be viewed as adequate.

Amidst the cacophony of calls for assessment of student learning, it is hard to discern any coherent theoretical framework for measuring it. Thus, an important first step is to develop or adapt a framework to capture the range of knowledge, skills, and dispositions that are important to the institution, students, parents, policymakers, and society. Addressing the concerns of these different audiences is a difficult task. On one hand, the assessment framework must provide the kind of feedback that institutions can use to improve the quality of their academic programs. On the other hand, the assessment framework must provide the kind of information that enables students, parents, and policymakers to make comparisons among peer institutions. Implicit in the goal of providing feedback as means of improvement is an assessment framework that distinguishes between those abilities that can be affected by the collegiate experience and those that are influenced by processes not under the control of the students or the institution (e.g., heredity, experiences outside of school). One framework for understanding this distinction is adapted from Shavelson and Huang in figure 15-2.[47]

The cognitive abilities listed in figure 15-2 interact in complex ways through inherited characteristics and experiences inside and outside of educational settings. More important for this discussion is that the abilities on the left side of the diagram remain relatively stable over a broad range of attempts to modify them.[48] Thus, in designing assessments for collegiate learning, it is important to ask where along this continuum the abilities they

FIGURE 15-2

A SIMPLIFIED TAXONOMY OF COGNITIVE ABILITIES

Gradual <<<<<<< *Influence of education and experience* >>>>>> Rapid

General intelligence:	Broad reasoning abilities:	Problem solving, reasoning, and writing across domains:	Subject matter knowledge and skills:
Fluid	*Verbal*	*Humanities*	*World History*
Crystallized	*Quantitative*	*Social sciences*	*Physics*
	Spatial	*Science*	*Use of technology*
IQ tests	*Graduate Record Exam (GRE)*	*Collegiate Learning Assesment (CLA)*	*ETS field tests*

Broad <<<<<<<<<<<<<<<<< *Specificity of outcome* >>>>>>>>>>>>>>> Narrow

SOURCE: Adapted from Shavelson and Huang, "Responding Responsibly."

assess actually lie. As desirable as it may be to improve students' general intelligence and broad reasoning abilities, they are not likely to be affected within the time frame of postsecondary education, nor are any changes likely to be directly attributable to it. For the purposes of accountability, attention should be directed to direct measures of knowledge, skills, dispositions, and abilities that are modifiable through the college experience rather than simply being measures of students' native abilities brought to the experience.

The development of the knowledge and skills listed on the right-hand side of figure 15-2 is much more sensitive to postsecondary education experiences that are more within the control of the faculty, students, and administrators. Generally speaking, knowledge in these domains is the most easily identifiable component of the college curriculum. Also included in this category is the broad array of skills students are expected to acquire with regard to use of technology. These skills may range from the use of discipline-specific software for performing symbolic/numeric computations and visualization of functions in a calculus class, to use of standard office productivity software for composing reports and making presentations.

Assessment of students' mastery of these areas, particularly as they relate to the major and professional licensure programs, can provide useful information about the effectiveness of practices by academic programs across institutions. The usefulness depends on comparability of the assessment instruments, sampling methods, and students' general abilities when they enter the program. Where there are differences in selectivity, it is possible to hold constant differences in students' precollegiate abilities. That is, the most effective programs are not necessarily those whose students earn the highest scores, but the programs whose students perform better than expected on the basis of their precollegiate abilities. In essence, we want to know what value is added by a collegiate experience. Licensure test score results, such as an institution's pass rate on the CPA exam, obviously matter. From the standpoint of comparing institutions, however, it would be important to examine pass rates based on students' characteristics upon entering the institution. This approach allows the possibility of identifying less selective institutions that may have a higher pass rate than expected based on their students' entering characteristics, and that may thus be considered more effective than a much more selective institution whose students perform only as well as expected.[49] We will discuss the value-added approach to assessment further below.

Development of the knowledge, skills, and dispositions to comprehend prose across a variety of domains, to reason and to solve novel problems involving multiple domains, and to communicate the outcome of those processes in writing is a ubiquitous goal of higher education. The framework in figure 15-2 identifies these skills as broader and developing more slowly than the development of specific subject-matter expertise. These skills are also likely to be influenced by processes external to postsecondary education experiences. Nonetheless, the development of these abilities is often the crux of the goals of higher education, and there is some evidence that U.S. colleges and universities may not be achieving these goals. The 2003 National Assessment of Adult Literacy (NAAL) reports that the average score in prose literacy for a baccalaureate graduate is in the intermediate, not proficient, range: the 2003 average of 314 out of 500 points was also eleven points lower than the average of a similar survey in 1992. A person with intermediate-level skills in prose literacy would typically be unable to "compare viewpoints in two editorials with contrasting interpretations of scientific and economic evidence" or "evaluate information to determine which legal document is applicable to a specific healthcare situation."[50] Results for quantitative and documentary literacy were similarly lackluster: average scores for baccalaureate graduates were in the intermediate range, and persons with skills at that level would typically not be capable of "interpreting a table about blood pressure, age, and physical activity" or "computing and comparing the cost per ounce of food items."[51]

There are some promising approaches to assessment in this area; however, we do not recommend specific instruments. The Collegiate Learning Assessment (CLA), for example, lends itself to large-scale implementation, although it may not be appropriate for every type of institution. It does not use multiple-choice items, but rather relies on performance-based tasks that require use of resources one would normally have access to in the real world. In addition, there are two realistic analytic writing tasks. One probe requires students to critique an argument and the other probe requires students to construct an argument. Similar to the NSSE, it takes the institution as the unit of analysis rather than the individual, although a longitudinal study of students is an option of the CLA. The assessment is typically administered to a cohort of freshmen and a cohort of seniors and thereby provides an indication of the value that is added by the institution to the development of the knowledge, skills, and dispositions assessed by the CLA. This is a powerful tool for colleges and universities, enabling them to measure the effectiveness of their investment in the core curriculum and general collegiate-level skills.

The secretary of education should continue to encourage U.S. colleges and universities to be open about their goals for students, transparent in their measurement and assessment of those goals, and accountable for progress toward meeting the goals. Otherwise, a public accustomed to large-scale clinical trials and to a heavily accountable and transparent K–12 system will be increasingly impatient with what it perceives to be higher education's evasiveness. In an era when public elementary and secondary schools must publish data concerning their teaching force and student achievement tests, colleges and universities cannot continue to assert that the individual judgment of faculty in their classrooms is adequate assurance of the acquisition of core skills.

The federal government will need to develop careful procedures that ensure accurate, good-faith reporting of results. The experience of a very worthy attempt to create transparent reporting of the quality of teacher education programs stands as a warning that institutions—and indeed state agencies—can be highly evasive in approaching such requirements. The

Education Trust's study of the quality of teacher preparation indicated that many institutions and some state licensure bureaus sidestepped the law's requirement to disclose the pass rates on teacher licensure exams by reporting the results only for "program completers," whom they defined as those who have completed all requirements, including passing the licensure exam. The report observed: "Reporting pass rates in these circumstances reveals nothing about how many aspiring graduates took the test but failed. As a result, the burden of accountability shifts away from the institution."[52] (The Higher Education Opportunity Act of 2008 has now closed this reporting loophole.)

Conclusion

Although the United States has a system of higher education that has been the envy of the world, public support for institutions of higher learning is eroding. These institutions can restore the public's trust by measures entirely within their own tradition of academic freedom, the pursuit of truth, and scientific measurement and analysis. Colleges and universities must make meaningful data available to the federal government so that the taxpayers who pay for these institutions have access to the facts about them. There is everything to gain, and nothing to lose, by confronting the complex challenges that come with a commitment to openness, transparency, and accountability.

Notes

1. John Immerwahr and Jean Johnson, *Squeeze Play: How Parents and the Public Look at Higher Education Today*, National Center for Public Policy and Higher Education, May 2007, report #07-4, http://www.highereducation.org/reports/squeeze_play/index.html.

2. The authors of this chapter have firsthand experience of this crisis: former senator Hank Brown is the immediate past president of the University of Colorado; John B. Cooney is associate vice president of adminstration at the University of Colorado and professor emeritus of the University of Northern Colorado; and Michael B. Poliakoff is the vice president for academic affairs and research at the Unversity of Colorado.

3. Integrated Postsecondary Education Data System, http://nces.ed.gov/IPEDS/about/.

4. Michael. F. Middaugh, *Understanding Faculty Productivity: Standards and Benchmarks for Colleges and Universities* (San Francisco: Jossey-Bass, 2001).

5. Donald Kagan, "As Goes Harvard . . . ," *Commentary*, September 2006, 37.

6. Boyer Commission on Educating Undergraduates in the Research University, *Reinventing Undergraduate Education: A Blueprint for America's Research Universities* (Stony Brook, NY: State University of New York, 1998). See also Clark Kerr, *Troubled Times for American Higher Education: The 1990s and Beyond* (New York: State University of New York Press, 1994).

7. U.S. Department of Education, National Center for Education Statistics, *Teaching Undergraduates in U.S. Postsecondary Institutions: Fall 1998* (NCES 2002–209) (Washington, DC: U.S. Department of Education, 2002), http://nces.ed.gov/pubs2000/2000186.pdf.

8. See Paul. T. Brinkman and Deborah. J. Teeter, "Methods for Selecting Comparison Groups," *New Directions for Institutional Research* 14, no. 53 (1987): 5–23; Paul T. Brinkman, "Effective Inter-institutional Comparisons," *New Directions for Institutional Research* 14, no. 53 (1987): 103–8.

9. See Kevin Carey, *College Rankings Reformed: The Case for a New Order in Higher Education* (Washington, DC: Education Sector, 2006), http://www.educationsector.org/usr_doc/CollegeRankingsReformed.pdf.

10. Neil Gross and Solon Simmons, "The Social and Political Views of American Professors" (paper presented at the Harvard University Symposium on Professors and Their Politics, Cambridge, MA, October 6, 2007).

11. John D. Gartner, "Antireligious Prejudice in Admissions to Doctoral Programs in Clinical Psychology," *Professional Psychology: Research and Practice* 17 (1986): 473–75.

12. See Raymond S. Nickerson, "Confirmation Bias: A Ubiquitous Phenomenon in Many Guises," *Review of General Psychology* 2, no. 2 (1998): 175–220.

13. Drew Westen, Pavel Blagov, Keith Harenski, Clint Kilts, and Stephen Hamann, "The Neural Basis of Motivated Reasoning: An fMRI Study of Emotional Constraints on Political Judgment during the U.S. Presidential Election of 2004," *Journal of Cognitive Neuroscience* 18 (2006): 1947–58.

14. Richard E. Redding, "Sociopolitical Diversity in Psychology: The Case for Pluralism," *American Psychologist* 56, no. 3 (2001): 205–15.

15. Nickerson, "Confirmation Bias," 211.

16. Baruch Fischhoff, "Debiasing," in *Judgment under Uncertainty: Heuristics and Biases*, ed. Daniel Kahneman, Paul Slovic, and Amos Tversky (Cambridge: Cambridge University Press, 1982), 422–44.

17. Paul E. Tetlock and Jae I. Kim, "Accountability and Judgment Processes in a Personality Prediction Task," *Journal of Personality and Social Psychology* 52 (1987): 700–9.

18. See Deiter Frey and Stefan Schulz-Hardt, "Confirmation Bias in Group Information Seeking and Its Implications for Decision Making in Administration, Business and Politics," in *Social Influence in Social Reality: Promoting Individual and Social Change*, ed. Fabrizio Butera and Gabriel Mugny (Ashland, OH: Hogrefe and Huber Publishers, 2001), 53–73; Lyn M. Van Swol, "Perceived Importance of Information: The Effects of Mentioning Information, Shared Information Bias, Ownership Bias, Reiteration, and Confirmation Bias," *Group Processes & Intergroup Relations* 10, no. 2 (2007): 239–56.

19. Jonathan A. Fugelsang, Courtney B. Stein, Adam E. Green, and Kevin N. Dunbar, "Theory and Data Interactions of the Scientific Mind: Evidence from the Molecular and the Cognitive Laboratory," *Canadian Journal of Experimental Psychology* 58, no. 2 (2004): 86–95.

20. Charles G. Lord, Mark R. Lepper, and Elizabeth Preston, "Considering the Opposite: A Corrective Strategy for Social Judgment," *Journal of Personality and Social Psychology* 47 (1984): 1231–43.

21. Ibid., 1233.

22. Peter R. Furlong, "Personal Factors Influencing Informal Reasoning of Economic Issues and the Effect of Specific Instructions," *Journal of Educational Psychology*, 85, no. 1 (1993): 171–81.

23. See, for example, Diane F. Halpern and Heidi Riggio, *Thinking Critically about Critical Thinking*, 4th ed. (Mahwah, NJ: Lawrence Erlbaum Associates, 2003). This text includes a separate instructor's manual.

24. American Council of Trustees and Alumni, *Politics in the Classroom: A Survey of Students at the Top 50 Colleges and Universities* (Washington, DC: American Council of Trustees and Alumni, 2004).

25. *NSSE 2007: National Benchmarks of Effective Educational Practice* (Bloomington: Indiana University Center for Postsecondary Research and Planning, 2007).

26. American Council of Trustees and Alumni, *Politics in the Classroom*, 11–18.

27. See Hank Brown, "Tenure Reform: The Time Has Come," *Inside Higher Ed*, March 26, 2007, http://www.insidehighered.com/views/2007/03/26/brown.

28. Neil Gross and Solon Simmons, "Americans' Views of Political Bias in the Academy and Academic Freedom" (working paper, May 2006), http://www.aaup.org/NR/rdonlyres/DCF3EBD7-509E-47AB-9AB3-FBCFFF5CA9C3/0/2006Gross.pdf.

29. Maragret A. Miller, "State-Level Post-Tenure Review Policies," *Innovative Higher Education* 24, no. 1 (2004): 17–24.

30. Brown, "Tenure Reform."

31. See *Independent Report on Tenure-Related Processes at the University of Colorado*, 2006, https://www.cu.edu/tenurereview/docs/Report-Final.pdf.

32. Brown, "Tenure Reform."

33. Harvey C. Mansfield, "Grade Inflation: It's Time to Face the Facts," *Chronicle of Higher Education*, April 6, 2001, B24; "Ivy League Grade Inflation," *USA Today*, February 7, 2002, http://www.usatoday.com/news/opinion/2002/02/08/edtwof2.htm; Daniel Pedersen, "When an A Is Average" *Newsweek*, March 3, 1997, 64; William M. Abbott, "The Politics of Grade Inflation: A Case Study," *Change* 40, no. 1 (2008): 32–38.

34. James E. Prather, Glynton Smith, and Janet E. Kodras, "A Longitudinal Study of Grades in 144 Undergraduate Courses," *Research in Higher Education* 10, no. 1 (1979): 11–24; Richard M. Summerville, Dennis R. Ridley, and Terry L. Maris, "Grade Inflation: The Case of Urban Colleges and Universities," *College Teaching* 38, no. 1 (1990): 33–38; Jack R. Wegman, "An Economic Analysis of Grade Inflation Using Indexing," *College and University* (Winter 1987): 137–46; Stuart Rojstaczer, "National Trends in Grade Inflation, American Colleges and Universities," http://gradeinflation.com/.

35. Isaac I. Bejar and Edwin O. Blew, "Grade Inflation and the Validity of the Scholastic Aptitude Test," *American Educational Research Journal* 18, no. 2 (1981): 143

36. Ibid., 143–56.

37. George D. Kuh and S. Shouping Hu, "Unraveling the Complexity of the Increase in College Grades from the Mid-1980s to the Mid-1990s," *Educational Evaluation and Policy Analysis* 21, no. 3 (1999): 297–320.

38. B. C. Hansford and John A. Hattie, "The Relationship between Self and Achievement Performance Measures," *Review of Educational Research* 52 (1982): 123–42.

39. Clifford Adelman, *Principal Indicators of Student Academic Histories in Post-Secondary Education, 1972–2000* (Washington DC: Department of Education, Institute of Education Sciences, 2004).

40. Hank Brown, "Grade Inflation Is Real and Growing," *Denver Post*, December 2, 2001.

41. Alexander W. Astin, *Assessment for Excellence: The Philosophy and Practice of Assessment and Evaluation in Higher Education* (New York: Macmillan, 1991), 3.

42. *University of Colorado at Boulder 2007 Catalog*, http://www.colorado.edu/catalog/catalog07-08/index.pl?s=2-6-4-2.

43. *University of Colorado at Colorado Springs 2007 Catalog*, http://www.uccs.edu/~pubs/bulletin07_08/General%20Info.pdf.

44. *University of Wisconsin–Madison 2007-2009 Undergraduate Catalog*, http://www.wisc.edu/pubs/ug/study.html#ger.

45. Blake A. Naughton, Anita Y. Suen, and Richard J. Shavelson, "Accountable for What? Understanding the Learning Objectives in State Higher Education Accountability Programs" (paper presented at the annual meeting of the American Educational Research Association, Chicago, April 21–25, 2003).

46. *Measuring Up 2006: The National Report Card on Higher Education* (Washington, DC: The National Center for Public Policy and Higher Education, 2006).

47. Richard J. Shavelson and Leta Huang, "Responding Responsibly to the Frenzy to Assess Learning in Higher Education," *Change* (January/February 2003): 11–19.

48. Douglas K. Detterman and Robert J. Stemberg, eds., *How and How Much Can Intelligence Be Increased?* (Norwood, NJ: Ablex, 1982).

49. Astin, *Assessment for Excellence*.

50. Mark Kutner, Elizabeth Greenberg, Ying Jin, Bridget Boyle, Yung-chen Hsu, and Eric Dunleavy, *Literacy in Everyday Life: Results from the 2003 National Assessment of Adult Literacy* (Washington, DC: U.S. Department of Education, National Center for Education Statistics, 2007): 3–6, http://nces.ed.gov/Pubs2007/2007480.pdf.

51. National Center for Education Statistics, *A First Look at the Literacy of America's Adults in the 21st Century*, NCES 2006-470, December 2005, http://nces.ed.gov/NAAL/PDF/2006470_1.PDF.

52. Sandra Huang, Yun Yi, and Kati Haycock, *Interpret with Caution: The First State Title II Reports on the Quality of Teacher Preparation* (Washington, DC: Education Trust, 2002), 6–8.

16

To Reform the Politically Correct University, Reform the Liberal Arts

John Agresto

I don't doubt for a moment that our universities and our teaching have become thoroughly politicized—and probably in far deeper ways than are suggested by the egregious examples that pop up every week in the journals and newsletters of the anti-PC stalwarts.

Still, there's something a little bit odd about the picture of our current politicization: it virtually all takes place in the liberal arts, and primarily in the humanities segment of the liberal arts. I know that statement is overbroad: what about the daily indoctrination we find in schools of education and social work, for example, or in departments, like geography, that are only tangentially related to the liberal arts? I'm in no position to deny these claims. Still, when we in and out of the academy complain that our students are being indoctrinated rather than educated, our main examples all seem to come from areas like literature or history or classics or philosophy, and rarely from engineering or the mechanical arts. Or even, let me venture, from the plastic and fine arts, at least not to the extent we all see every day in English departments or, God help us, in the various subdepartmental "studies"—women's, gay, Chicano, and so on.

Parents and students all understand this in an almost intuitive way. We used to bemoan the existence of the "Two Cultures" in the academy—how the sciences looked down on the humanities, how the humanities couldn't speak the language of the hard sciences, and how neither could really understand the other—though none of this stopped them from being suspicious of each other or even holding each other in contempt.

Now we seem to have a different two cultures around us—American citizens, ordinary people and their children on one hand, and the academic elites, especially the liberal arts elites, on the other. One side often thinks the other effete, useless, smug, and vaguely un-American. The other sometimes holds the great mass of more ordinary folk to be, well, crass, materialistic, jingoistic, benighted, shallow, ignorant, red-necked, homophobic, racist, sexist, reactionary . . . .

Legions of academicians will now jump to the defense of their trade and tell me that they think no such thing; or if they think it they don't say it; or if they say it, well, hell, it's true, isn't it? In any event, I'm only talking now about perceptions, not reality; and the perception on the part of the crass and materialistic is that if they want to be browbeaten by someone's political opinions, they'll watch the Sunday talk shows, thank you very much, and spend their tuition money on something that will give them a reasonable return on their investment, like electrical engineering, pre-med, or business administration. Today 47 percent of all students in higher education have opted to attend their local community college for two years, and the great majority of these do so without plans to parlay this diploma into a four-year liberal arts degree. Yet, oddly, one hears very little about the politicization of professional or vocational education. On the other hand, while community colleges and technical and vocational education flourish, Antioch has closed its doors.

One strange part of all this is that while there are accountants and electricians at community colleges and teaching scientists and mathematicians in our universities who hold very strong political views and social opinions, these views and opinions seem only rarely to lend themselves to classroom proselytizing or political indoctrination.

So, what is it about the liberal arts rather than more professional, vocational, or technical fields that they offer themselves as the handmaidens of indoctrination, and why the humanities more than math or science?[1] It's not actually that hard a question, though the remedies to overcome indoctrination in the liberal arts classroom might turn out to be more difficult than we had hoped.

But, first, let's put aside the notion that "relativism" has captured the spirit of higher education and is the cause of all our grief. I never met a relativist in academe in all my life, at least not in the humanities and social sciences. In fact, those most bent on proselytizing their students are always the farthest from relativism that one can find. They know what is true and what is false, what is just and unjust, good and bad, and if they have their way, their students will soon know it, too. Proselytizing is, in a way, their "job." Oddly enough, as I'll explain later, any practicing relativists left in the universities are to be found on the libertarian right, among the most vociferous critics of PC, rather than on the left.

Let me say something that might seem vaguely exculpatory about the politicizers and indoctrinators I've met in our colleges, though I don't mean it that way: there actually may be something in the nature of the liberal arts that invites their misbehavior.

First, there are lots of ways of looking at the liberal arts. Some understandings have a more antique sound, some more contemporary. Some seem a bit banal, as when we talk of the liberal arts as those studies that make our students "well rounded." Some don't seem to get us all that far, as when we describe the liberal arts as a collection of disciplines or fields, such as philosophy or literature, or the old *trivium-quadrivium* list.

What, we might then ask, sets these disciplines apart; what makes them "liberal"? It is said that a liberal study is one with no professional or pecuniary aim. Thus, the study of nursing is a nonliberal art, a "servile" art (as the snooty might allow), since people do pay for its application, thinking, quite rightly, that it might have some real and practical value. The study of Restoration poetry then becomes a liberal art, since no one would pay all that much for your knowledge of it.

Abstracting from this idea of separating knowledge from labor, we are also told that the liberal arts are those studies that are fit for free men and women. Or, as we are more likely to say these days, they are those studies that help *make* us free. When asked, "In what sense do they make us free?" we sometimes hear, "Well, they free us from the opinions of others and help us come into the possession of our own minds." The liberal arts bring us out of the cave of mere opinion—out of the cave of the myths handed down by our poets, priests, and parents—and help us approach the light of the sun, the light of things as they actually are, not as mere opinion holds them to be. That, to be sure, is an answer at a very high level. It may also, as I will suggest, have in it an insight into the problem we're facing.

A second definition or perspective on the meaning of the liberal arts, one that builds on the cave-sun understanding, one that I believe is also true, but that also has within it a political problem, is this: *The liberal arts are those studies that help us discover the truth about the most important human matters through reason and reflection.* To say we learn these matters through reason and reflection means we don't learn them through authority or revelation. More importantly, this understanding of the liberal arts directs our attention to the idea that what we are about in the liberal arts isn't some kind of adornment, isn't the acquisition of a veneer of culture or refinement, but the study of the most important issues facing us as human beings: What is justice? What's the relation of power to justice? How should I live? How should *we* live? What is beautiful and why? Is the universe a cosmos or is it something more random? What is love? What should I love? What should I hate? Does God exist, and what does he ask of me? No one could reasonably deny that these and scores of other similar questions concern the most important matters of human life. Finally, this understanding says to us that the liberal arts aim at knowing the truth about these matters. Not just a catalogue of different nice opinions on these matters but the actual Truth about them, as best we humans might come to discern the truth.

Despite the push-back I get from academics across the political spectrum when I mention this—since there's often a feeling that I am trying in some underhanded way to impose on them my own view of what's true and what's not—the fact is that most professors who politicize their classrooms have a sense that this definition is not far off the mark. Hardly relativists, they entered the profession in the first place because they already saw themselves as having a certain handle on the truth and wanted to promote their vision of it to the next generation and all succeeding generations of students.

To use the classroom to propagandize for your own views of right or social justice or faith is, of course, a highly partial understanding of what liberal arts instruction might be. It overlooks the notion that the liberal arts promise a *search* for the truth; it hardly validates the imposition of a professor's particular understanding. The liberal arts are, moreover, *arts*, involving the acquisition of skills, the acquisition of various habits and facilities of mind, all in the service of more serious and substantive learning. These arts are hardly promoted by our being asked to prattle back particular answers suggested, promoted, or imposed by one's professor.

Notice, of course, that these are equal-opportunity rules, rules that apply alike to all parts of the political spectrum. The religious sectarian committed to showing his students in Western Civ that everything done since the Enlightenment has been little more than a diabolical plot trying to separate men from their Creator is no less illiberal, no less political and politicized, than the shrill feminist out to prove that the history of the West is little more than the history of male hegemony and power, or the sexual enslavement of women.

While it is tempting to give a fuller catalogue of all the horrors perpetrated these days in the name of liberal education, I don't think I can even begin. Sorry to say, while the varieties of truth may be limited, the varieties of error and ideology are infinite. Worse, while the most egregious examples make the headlines, the situation is significantly more serious than even these imply because of the subtler politicization that imbues so many courses, often without the professor, much less the students, seeing it. In some places, a Marxist or feminist analysis just seems natural. That's the way the professor was taught in graduate school, that's what he thinks constitutes analysis, and that's the basis on which he constructs his syllabus. He doesn't see it as political, because he thinks that way of looking at the material is what professors *do*. Truly to begin to break the back of the PC university would involve reforming graduate education, reforming the nature of the PhD, and breaking the nexus between "cutting-edge scholarship" and earning a doctorate. Yet hardly any of the foes of political correctness seem prepared to talk about this.[2]

Yet even though the varieties of doctrine might be myriad, and even if most are unconventional, even inane and false, it is precisely because they seem so eminently true and reasonable to the one professing them—and present themselves as truths concerning the most important human matters!—that such politicizing finds a ready home in the liberal arts. If the liberal arts purport to help us understand the truth about the most important human matters, well then, the indoctrinator says, I have exactly what you've been looking for! Indeed, the reason I became a teacher, he or she might say, was so I could bring the truth to the great unwashed.

Thus, we should not be surprised when every rag-tag opinion that thinks itself true, and every ideologue who sees himself with a calling to teach everyone what he knows, comes knocking at the door of the liberal arts. It doesn't mean we shouldn't be distressed. It doesn't mean we shouldn't mightily resist. But it does mean we shouldn't be surprised.

There are, of course, those who look in horror at this anti-intellectual browbeating of students and at the constant barrage of accusations, fulminations, and even reeducation classes designed to suppress opposition and lead students and recalcitrant faculty to a new "belief." Those who point out these horrors are among our finest professors, though, sadly, sometimes they find themselves outside the academy, looking in. Still, I've noticed that sometimes their answers are incommensurate with the problem. And some of their answers I find unhelpful. Here's where that ol' debbil "relativism" often starts to creeps in.

The problem is, we are told, that when we put our emphasis on finding the "truth," we let all kinds of ideologues, dogmatists, authoritarians, and totalitarians, not to mention outright nut-jobs, into the profession. Once we place our emphasis on truth, we are told, we should not be surprised that ideologues find a ready home in the liberal arts. Better we should put the emphasis on liberty, on freedom, on fairly absolute freedom not only of inquiry but of expression. Emphasize freedom, cultivate liberty; but deemphasize truth, for the toll keepers on the way to truth are the dogmatists. Besides, in making freedom, not truth, the core of our educational experience, it might well then turn out that real truth will ultimately win out, given the marketplace of ideas.[3]

Well, perhaps. Though the belief that truth will win out given a free market of ideas might itself be merely a conventional opinion, a nice hope, a dogma. For truth actually to win out might require an atmosphere of civility, rules, ordered study, requirements, and self-restraint. It might require the acceptance of certain conventions—for example, that reason is superior to intuition or feeling if one is truly to know—even though such conventions might ultimately be questioned. In any event, while it seems fairly clear that the truth, if approached, will make us free—that is, free from false beliefs and mere opinion—it's not so certain that freedom will, in itself, make us wise.

All this is to say that we have a problem. We should not wish to abandon the search for truth, for wisdom, for solid knowledge of the most important human things, as the very basis of the liberal arts, even though we know that such a project seems an open invitation to proselytizers and dogmatists. Nor can we easily say that only those who are merely open, who profess nothing but ignorance, are fit teachers of the liberal arts. Some things are seemingly closed, and properly so, at least as starting points for our inquiry—for example, that incivility will not be tolerated in class, that plagiarism is theft and theft is wrong, that argument is superior to assertion, that opinion is inferior to knowledge, and that reason trumps emotion.

Still, in asserting that a truly liberal education concentrates on knowledge of the most important human things, we have probably already made assumptions that are ineluctably political. "Your 'important questions' are not necessarily *my* important questions," we are told. "Your ordering of what's important already involves an implicit judgment of what's better and what's worse, of what's worthy of study and what's peripheral, and is therefore *intrinsically* political. When you say it's more important to examine Shakespeare's view of the best social order rather than homoerotic themes in Julius Caesar, you've made a *political* decision." It may be that Socrates claimed he knew nothing, but we are always left with the impression, first, that he really had some inklings of what was true and what was false, and, second, in the questions he both asked and didn't ask, he had more than just a hunch about what was better and what was worse. Liberal education is, *per necessitate*, much like that.

Still, to say that there is an inherent and necessary bias in the liberal arts regarding the centrality of truth and its superiority over opinion does not excuse professorial indoctrination of students nor, perhaps above all, does it ever excuse silencing serious thoughts or arguments because they're at variance with an instructor's cherished views. To say that the liberal arts contain within them the search for the truth about the most important human matters may help explain why professors are often tempted to impose their views on students, but it does not forgive it.

I would hardly want to break the connection between the liberal arts and the pursuit of truth simply because it lends itself to corruption by those who prefer to proselytize rather than to teach. To unmoor liberal learning from the search for truth would be to make it frivolous and unimportant. At the same time, if the connection of the liberal arts at their best with truth is seemingly unavoidable despite all the troubles it brings, the connection of the liberal arts with questioning, with criticism, might well bear some salutary rethinking.

I said earlier that the liberal arts bring us out of the cave of mere opinion—out of the cave of the myths handed down by our poets, priests, and parents—and help us approach the light of the sun, the light of things as they actually are, not as mere opinion holds them to be. Who among us has not used these or similar words when describing the workings of the liberal arts? The liberal arts teach us to put all ideas to the test. The liberal arts call our traditions, our religion, our country, and our most cherished beliefs into account. "You will," I have told incoming freshmen any number of times, "have your values questioned, your beliefs criticized, and your minds changed repeatedly over the next four years." Yes, I have said such things, and I now repent of my having said them.

In saying that we in the liberal arts are essentially critics, essentially challengers and questioners, we begin the shallow activity of puffing ourselves up. We think to ourselves, we surely aren't Socrates, but if we teach our students to challenge everything, maybe we're on the way towards being a pretty fair imitation. We no longer promise to help answer all questions—we now proclaim it our job to question all answers. Insofar as that becomes apparent, is it any wonder that so many decent people look askance at our trade: I should pay all that money just to have my most cherished beliefs undermined, my faith cast into doubt, and my parents and country undermined? I don't think so.

Still, we persist. In order to reach the truth about the most important things, we professors pronounce that we must encourage *critical* intelligence. We think questioning, criticizing, undermining, have become our sacred duty. After all, didn't Socrates go around showing people how little they knew, pointing out the weakness in their thoughts, making a fool of everyone he met, all the better to prepare us to leave the cave of opinion and enter the light of truth? Aren't we to be like him?

Well, aside from the fact that most professors rarely turn their criticism on their own cherished orthodoxies, this is a partial and self-serving view of the Socratic enterprise. To take Socrates at his word, the reason he would question men was *to find out what they knew.* It was the search for knowledge, not particularly the desire to undermine, that animated the questioning. To be certain, most of the people Socrates spoke with very often did not know all they claimed to know. Their notions of justice, piety, and ethics were almost always partial or contradictory. But it was not radical doubt that pushed Socrates but, rather, a desire to find out what people actually did know and could defend. Socrates is not Descartes.

What this means is that we who profess the liberal arts have one of the hardest but perhaps most noble of jobs—we cannot be content with being critics, we have to be searchers after the truth. Our job is not to point and ridicule or snicker but to try to understand, to try to *learn* and to *know*. Yes, Jefferson wrote that all men were created equal and, yes, Jefferson owned slaves. But what can we learn from that? Shall we read Jefferson with even greater care to see why this was so, or will we be content simply to be critical or smug? Shall we start to understand the complex political and even spiritual problem Jefferson forced himself to face when he refused to hide the fact that there were certain self-evident truths that called into question his own actions? Or is labeling Jefferson a racist good enough? Shall we try to understand what Genesis is trying to teach, or will we be happier trying to undermine our students' religious beliefs by saying that everyone knows such writings are just myths or fables?[4]

Let me try to offer a small antidote to at least some of the varieties of indoctrination in our classrooms: Let's go back to an older understanding of the liberal arts as the home not of sophistication but of naiveté. Let us again see the liberal project as an attempt to draw from books and ideas and statesmen and philosophers all the wisdom they might offer. If we wish to be like Socrates and question everyone, let us at least be open to the answers they might give. Let us, if we see something contrary to our sensibilities, *ask why someone might hold such a view.*

Yes, Socrates questioned everybody, and this attitude of questioning seems to be so ingrained in the soul of the liberal arts that it seems almost to define their very core—question everything, dispute everything, deflate everything, perhaps even degrade everything. Begin with radical doubt and see what ideas and institutions are left standing after you've called them into account. Church, family, government, charity . . . question them all. Then perhaps one's own views will shine.

But there's another part of Socrates that begins not with doubt but with wondering, with marveling. In what I think should become the paradigmatic metaphor for liberal education, those who leave the cave of ignorance and mere opinion and see objects as they are in the light of day are not cynics but wonderers, marvellers. They marvel at seeing things clearly, and for the first time. There's a joy of discovery in this education, not the sadness of constant skepticism.[5] There's a real happiness that no other earthly creature seems able to have, of knowing how things work, and why they work, and the reasons and arguments behind things.

I realize in saying this that I am saying something considerably more fundamental, perhaps more radical, than most of the other fine essayists in this volume. I do not believe that the depoliticization of our universities will come about by hiring more "conservatives" or by demanding intellectual diversity or trying to counteract some political views with others. Maybe, especially in some of the social sciences, making sure students see the full array of opinions on a topic is appropriate and sufficient. But the liberal arts in general, including the sciences and mathematics, are not really collections of variant opinions, but something far more subtle and grand. They are an attempt to reason our way, with our students, to a better and clearer understanding of what's beautiful, what's ennobling, and what might be actual or true or just or right. This undertaking has to do with reason and insight, not assertion or opinion.

This perspective not only makes this essay more radical: it also, given the degraded character of contemporary higher education, makes the solution more difficult, perhaps in some places impossible. Still, even if unattainable, what it asks for is simple: Let us begin again to look at the world of learning with a kind of openness and wonder. Let us see what we can discover rather than what we can impose or exclude. In so doing, we will find arguments where others might only see excuses. We will see reasons where others see only rationalizations. We might soon see the reasons for things, see the ideas behind things, see the complexity of humans and the universe, and see the limits and limitations of things. And we can do it by being open to arguments and following things through to their conclusions, and always asking important questions, not small ones.

None of this will change the mind of even one professor who thinks that deconstructing literature, debunking history, or dethroning all idols but his own is what his job is all about. But at least we can tell students that those professors who think that their views are wisdom itself are the enemies of their education. We can tell students that the purpose of a real education is to have them marvel at things they never saw before, perhaps come to a better and surer understanding of beliefs they already hold, and learn better how to think, analyze, and weigh evidence so as to come into the possession of their own minds. And tell them that those who would have them do otherwise are not true teachers but frauds, charlatans, and crooks. Or tell them that we would say this, except that the thought police won't allow it.

Notes

1. To be sure, the new Religion of Global Warming has had some effect in some science departments; but my guess is that even this issue is handled in a more rational and evaluative way in the sciences than in the more politicized, mocking, and self-righteous atmosphere of the humanities. Along these same lines, please note Steve Balch's remarks in this volume on the greater politicization of the humanities over the sciences.

2. See John Agresto, "Narrowness and Liberality," *Academic Questions* 17 (Winter 2003–4): 83–86, for an attempt to begin a discussion of graduate school and PhD reform.

3. Perhaps the best contemporary expression of this position is Alan Charles Kors and Harvey A. Silverglate, *The Shadow University: The Betrayal of Liberty on America's Campuses* (Free Press, 1998). But see John Agresto, "Truth v. Liberty: A Confusion of Priorities," *Academic Questions* 12 (Summer 1999): 16–20, with a rejoinder by Kors and Silverglate, 30–35.

4. In a slightly different vein, my friend Jon Moline once noted that maybe it was true that all great people had feet of clay, but that was no reason why all professors had to be foot fetishists.

5. See Josef Pieper, "The Philosophic Act," in *Leisure: The Basis of Culture*, trans. Gerard Malsbary (1948; South Bend, IN: St. Augustine's Press, 1998).

Index

About the Authors

John Agresto was most recently a visiting fellow at the Madison Program in American Ideals and Institutions at Princeton University, where he was writing a book on liberal education. Prior to this, he was provost and acting chancellor at the new American University of Iraq in Sulaimani, which he helped found. In 2004, he returned from Iraq, where he had served as the senior advisor for higher education and scientific research for the Coalition Provisional Authority. Before going to Iraq, he was, for eleven years, president of St. John's College in Santa Fe. Mr. Agresto has taught at the University of Toronto, Kenyon College, Duke University and the New School University, and, in 2002–3, was Lily Senior Research Fellow at Wabash College. In the 1980s, Mr. Agresto served as both administrative and policy head of the National Endowment for the Humanities. Widely published in the areas of politics, law, and education, Mr. Agresto is the author or editor of a number of books, including *Mugged by Reality: The Liberation of Iraq and the Failure of Good Intentions*; *The Supreme Court and Constitutional Democracy*; and *The Humanist as Citizen: Essays on the Uses of the Humanities*.

Stephen H. Balch is founder and chairman of the National Association of Scholars, America's largest and most active membership organization of scholars committed to higher education reform. He was a member of the government faculty at John Jay College of Criminal Justice of the City University of New York for fourteen years. He is a member of the board of directors of the American Council of Trustees and Alumni and has played a central role in the founding of four other higher education reform organizations. Mr. Balch is the author of a variety of articles on reopening the campus marketplace of ideas and is a leader in the national movement to foster greater intellectual pluralism through the creation of new academic programs. In 2007 he received the National Humanities Medal from President George W. Bush.

Hank Brown joined the political science department at the University of Colorado, Boulder in fall 2008 as a full professor and as the first holder of the Quigg and Virginia S. Newton Endowed Chair in Leadership. Prior to joining the department, he served as president of the University of Colorado system from 2005–8. He has served as the president and CEO of the Daniels Fund, president of the University of Northern Colorado, U.S. Senator from Colorado, member of the U.S. House of Representatives for Colorado's 4th Congressional District, and state senator. He has also served as vice president of Montfort of Colorado. He is an attorney, with degrees from the University of Colorado Law School and George Washington University Law School. He served in the U.S. Navy from 1962–66 and was decorated for his combat service in Vietnam as a forward air controller. He is also a CPA, having graduated with a degree in accounting from the University of Colorado, Boulder in 1961.

Paul A. Cantor is the Clifton Waller Barrett Professor of English at the University of Virginia. He was assistant professor of English at Harvard University from 1971 to 1976. He served on the National Council on the Humanities from 1992 to 1999. He is the author of *Shakespeare's Rome: Republic and Empire* (Cornell University Press, 1976), *Creature and Creator: Myth-making and English Romanticism* (Cambridge University Press, 1984), and the *Hamlet* volume in the Cambridge Landmarks of World Literature series (1989; 2004). His book *Gilligan Unbound: Pop Culture in the Age of Globalization* (Rowman & Littlefield, 2001) was named one of the best nonfiction books of the year by the *Los Angeles Times*. Mr. Cantor is a regular contributor to national journals such as the *Weekly Standard*, *Reason*, and the *Claremont Review of Books*.

James W. Ceaser is a professor of politics at the University of Virginia, where he has taught since 1976. He has written several books on American politics and political thought, including *Presidential Selection: Theory and Development* (Princeton University Press, 1979), *Liberal Democracy and Political Science* (The Johns Hopkins University Press, 1990), *Reconstructing America: The*

Symbol of America in Modern Thought (Yale University, 1997), and *Nature and History in American Political Development: A Debate* (Harvard University Press, 2006). Mr. Ceaser has held visiting professorships at the University of Florence, the University of Basel, Oxford University, the University of Bordeaux, and the University of Rennes. He is a frequent contributor to the popular press, and he often comments on American politics for the *Voice of America*.

John B. Cooney is associate vice president for the University of Colorado System Administration and professor emeritus at the University of Northern Colorado, where he was a member of the faculty from 1980 to 2005. Mr. Cooney specializes in cognitive psychology, applied statistics, and research methodology. His work has appeared in numerous journals, including the *American Educational Research Journal*, *Cognition & Instruction*, *Intelligence*, *Journal of Educational Psychology*, *Journal of Experimental Child Psychology*, *Journal of School Psychology*, and *Learning Disability Quarterly*. He is the past editor of *Learning and Individual Differences* and a member of the editorial board for *Learning Disability Quarterly*. Current work includes a five-year longitudinal investigation of school choice on educational attainment.

Victor Davis Hanson is the Martin and Illie Anderson Senior Fellow at the Hoover Institution. Mr. Hanson is the author of some 170 articles, book reviews, and newspaper editorials on Greek, agrarian, and military history and essays on contemporary culture, and is currently a weekly columnist for the *National Review Online*. He has written or edited thirteen books, including *Warfare and Agriculture in Classical Greece* (University of California Press, 1998), *The Western Way of War* (Alfred Knopf, 1989; 2d paperback ed. University of California Press, 2000), *Hoplites: The Ancient Greek Battle Experience* (Routledge, 1991; paperback ed. 1992), *The Other Greeks: The Family Farm and the Agrarian Roots of Western Civilization* (Free Press, 1995; 2d paperback ed. University of California Press, 2000), *Fields without Dreams: Defending the Agrarian Idea* (Free Press, 1996; paperback ed. Touchstone, 1997), *The Land Was Everything: Letters from an American Farmer* (Free Press, 2000); *The Wars of the Ancient Greeks* (Cassell, 1999; paperback ed., 2001), *The Soul of Battle* (Free Press, 1999, paperback ed. Anchor/Vintage, 2000), *Carnage and Culture* (Doubleday, 2001; Anchor/Vintage, 2002), *An Autumn of War* (Anchor/Vintage, 2002); *Mexifornia: A State of Becoming* (Encounter, 2003), *Ripples of*

Battle: How Wars of the Past Still Determine How We Fight, How We Live, and How We Think (Random House, 2004), and *The Immigration Solution: A Better Plan Than Today's* (Ivan R. Dee, 2007). Mr. Hanson coauthored, with John Heath, *Who Killed Homer? The Demise of Classical Education and the Recovery of Greek Wisdom* (Free Press, 1998; paperback ed. Encounter Press, 2000) and, with Bruce Thornton and John Heath, *Bonfire of the Humanities* (ISI Books, 2001). Mr. Hanson was a full-time farmer before joining California State University, Fresno, in 1984 to initiate a classics program. He has won numerous awards, including an American Philological Association Excellence in Teaching Award in 1991, and the National Humanities Medal in 2007. He currently lives and works with his family on their forty-acre tree and vine farm near Selma, California, where he was born in 1953.

Frederick M. Hess, AEI's director of education policy studies, is an educator, political scientist, and author. At AEI, Mr. Hess studies a range of K-12 and higher education issues. He has authored influential books such as *Common Sense School Reform*, *Revolution at the Margins*, and *Spinning Wheels*. A former public high school social studies teacher, he has also taught education and policy at universities including Georgetown, Harvard, Rice, the University of Virginia, and the University of Pennsylvania. He is executive editor of *Education Next* and a faculty associate with Harvard's Program on Education Policy and Governance, and he serves on the board of directors for the National Association of Charter School Authorizers and on the review board for the Broad Prize in Urban Education.

April Kelly-Woessner is an associate professor of political science at Elizabethtown College. Her research interests involve a range of topics in political behavior and political psychology. Most recently, she has published a series of articles with coauthor Matthew Woessner on the effect of partisanship on communication in the classroom, which have appeared in *PS: Political Science and Politics* and *The Journal of Political Science Education*. She is currently working on a book with coauthors Stanley Rothman and Matthew Woessner on conflict in the American University (forthcoming, Johns Hopkins University Press). Ms. Kelly-Woessner's research has been featured in stories in the *New York Times*, the *Chronicle of Higher Education*, the *Guardian*, and *InsideHigherEd.com*.

Daniel B. Klein is a professor of economics at George Mason University. Mr. Klein has published research on policy issues including toll roads, urban transit, auto emission, credit reporting, and the Food and Drug Administration (FDA). He has also written on spontaneous order; the discovery of opportunity; the demand and supply of assurance; why government officials believe in the goodness of bad policy; and the relationship between liberty, dignity, and responsibility. Mr. Klein is the chief editor of *Econ Journal Watch*, an online journal dedicated to economic criticism from a Smith-Hayek viewpoint. He is the coauthor of *Curb Rights: A Foundation for Free Enterprise in Urban Transit* (Brookings Institution Press, 1997), editor of *Reputation: Studies in the Voluntary Elicitation of Good Conduct* (University of Michigan Press, 1997), and editor of *What Do Economists Contribute?* (Macmillan, 1999). He has coauthored a website on the FDA and coedited *The Half-Life of Policy Rationales: How New Technology Affects Old Policy Issues* (New York University Press, 2003). He also is affiliated with the Ratio Institute as an academic advisor and associate fellow.

S. Robert Lichter is professor of communication at George Mason University, where he directs the Center for Media and Public Affairs and the Statistical Assessment Service (STATS). Mr. Lichter is the author or coauthor of a dozen books and numerous popular and scholarly articles and monographs on politics and the media. His most recent books are *The Nightly News Nightmare* (2007, 2nd ed.) and *The Mediated Presidency* (2005), both coauthored with Stephen Farnsworth. Mr. Lichter previously served on the faculties of Yale, Princeton, Columbia, Georgetown, and George Washington University. He has also served as an expert witness and testified before Congress on media content and effects.

Robert Maranto is the 21st Century Chair in Leadership in the Department of Education Reform at the University of Arkansas and previously served as associate professor of political science and public administration at Villanova University. He has taught at numerous colleges, and served President Clinton's administration. Mr. Maranto has done extensive research on education reform, political leadership, and civil service reform. In concert with others, he has written or edited scholarly books which have sold dozens of copies and are so boring that his own mother refused to read them. These include

Judging Bush (Stanford University Press, 2009), *A Guide to Charter Schools* (Rowman and Littlefield Education, 2006), *Beyond a Government of Strangers: How Career Executives and Political Appointees Can Turn Conflict to Cooperation* (Lexington, 2005), *School Choice in the Real World: Lessons from Arizona Charter Schools* (Westview 2001), and *Radical Reform of the Civil Service* (Lexington 2001). He is now researching urban school reform. His several dozen refereed articles have appeared in journals including *Teachers College Record*, the *American Review of Public Administration*, the *American Journal of Education*, and *Policy Studies Journal*. His op-eds have appeared in newspapers including the *Washington Post*, *Philadelphia Inquirer*, *Philadelphia Daily News*, and *Baltimore Sun*, and *WallStreetJournal.com*.

John McWhorter is a senior fellow at the Manhattan Institute, columnist for the *New Republic*, and adjunct professor at Columbia University. His academic specialty is language change and language contact. He is the author of *The Power of Babel: A Natural History of Language* (Times Books, 2001), on how the world's languages arise, change, and mix. He is also the author of *Doing Our Own Thing: The Degradation of Language and Music and Why We Should, Like, Care* (Gotham Books, 2003). He has written a book on dialects and Black English, *The Word on the Street: Fact and Fable about American English* (Plenum, 1998), and three books on Creole languages. The Teaching Company has released two of his thirty-six-lecture audiovisual courses. Beyond his work in linguistics, he is the author of *Losing the Race: Self-Sabotage in Black America* (Free Press, 2000), an anthology of race writings, *Authentically Black* (Gotham Books, 2003), and *Winning the Race: Beyond the Crisis in Black America* (Gotham Books, 2006). His academic linguistic book *Language Interrupted: Signs of Non-Native Acquisition in Standard Language Grammars* appeared in 2007; for the general public, *Our Magnificent Bastard Tongue: The Untold History of English* appeared in the fall of 2009.

Anne D. Neal is president and a founder of the American Council of Trustees and Alumni, a national nonprofit dedicated to academic freedom, excellence, and accountability in higher education. She is a graduate of Harvard College and Harvard Law School and for a number of years specialized in First Amendment law. In the early 1990s, Ms. Neal served as general counsel and congressional liaison for the National Endowment for the Humanities. She has had extensive involvement with cultural and civic organizations supporting the arts and humanities; currently she serves on the boards of the Mount Vernon Ladies' Association, Casey Trees, and the U.S. Capitol Historical Society. She is a frequent public speaker and commentator, and is widely published on higher education, the arts and humanities, landscape architecture, and the law. She is also the higher education consultant to the Philanthropy Roundtable and coauthor of *The Intelligent Donor's Guide to College Giving*.

William O'Donohue is the Nicholas Cummings Professor of Organized Behavioral Healthcare Delivery, an adjunct professor of philosophy, and an adjunct professor of psychiatry at the University of Nevada, Reno. His main research areas include behavioral health care delivery, male sexual misbehavior, behavior therapy, and philosophy of psychology. He has worked on many books on human sexuality, behavior, and treatment, including *Learning and Behavior Therapy* (Allyn and Bacon, 1997) and *Handbook of Behaviorism* (Academic Press, 1998). Mr. O'Donohue has also published articles in multiple journals, including the *Journal of Psychotherapy Practice and Research*, *Journal of Abnormal Psychology*, and *Behavior and Philosophy*.

James Piereson is president of the William E. Simon Foundation, a private grant-making foundation based in New York City. He is also a senior fellow at the Manhattan Institute, where he is director of the Center for the American University. Mr. Piereson was previously executive director and trustee of the John M. Olin Foundation from 1985 until the end of 2005 when, following longstanding plans, the foundation disbursed its remaining assets and closed its doors. He previously served on the political science faculties of Iowa State University, Indiana University, and the University of Pennsylvania, where he taught courses in the fields of U.S. government and political theory. Mr. Piereson is the author of *Political Tolerance and American Democracy* (University of Chicago Press, 1982) and *Camelot and the Cultural Revolution: How the Assassination of John F. Kennedy Shattered American Liberalism* (Encounter, 2007). He has published articles and reviews in numerous periodicals, including *Commentary*, the *New Criterion*, the *Wall Street Journal*, *Philanthropy*, and the *Public Interest*.

Michael B. Poliakoff served from 1996–99 as Pennsylvania Deputy Secretary of Education, where he was responsible for the development of rigorous and streamlined teacher preparation and certification systems, the creation of statewide professional development opportunities, and the reorganization of the Higher Education for the Disadvantaged program. Between 2002 and 2007, he was Director of Education Programs at National Endowment for the Humanities, where he led his division in creating the Landmarks of American History and Culture program. In January 2007, he was appointed Vice President for Academic Affairs and Research at the University of Colorado. His career in higher education began as a professor of classical studies. He is the author of *Combat Sport in the Ancient World: Competition, Violence, and Culture*, published by Yale University Press, and many articles and reviews on education and culture, in addition to scholarly studies of the ancient world.

Richard E. Redding is an associate dean and professor of law at Chapman University School of Law. Previously, he was professor of law at Villanova University School of Law, research professor of psychology at Drexel University, and director of the JD/PhD Program in law and psychology at Villanova and Drexel Universities. He has also taught at the University of Virginia. He is a fellow of the American Psychological Association and serves on the editorial boards of numerous journals. Mr. Redding has published over seventy-five book chapters and articles in leading scientific, legal, and policy journals and has coauthored or coedited four books, including *Juvenile Delinquency: Assessment, Prevention, and Intervention* (Oxford University Press, 2005). He specializes in forensic issues in criminal law, juvenile justice, the use of social science in law and public policy, the ways in which social and political attitudes influence how science is used in policymaking, and sociopolitical diversity. His work in these areas is both theoretical (or policy-oriented) and empirical. In addition to practicing law, he has worked as a clinician with children and families, has directed R&D projects for the U.S. Air Force and Navy, and periodically serves as a consultant to the U.S. Justice Department, Office of Juvenile Justice and Delinquency Prevention.

Stanley Rothman is emeritus Mary Huggins Gamble Professor of Government at Smith College and the director of the Center for the Study of Social and Political Change. He is the author or coauthor of fifteen books, including *European Society and Politics* (Bobbs-Merrill, 1970), *Roots of Radicalism: Jews, Christians, and the New Left* (Oxford University Press, 1982), and *The Media Elite* (Adler & Adler, 1986). His more recent books include *American Elites* (Yale University Press, 1996), *Hollywood's America: Social and Political Themes in Motion Pictures* (Westview, 1996), *Environmental Cancer: A Political Disease?* (Yale University Press, 1999) and *The Least Dangerous Branch? The Consequences of Judicial Activism* (Praeger, 2002). The major focus of his work in recent years has been on elites and elite conflict in the United States as part of a project concerned with the analysis of social and political change.

Charlotta Stern is an associate professor at the department of sociology at Stockholm University. She has studied how social networks influence the recruitment into and the diffusion of social movement organizations and the influence of social networks on welfare outcomes. At present, Ms. Stern is involved in two projects about policy views of academics. One is based on data about American social scientists, in collaboration with Daniel Klein. The other study is based on data about Swedish social scientists, in collaboration with Niclas Berggren and Henrik Jordahl.

Matthew Woessner is an associate professor of political science and public policy at Penn State Harrisburg. He pursues teaching and research interests in American politics. His specializations include political behavior and research methodology. Along with his wife, April Kelly-Woessner, Mr. Woessner coauthored a number of articles on politics in the classroom including "My Professor Is a Partisan Hack: How Perceptions of a Professor's Political Views Affect Student Course Evaluations" (*PS: Political Science and Politics*), "Conflict in the Classroom: Considering the Effects of Partisan Difference on Political Education" (*The Journal of Political Science Education*) and "I Think My Professor Is a Democrat: Considering Whether Students Recognize and React to Faculty Politics" (*PS: Political Science and Politics*). Along with his coauthors April Kelly-Woessner and Stanley Rothman, Mr. Woessner is currently writing a book tentatively titled *Conflict and Consensus in the American University* (Johns Hopkins University Press), which examines differing perspectives on social equity, partisan politics, and institutional power among students, faculty, and college administrators. His work on politics in academia has been featured in the *Chronicle of Higher Education*, the *Christian Science Monitor*, the *Guardian*, the *Wall Street Journal* and the *New York Times*.

Peter Wood is president of the National Association of Scholars. He is the author of *A Bee in the Mouth: Anger in America Now* (Encounter, 2007) and *Diversity: The Invention of a Concept* (Encounter, 2003), which won the Caldwell Award for Leadership in Higher Education from the John Locke Foundation. He previously served as provost of the King's College in New York City and as associate provost and president's chief of staff at Boston University, where he was also a tenured member of the anthropology department. His essays on American culture have appeared on *National Review Online* and in *Partisan Review*, *FrontPage Magazine*, *Minding the Campus*, the *Claremont Review of Books*, the *American Conservative*, *Society*, and other journals.